AF594376

KIMONO COUTURE

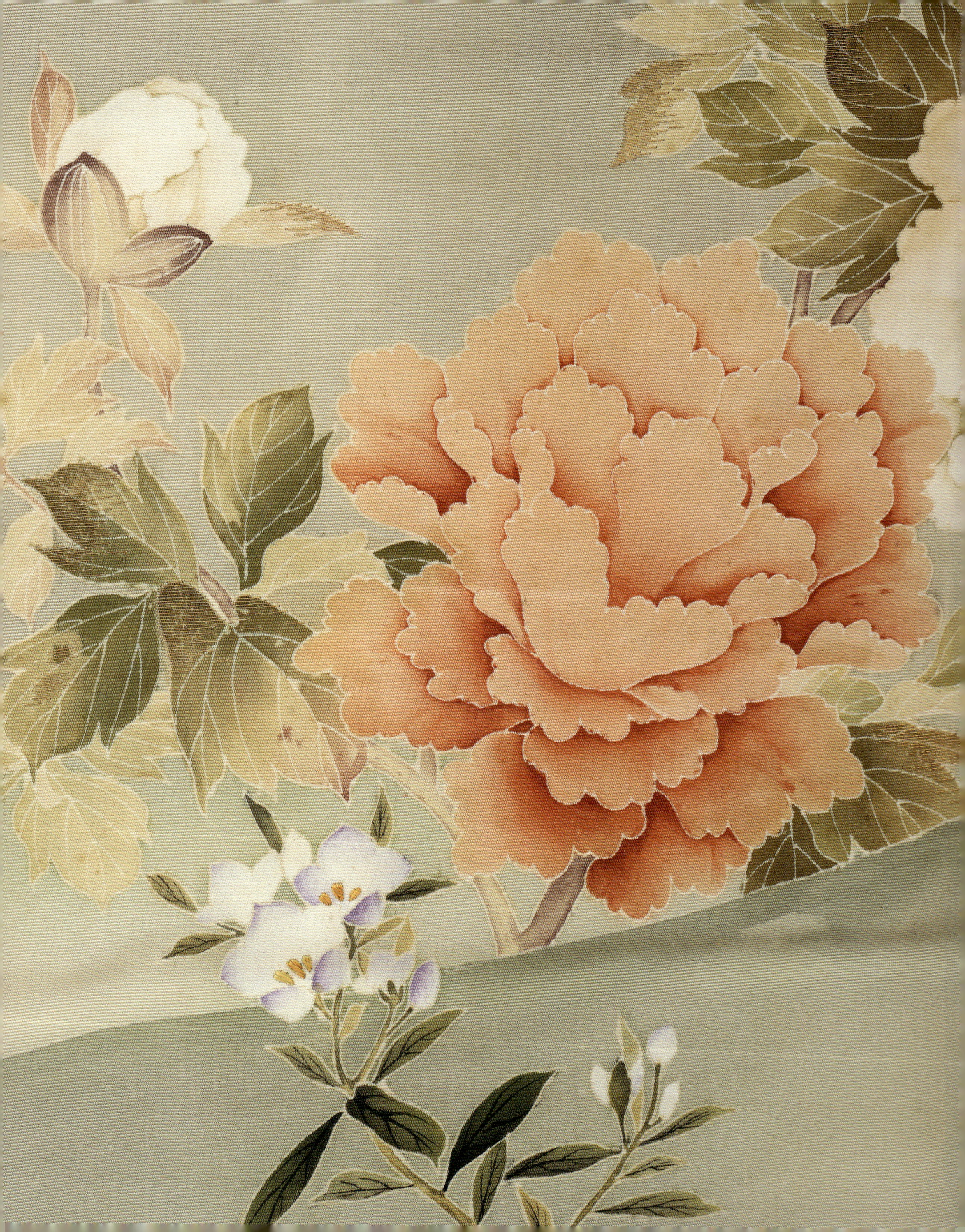

KIMONO COUTURE

The Beauty of Chiso

Edited by Vivian Li and Christine D. Starkman

With contributions by Monica Bethe, Kikuchi Riyo, Yukio Lippit, Nagasaki Iwao, Nii Rie, and Stephanie Su

WORCESTER ART MUSEUM

g

Kimono Couture: The Beauty of Chiso is supported by the Fletcher Foundation and Michie Family Curatorial Fund. Research for this project was made possible by the Japan-United States Friendship Commission and the Northeast Asia Council of the Association for Asian Studies.

Worcester Art Museum expresses gratitude for the operating support provided by the Mass Cultural Council, a state agency supported by the National Endowment for the Arts, Patrick and Aimee Butler Family Foundation, and the Carl Lesnor Family Foundation.

This catalogue accompanies the exhibition *Kimono Couture: The Beauty of Chiso* on display at the Worcester Art Museum, April 25 – July 26, 2020

First published in 2020 by GILES
An imprint of D Giles Limited
66 High Street,
Lewes, BN7 1XG, UK
gilesltd.com

ISBN: 978-1-911282-66-2

The exhibition was curated by Vivian Li and Christine D. Starkman

For Worcester Art Museum
Edited by Vivian Li and Christine D. Starkman
Copyedited by Amy Reigle Newland

For D Giles Limited
Designed by Alfonso Iacurci
Produced by GILES, an imprint of D Giles Limited
Printed and bound in Slovenia

Front and back cover illustrations: *Worcester Wedding Kimono* design, 2020 (detail)
Chiso Co., Ltd.
Frontispiece: Detail of cat. 1

Contents

Forewords

Japanese art was introduced and cultivated in the United States by prominent collectors in Gilded-Age New England at the close of the nineteenth century. Many of the fine museum collections of Japanese art in the region today attest to this legacy, including that at the Worcester Art Museum. Soon after its founding in 1896, the Museum's first major acquisition consisted of approximately 3,000 *ukiyo-e* woodblock prints from the collector John Chandler Bancroft (1835–1901) in 1901. This significant gift included rare early prints by seventeenth- and eighteenth-century artists such as Hishikawa Moronobu and Okumura Masanobu as well as nineteenth-century works by Katsushika Hokusai and Utagawa Hiroshige. Important additions since the foundational Bancroft bequest have expanded the Japanese art collection to include paintings and prints by Ōbaku Dokuryū, Sakai Hōitsu, and Tsukioka Yoshitoshi, among others.

Our special partnership with Chiso continues this intimate aesthetic relationship and dialogue between Worcester and Japan. A prestigious maker of Buddhist vestments since 1555, Chiso shifted to the design and production of luxury kimono in the latter half of the nineteenth century. Besides supplying kimono to the Japanese imperial court, they were active participants at several international expositions during this time and were recognized with numerous awards for their artistic caliber and technical advancements in the textile arts.

Introducing Chiso's art to contemporary American audiences in the show *Kimono Couture: The Beauty of Chiso* continues the Worcester Art Museum's long tradition of supporting and exhibiting international creative leaders—the museum was, for example, an early champion of Claude Monet and Paul Gauguin in the United States. The special commission for Chiso to produce a "Worcester Kimono" inspired by the shared love for nature in New England and Japan, particularly Worcester's iconic "Seven Hills," will bring together Chiso's almost five centuries of innovation, beauty, and technical achievement. This first museum commission for Chiso is also the first kimono to enter the Worcester Art Museum's collection, thus solidifying our commitment to Chiso and the sophisticated arts of the kimono in Japan today.

We are completely indebted to Chiso for being dedicated collaborators, especially Nishimura Sōzaemon XV of the founding family of Chiso, President Nakata Yasushi and Senior Managing Director Isomoto En as well as Katō Yuriko, Director of the Institute for Chiso Arts and Culture, and senior designer Imai Atsuhiro who created the one-of-a-kind kimono commission for Worcester. Special thanks are also due to the co-curators Vivian Li and Christine D. Starkman for spearheading this exhibition and its publication, and Claire Whitner, Director of Curatorial Affairs and James A. Welu Curator of European Art, for her steadfast guidance. Our gratitude goes also to the Fletcher Foundation and the Michie Family through their endowed fund for generously supporting the realization of this exhibition project, and the Japan-United States Friendship Commission and the Northeast Asia Council of the Association for Asian Studies for making possible the necessary critical research.

Matthias Waschek
Jean and Myles McDonough Director

Over 140 years ago, in 1876, Chiso first displayed its artworks in America at the Centennial International Exhibition in Philadelphia, and *Kimono Couture: The Beauty of Chiso* represents the first occasion since then that the Chiso Collection will be viewed by audiences in the United States. For us, it is a great pleasure that we are once again connected, and we are delighted to see an exhibition that will introduce twenty-first century American audiences to Chiso.

The year 2020 marks 465 years since the founding of Chiso in Kyoto. The Chiso Collection was not amassed for viewing, but rather as historical research and study materials for the production of kimono. Even today, it continues to be the creative source for our own aesthetic, inspiring an enduring passion and resolve to pass on tradition and at the same time fashion new "beauty."

This exhibition was made possible because the Worcester Art Museum, the organizer of *Kimono Couture: The Beauty of Chiso*, deeply connected with our spirit. I would like to express my heartfelt appreciation to the Museum, its curators, and all those involved who assisted in the realization of this project and for their enormous support. We hope Chiso's beauty, which we have built and continue to develop, will touch people's hearts.

Nishimura Sōzaemon XV
Chairman of Chiso

Acknowledgments

In 2015, on an autumn night in Kyoto, Christine D. Starkman came upon a curious, nondescript building next to the Mitsui Garden Hotel where she was staying. Finding it still open, she went inside and found a woman conducting a late-night inventory of kimono accessories. She learned that this was the retail store of Chiso, one of the premier kimono makers in Japan. Astounded by the history and artistry of Chiso's kimono, Christine wondered about the possibilities of collaborating with the company on a museum exhibition in the United States. Months later, during Asia Week in New York in March 2016, Christine told Vivian Li about Chiso, and from that time onward discussions began regarding a kimono exhibition with this respected company. *Kimono Couture: The Beauty of Chiso* is the result of that serendipitous night and the transformative four-year journey of this project for both us and Chiso.

This exhibition would not have been possible without the generous spirit and kindness of an international team of dedicated people. We would like to thank the Jean and Myles McDonough Director of the Worcester Art Museum, Matthias Waschek, and the president of Chiso, Nakata Yasushi, for their vision of bringing to US audiences the dynamic art and beauty of Chiso's kimono via the exhibited works and the special "Worcester Kimono" commission. Our heartfelt appreciation also to the current head of the founding Nishimura family, the fifteenth-generation Nishimura Sōzaemon, for his commitment to the project. From the beginning, the incredible support of Isomoto En, Chiso's Senior Managing Director, likewise made possible the effortless collaboration between Chiso and the Worcester Art Museum.

We are completely indebted to Katō Yuriko, Director of the Institute for Chiso Arts and Culture, in her tireless support of our research of the Chiso collection. She was key in introducing us to the history of Chiso, the inner workings and organization of the company, and providing us access to the firm's exquisite art and kimono collection. She, along with Imai Atsuhiro, Chiso's Senior Designer, and Ishida Naoko, Chiso's Gallery Curator, made the special arrangements for our studio visits with the firm's kimono artisans during our final research trip in the summer of 2019. Our sincere thanks to Ms. Ishida for also enabling our research into the Chiso art collection and archives and our obtaining the vital photography for this publication.

We are equally grateful to Imai Atsuhiro for his remarkable design of the "Worcester Kimono" commission. He carefully considered the Japanese tradition of kimono in keeping with Chiso's core value of beauty and the contemporary woman in the final design that could represent twenty-first century kimono fashion and design. Isomoto En and Shiba Daisuke, Chiso's Communications Director, supported Mr. Imai's design process and offered valuable counsel and encouragement in imagining the vision of Chiso kimono.

Many thanks to Melissa Rinne for introducing us to Monica Bethe, and Monica Bethe for agreeing to serve as our translator for the interview with Imai Atsuhiro. Bethe's over fifty years of experience in Japan as a scholar and lecturer in Japanese textiles enlightened us on the history of Japanese kimono and textile traditions. Her daughter, Miyo Sugimoto, a professional translator, deftly translated the interview into English. The contributors to the publication—Kikuchi Riyo, Yukio Lippit, Nagasaki Iwao, Nii Rie, and Stephanie Su—each masterfully contributed their expert knowledge to ensure that their texts encompass a broad range of Chiso history and kimono-making. Special thanks are due to Professor Lippit, who from the outset of this project enthusiastically offered his counsel, and rightfully impressed upon us the importance of producing the present volume. He also warmly hosted Katō Yuriko and Imai Atsuhiro at Harvard University during their visit to New England in 2019.

We also greatly benefited from the expertise and experience of other colleagues and textile specialists, particularly curators Hollis Goodall at the Los Angeles County Museum of Art, Anna Jackson at the Victoria and Albert Museum, London, and Lee Talbot at the Textile Museum of the George Washington University Museum in Washington, DC. Historian Henry D. Smith II, Professor Emeritus of Columbia University, generously met us during our early research trip in Kyoto in the summer of 2017. The Japan-United States Friendship Commission and the Northeast Asia Council of the Association for Asian Studies generously supported our last and critical research trip to Chiso in the summer of 2019. Eliza Spaulding, Paper Conservator at the Worcester Art Museum, traveled with us to visit Chiso during this time to plan for the safe transport of the textiles and books to Worcester. She was indispensable in assisting Katō Yuriko and Ishida Naoko in the final installation of the works at the Museum.

Countless other colleagues at the Worcester Art Museum helped cultivate and nurture our idea for *Kimono Couture*. We thank Jon L. Seydl, former Director of Curatorial Affairs and Curator of European Art, for his strong support in pursuing this project during its initial stages, followed by Claire Whitner, Director of Curatorial Affairs and James A. Welu Curator of European Art, who continued to provide encouragement and advice as the project developed. Exhibition designer Patrick Brown, along with the Museum's graphic designer Kim Noonan, complemented the splendor of the works with the elegant and brilliant gallery presentation. The exhibition production team, led by Trevor Toney and including Wes Small and Anne Greene, created the complex mounts and casework for the works and handled the works with their customary care.

Gareth Salway, Director of Museum Services, and Alison Rosenberg, Assistant Registrar, expertly managed this first major international travel of Chiso's collection to the United States, while Sarah Gillis, Associate Registrar, assembled the many images for the publication. Marnie Weir, Director of Education and Experience, and her team invented imaginative ways for the public to learn about the art of kimono. Julieane K. Frost, Senior Marketing Manager, worked vigorously and creatively with her team to introduce the exhibition to the public, and Christine Proffitt, Senior Manager of Institutional Giving, helped inspire benefactors to this project. Lear Curatorial Fellow, Rachael Kane, contributed special research in the latter stages of the exhibition, while Curatorial Assistant Olivia Kiers lent crucial administrative support with her usual reassuring confidence.

We extend our heartfelt gratitude to Amy Reigle Newland for her exhaustive editorial guidance and exceptional professionalism—especially in working to tight deadlines—that greatly improved the overall quality of this volume. We are also indebted to Dan Giles at D Giles Limited, for sharing our excitement for this exhibition and publication project and co-publishing this book with the Museum. Special thanks to Katherine Anne Paul for kindly introducing us to Dan Giles. Many thanks also to Louise Ramsay, Production Director, and Allison McCormick, Editorial Manager at Giles, as well as book designer Alfonso Iacurci for this stunning publication.

Vivian Li
Associate Curator of Asian Art and Global Contemporary Art, Worcester Art Museum

Christine D. Starkman
Independent Curator of Contemporary Art

Note to the Reader

Japanese terms and names have been rendered in keeping with the modified Hepburn system of Romanization. Most Japanese names follow traditional form with family name before given name. For authors and scholars working and acknowledged internationally this is sometimes reversed. Artists best known by their studio or art names are referred to accordingly, and this usually applies to historical figures (e.g., Kishi Chikudō as Chikudō or Imao Keinen as Keinen). Japanese terms, place designations, and personal names appear in their original accented form, unless they have entered into common English usage (e.g., Kyoto, not Kyōto; daimyo, not daimyō). The Chiso firm name is also seen written as Chisō.

Before the nineteenth century, there were many types of garments with different sleeve lengths, functions, and materials. Each had its own name but since the Meiji period (1868–1912) all have become described by the popular term *kimono*, which is a general designation for traditional Japanese dress. Unless otherwise specified, all works are from the Chiso Collection. Sizes are given in height × width (centimeters and inches). With books, the measurements provided are the height × width of the closed book. The contributors to the entries are identified as such: VL (Vivian Li), NI (Nagasaki Iwao), NR (Nii Rie), CS (Christine D. Starkman), and SS (Stephanie Su).

Detail of cat. 5

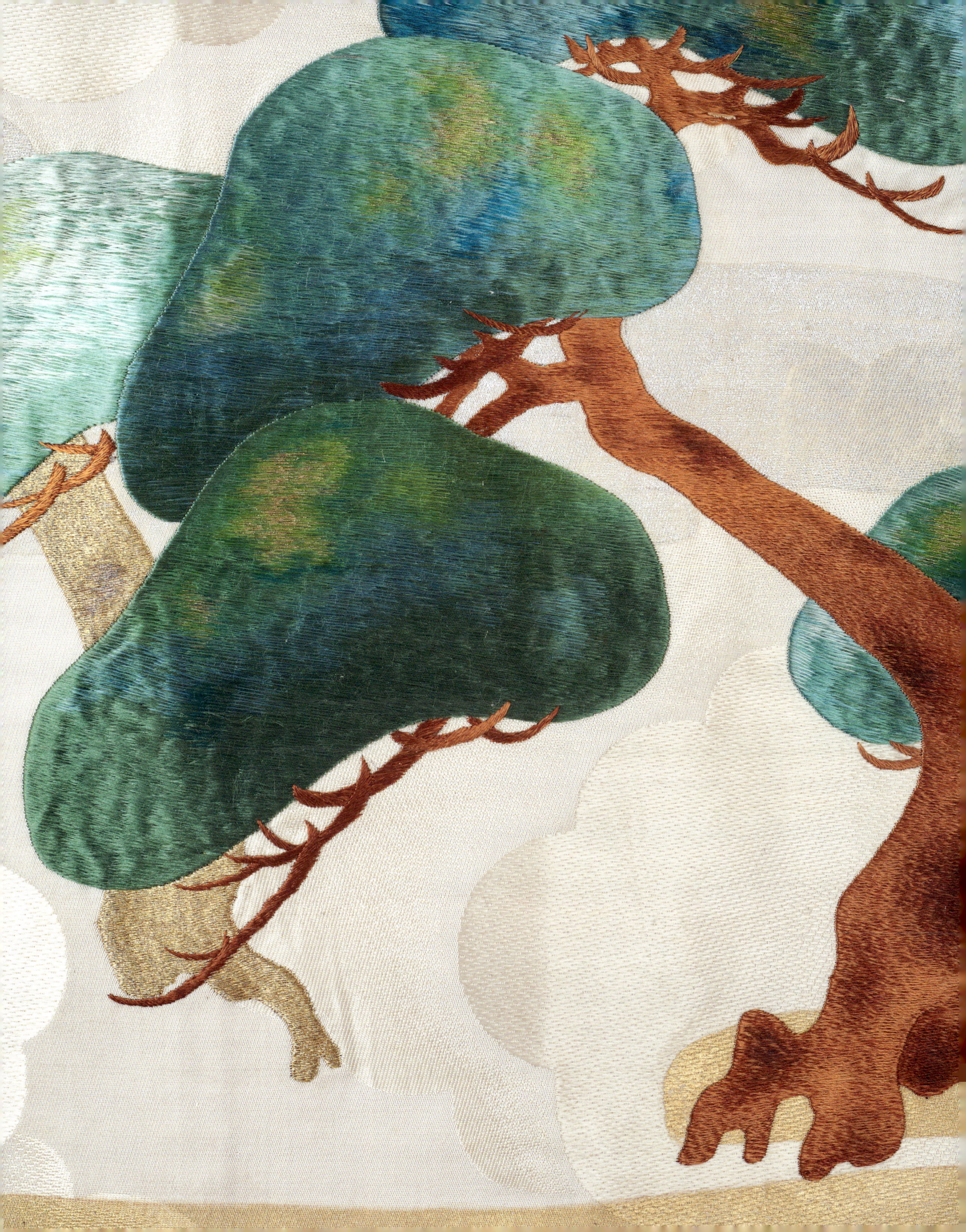

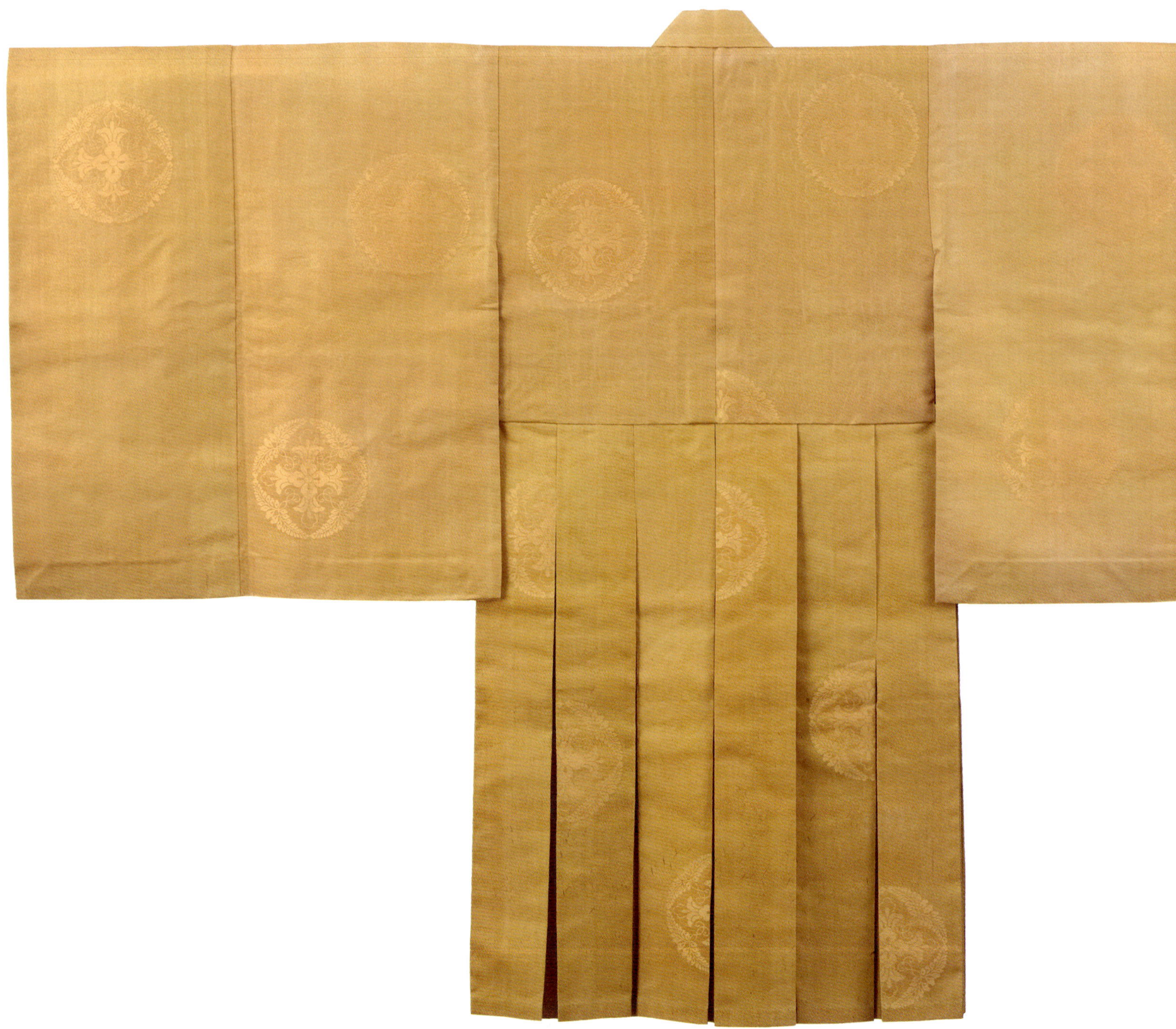

Fig. 1
Chiso Co., Ltd., *Priest's Robe*,
19th century, woven silk,
123.3 × 184.6 cm (48 1/2 × 72 11/16 in.),
Chiso Collection, Kyoto

FROM THE EVERYDAY TO COUTURE

Chiso and Contemporary Kimono

Vivian Li and Christine D. Starkman

The kimono has become the unmistakable international icon of Japanese art and culture, although its journey to reach such an esteemed status reveals a century of contentious debates surrounding clothing, modernity, and the handmade. In the second half of the nineteenth century, for example, the kimono was under scrutiny as a cultural relic as Japan embarked on its path to becoming a modern nation-state during the Meiji period (1868–1912). This stood in stark contrast to the appreciation of Japanese art and culture, including the kimono, during the wave of *Japonisme* sweeping through Europe and America at this time.[1]

In the 1940s, during World War II (1939–45), the kimono became a target of sumptuary laws as resources were diverted to the war effort. On July 7, 1940, the Japanese government issued the Wartime Command Economy and Regulations Limiting Manufacture and Sale of Extravagant Goods Law, also known as the "7-7 Law." Under this law, the kimono was banned, and in its place the Japanese were encouraged to wear "the clothing of the nation's people" (*kokuminfuku*), which comprised either a jacket and trousers for men or a top and trousers for women.[2] And with postwar austerities, kimono became increasingly unaffordable compared to less expensive, mass-produced alternatives. From this period onward the kimono completed its transformation from everyday clothing into an object of relative luxury and culture emblematic of Japan.

The artistic status of the kimono was acknowledged with its designation as a cultural property in 1950 (see Kikuchi Riyo's essay in this volume). Since this time, and even before, there have been countless art museum exhibitions featuring kimono that have addressed the timeless beauty and social associations of the kimono through the lens of a particular collector or on a historical theme. And more recently, exhibitions have also focused on the inspiration and appropriation of the kimono form by leading artists and fashion designers. The collaboration with the Kyoto kimono maker Chiso that culminated in the exhibition and publication *Kimono Couture: The Beauty of Chiso* thus offers a rare opportunity to approach the kimono as a contemporary practice. *Kimono Couture* endeavors to combine Chiso's 465 years of technical achievement, innovation, creativity, and artistry in the present and for the future.

Chiso, like many other established kimono houses in Japan, is known for its intensively private and tightly held operations.[3] Fortuitously, when we approached Chiso in 2016 about the possibility of an exhibition and publication, the company was open to collaboration. It had just celebrated its 460th anniversary and was contemplating the future twenty-first-century face of the company and the role of kimono therein. The subsequent research visits to Chiso's gallery and headquarters in Kyoto each summer beginning in 2017 shaped the contour and scope of the current exhibition and publication. At the same time, it deepened our understanding of the history of the kimono, informing and refining our motivations for the project.

Cultural Keepers of Modern Japan

Before our initial visit to Chiso in 2017 we knew relatively little about this premier kimono maker. Chiso was founded in 1555 and until the Meiji period was primarily involved in the manufacture of Buddhist vestments (fig. 1). In the Meiji period, the government targeted Buddhism in an attempt to separate Shintoism from Buddhism and to abolish Buddhism. This, combined with the decline of patronage due to the shifting political, social, and cultural situation at this time, forced Chiso to seek out new sources of patronage. It began the production of decorated textiles and kimono for the imperial family, luxury kimono for the diversifying domestic market, alongside ornamental tapestries and kimono-inspired garments for a foreign clientele.

From our first viewing of Chiso's art collection in 2017, we learned of the company's remarkable position as an art patron. Chiso collects art, not for exhibition, rather as sources to inspire original design. It was the first kimono firm to commission and collaborate with artists in the Meiji period who were themselves looking for new patrons. Chiso subsequently supported many celebrated *nihonga* (Japanese-style painting) artists at the time, starting with Kishi Chikudō (1826–97) (cats. 14–16), who taught painting to Chiso's owner Nishimura Sōzaemon XII (1855–1935)

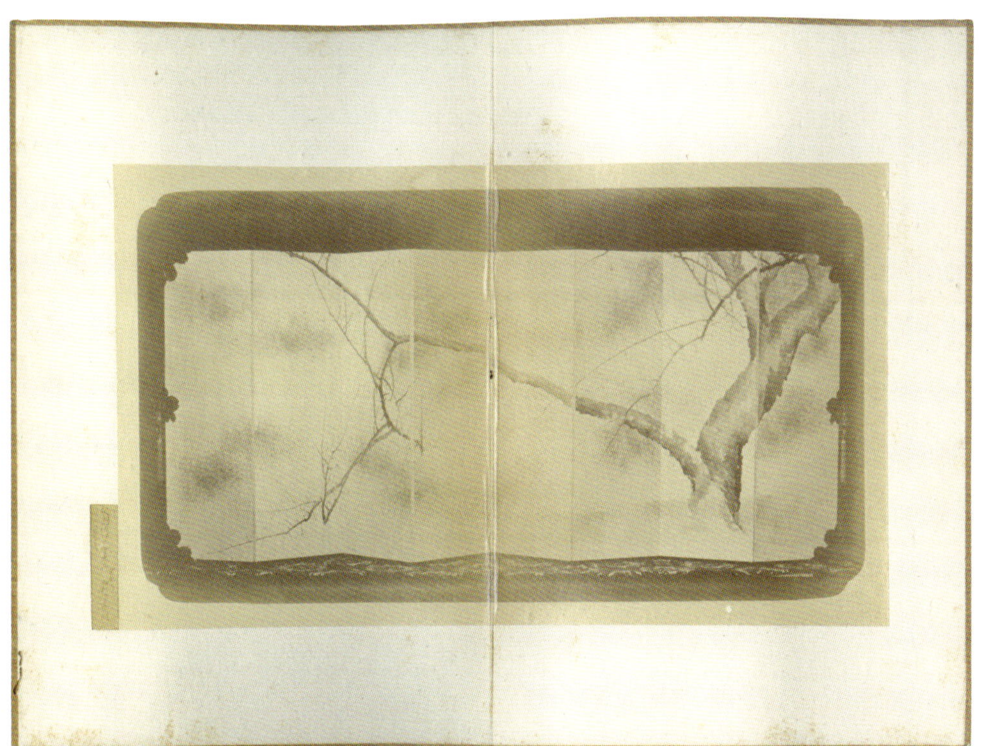

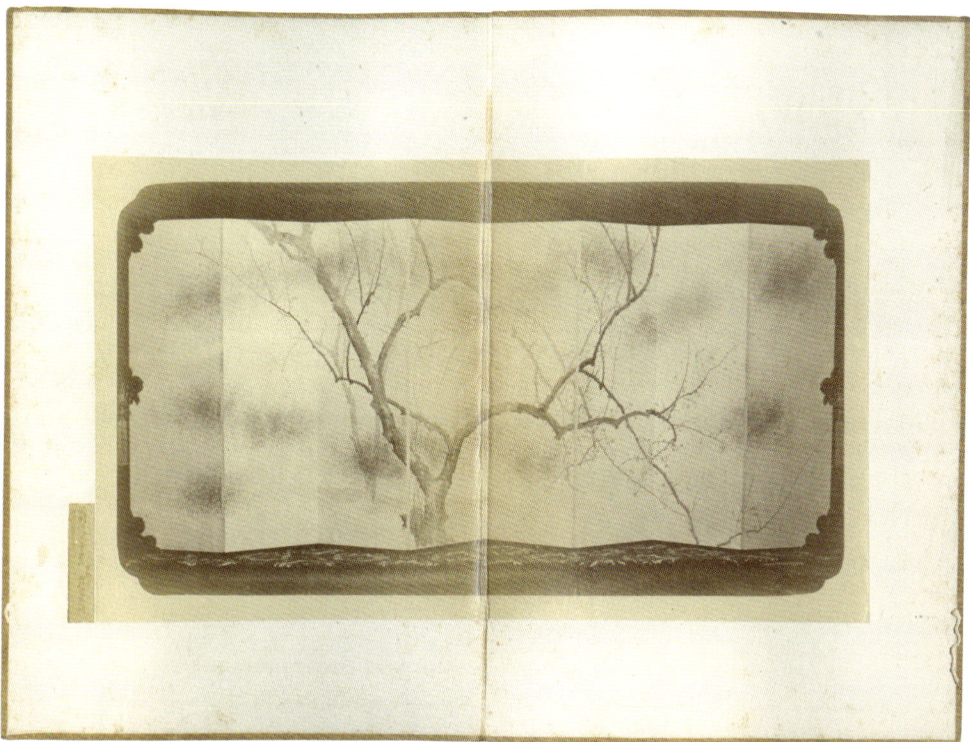

Figs. 2–3
Photographs of *Plum Tree* by Kishi Chikudō, from an unpublished album with a cover label reading "Meiji 8 [1875], Works for Display at the American Government Exposition," Chiso Collection, Kyoto

and who Nishimura later invited to instruct the company's designers in the creation of unique designs. Works by some of these *nihonga* artists are represented in this publication, including two pairs of folding screens by Chikudō that were shown with Chiso at the Philadelphia Centennial International Exhibition of May 10–November 10, 1876, the first world's fair in the United States (see figs. 2–3, cat. 15 & Yukio Lippit's essay in this volume) and *Keinen's Painting Album of Flowers and Birds* (*Keinen kachō gafu*), an 1891 work by Imao Keinen (1845–1924) that Chiso commissioned as a model book (cat. 23).[4]

Chiso's support of the arts extended to its commitment and sense of responsibility to its hundreds of highly skilled, independent artisans. In order to assist its artisans (and their respective métiers) during World War II, Chiso applied and was

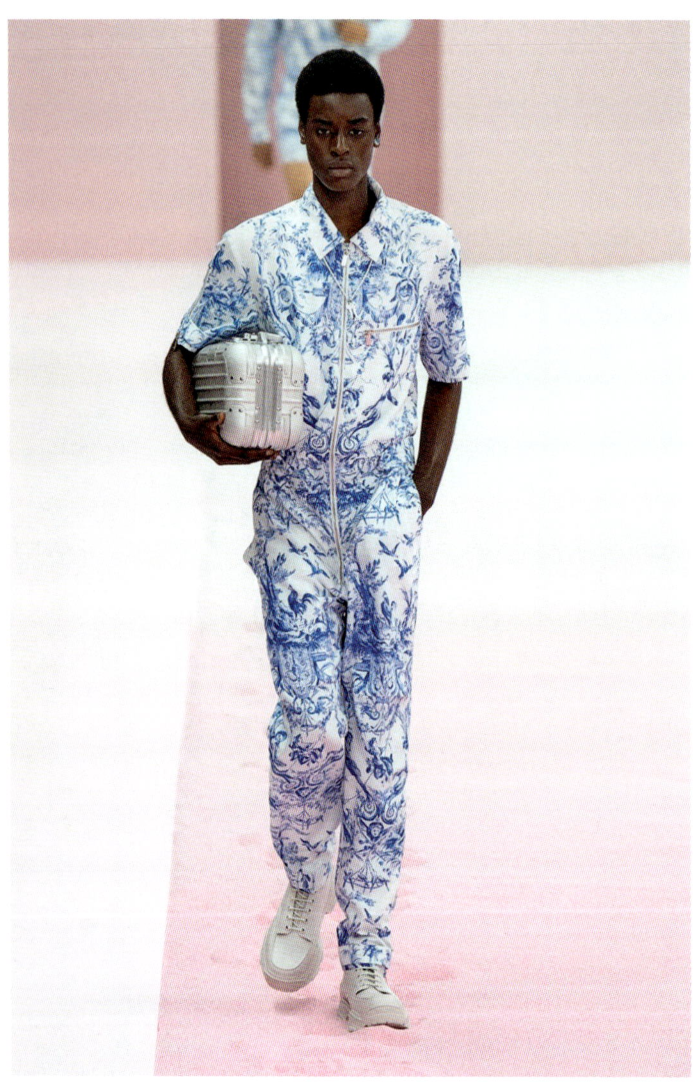

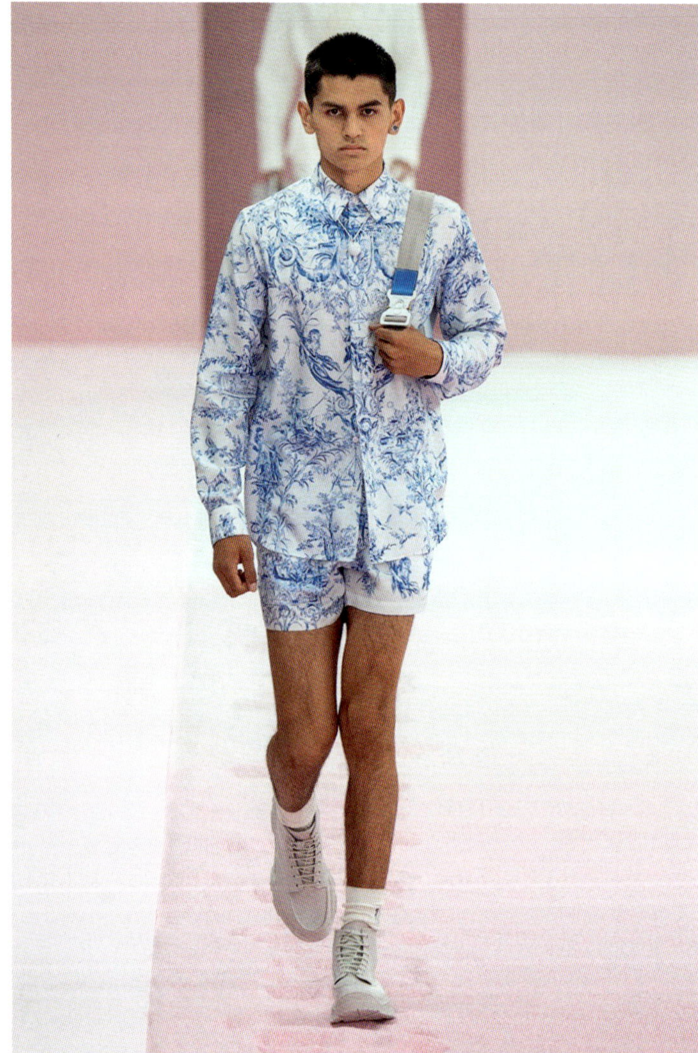

Figs. 4–5
Chiso for Dior, Spring/Summer 2020 Menswear Collection

granted permission to establish the Nishimura Weaving and Dyeing Centre (Nishimura Senshoku Kenkyūjo) in 1943, three years after the promulgation of the 7-7 Law outlawing the kimono. Under the educational mandate to preserve advanced textile skills and knowledge, Chiso was now sanctioned by the government to continue its signature *yūzen*-dyed silk kimono. This secured work for Chiso's artisans, thereby guaranteeing the survival of the complex skills of its weavers and dyers.[5] Even today, Chiso finds creative opportunities for its network of artisans, and this is not limited to kimono. Most recently, for instance, Chiso collaborated with its specialist in colored flour paste-resist dyeing (*iro utsushi itchin yūzen*) to contribute to Dior's Spring/Summer 2020 Menswear Collection (figs. 4–5). From the initial planning trip for this project, we realized the extraordinary significance of the kimono industry, especially such large and eminent drapers as Chiso in their roles as major champions of Japan's artistic traditions and their contribution to modern fashion. It was exactly these roles as kimono producers *and* as modern art patrons that we wished to convey in *Kimono Couture*.

What is Modern?: Commissioning Chiso

The purpose of our second research trip to Chiso's collection in the summer of 2018 was to choose works for the exhibition and this publication. Among the final selections from the Edo period (1603–1868) were five kimono (cats. 8–12), two important pairs of screens (cats. 14–15) and a pair of hanging scrolls (cat. 16) by Kishi Chikudō, and the five-volume *Patterns from the Shōtoku Era* (*Shōtoku hinagata*) by Nishikawa Sukenobu (1671–1750) from Chiso's design research collection (cat. 13). Later pieces include three twentieth-century formal overcoats worn during weddings (*uchikake*) created by Chiso that are today in the Nishimura family collection (cats. 1, 2, 5). Of all the kimono we viewed, the example that appeared the most modern and the one often studied by Chiso's designers—the seventeenth-century *Kosode with Overturned Flask Design* (cat. 8)—is in fact one of the earliest kimono in the firm's holdings. We began to question our expectations of what constituted the contemporary practice of kimono-making when we became aware that the most modern-looking kimono to inspire contemporary designs at Chiso is the oldest historically.

In order to fulfill our original intention to show the kimono as a form of contemporary art practice, it became apparent that a recent example by Chiso should complement the historical robes included in *Kimono Couture*. In our discussions about how best to include twenty-first-century kimono—as a commercial firm Chiso's kimono are often sold and not available—we arrived at the idea of commissioning a new kimono. Undertaking such a commission radically changed the approach and strategy of the exhibition. It became an exceptional opportunity for an art museum in the United States to collaborate, for the first time, with a Japanese kimono company. For Chiso, this commission also marked its first collaboration with an art institution—inside or outside Japan—in its 465 years of operation. (Chiso's collaborations with Japanese museums typically involve the loan of historical kimono from its collection of over 130 *kosode*.) The commission of a kimono as an *artwork* for an *art museum*, rather than for a specific client or occasion, and one by its own fashion designers, gave Chiso limitless creative space to give form to its ethos regarding the present and future art of the kimono.

In 2018, the Worcester Art Museum approved the special exhibition commission that would enter the Museum's permanent collection, and thereafter the process of realizing and fabricating the "Worcester Kimono" commenced. The senior kimono designer at Chiso, Imai Atsuhiro, conducted a site visit to Worcester in May of the following year. He made excursions to see New England's bucolic landscape as part of his research into our suggested theme of the iconic "Seven Hills" around Worcester (see interview with Imai Atsuhiro in this volume & fig. 3, p. 47). The selected Worcester kimono design (cat. 24) was inspired by the shared appreciation in Japan and New England for the seasonal change represented by maple leaves. It paid homage to the idyllic Seven Hills and the auspicious octagonal *chikiri* motif that is also prominently represented in the Chiso company crest (fig. 6).[6]

Imai's design comprised a repeated, allover pattern of an abstracted octagonal maple-leaf motif. Larger octagonal patterns appear on the back and sleeve panels of the kimono, and when folded, the two front panels also form a large

Fig. 6
Chiso's trademark in the form of three octagonal *chikiri* wooden pedestals

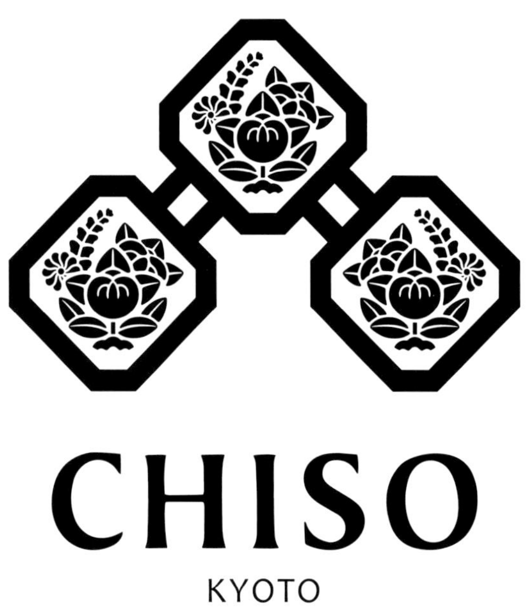

octagonal pattern. The complete shape of the octagon represents the bond and friendship between Chiso and the Worcester Art Museum. As a complement to the Seven Hills theme, the maple-leaf pattern shows seven gradations of color as a depiction of seasonal change and employs seven sophisticated textile techniques for the decoration: barrel tie-dyeing (*okedashi shibori*), standard paste-resist dyeing (*yūzen*), the more specialized colored flour paste-resist dyeing, threadline paste-resist dyeing (*itome-yūzen*), and "snowstorm" wax-resist dyeing (*fubuki rōketsuzome*) as well as gold leaf and embroidery (*shishū*). Some of these seven techniques are new while others are at risk of disappearing, not because they are "traditional" but because they are often labor-intensive, making it difficult to attract a younger generation of artisans. This approach to the decoration of the Worcester kimono reflects Chiso's awareness regarding the need for both the innovation and the preservation of highly evolved textile skills and the desire to honor the coexistence of these methods in contemporary kimono-making.

Our last research trip to Chiso in the summer of 2019 focused on reviewing the final list of pieces for the exhibition, and as Chiso's "clients" we were now granted rare access to the seven studios of the artisans who would work on the seven special techniques for the commissioned kimono. Chiso employs over six hundred, principally Kyoto, craftspeople, who are all part of a collaborative process that requires meticulous precision and quality control at every phase of the process. Our visit to these artisans' studios also offered a glimpse into Chiso's established relationships with the trusted kimono brokers who identify and recommend top talents to Chiso. This has resulted in a critical, close-knit network of artists, designers, artisans, salesmen, department stores, and finally the consumers who wear the kimono: each is therefore instrumental in the production and marketing of kimono.

Most of the studios we visited have collaborated with Chiso for generations, and some exclusively so. These long-term partnerships also encourage the invention of techniques unique to Chiso. That of colored flour paste-resist dyeing, for example, which allows for the colored paste-resist to be rubbed away from the cloth after the flour dries, was developed in the 1990s by Chiso and one of its *yūzen* artisans. The son of that artisan, Kamachi Yutaka, and his son, Kamachi Shota, carry on perfecting this technique, and they work solely with Chiso (fig. 7). Moreover, two of the seven textile specialists—one in barrel tie-dyeing, the other in "snowstorm" wax-resist dyeing—may be the last of their line since they are without apprentices to continue these exacting practices.

Our visit to the studio of the master barrel tie-dyer, Matsuyama Itsuo, revealed his dedication and commitment to the craft in a process that involves using a wooden barrel specifically made for dyeing large sections of fabric in this *shibori* technique. Once the design of the textile is isolated, or reserved, in the interior of the barrel, the barrel is sealed and sent to the dyer to immerse in a vat of color. New wooden barrels with a special sealing mechanism are no longer produced because the last craftsman who made them died without any successors. The studio, therefore, carefully uses (and maintains) the remaining nine wooden barrels, but Matsuyama is also the last barrel tie-dyeing specialist in Chiso's network (fig. 8). Chiso therefore conceived the commissioned wedding kimono as a symbol of the marriage between Japan and Worcester, as well as a sort of time capsule showcasing the range of textile techniques and artistry that the kimono industry supports today.

From our initial mission to explore the kimono as a form of contemporary art practice, our frame of reference was constantly challenged and always changing. Our understanding of the kimono began from the perception of it as a time-bound practice that is either premodern or contemporary to an appreciation of the ease with which designers work between time periods to present something exciting, something novel. The commissioning of a new kimono from Chiso permitted us to experience firsthand the intimate relationship between Chiso's curatorial and design team and their network of talented textile artists who mutually sustain (and are sustained) by the kimono industry. We also learned that for Chiso the notion of "contemporary" has more to do with aesthetic tastes than any temporal considerations. According to Isomoto En, Chiso's Senior Managing Director, the firm's core value is *bi hitosuji*, which in English translates to "nothing but beauty." Defining beauty from the perspective of Japanese women and as a

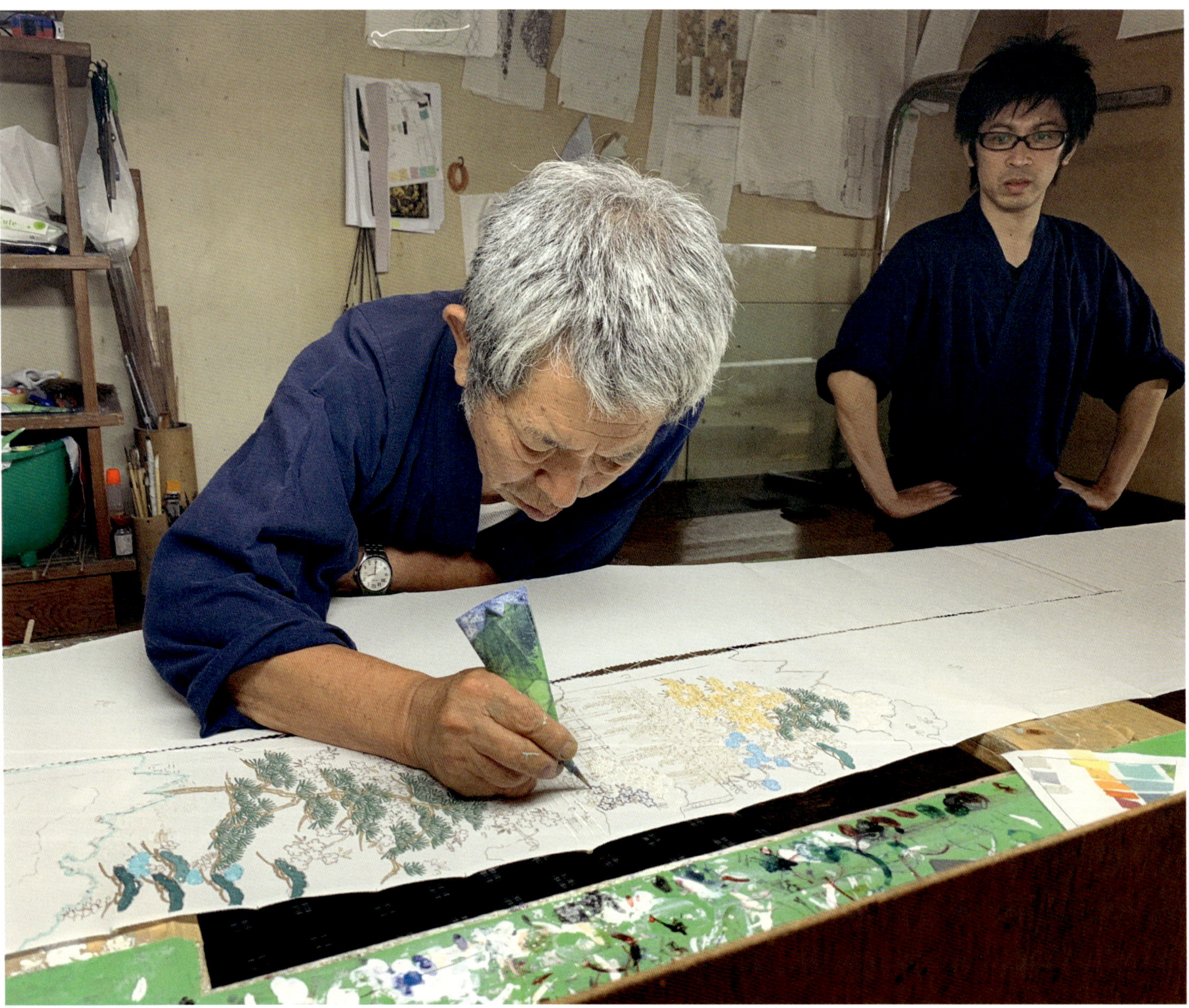

Fig. 7
Kamachi Yutaka and his son, Kamachi Shota, artisan specialists of colored flour paste-resist dyeing (*iro utsushi itchin yūzen*) for Chiso

reflection of their present-day lifestyles, Isomoto maintains that in its designs Chiso values what is beautiful above all else and as such they are always contemporary.[7]

The revered kimono, although no longer worn for the everyday, is today often associated with key celebrations as well as cultural events such as tea ceremonies. The kimono is most prominently worn at specific life milestones, such as a child's coming of age ceremony at three, five, seven, and twenty years, at weddings, and at death. *Kimono Couture: The Beauty of Chiso* captures the kimono not only as a contemporary art practice but also, and perhaps most crucially, the contemporary life it creates around it.

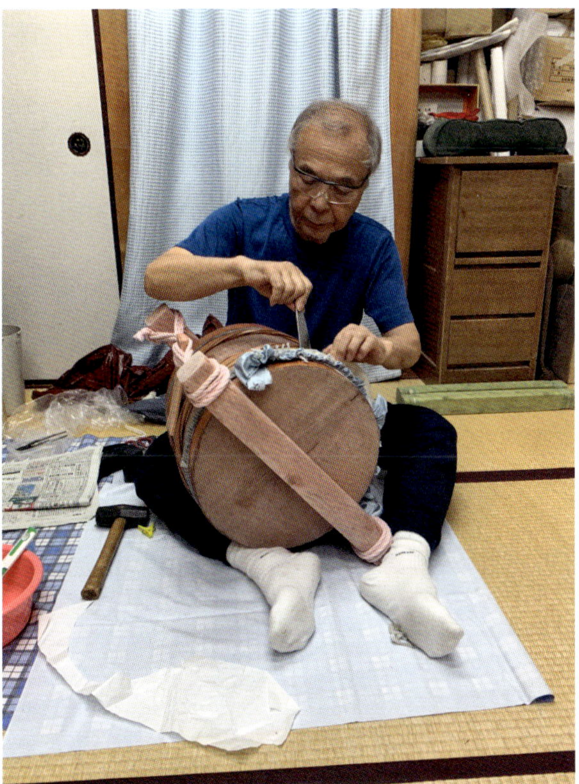

Fig. 8
Matsuyama Itsuo, artisan specialist of barrel tie-dying (*okedashi shibori*)

Notes

1. For more information on Meiji-period debates about the kimono, see Terry Satsuki Milhaupt, *Kimono: A Modern History* (London: Reaktion Books, 2014).
2. Ibid., 191.
3. Masakazu Ishikawa and Shin'ya Nagasawa, "Customer Experience of CHISO: The Centuries-old Business of Japanese Luxury Kimono Garments," in "Customer Experience Management/Marketing Branding," special issue, *Science Journal of Business and Management* 3, no. 2–1 (2015): 83–91.
4. For more information on Keinen's album, see Stephanie Su, "Weaving Art, Science, and Modern Design: *Keinen's Painting Album of Flowers and Birds*," in *The Kimono in Print: 300 Years of Japanese Design*, ed. Vivian Li (Leiden: Hotei Publishing, 2020), 75–88.
5. Today Chiso's design subsidiary, Sohya, markets itself as a general design firm "drawing on Japanese beauty." Sohya's designs range from drink labels for the large Japan-based beverage company Suntory, to shoes and sandals for the Brazil-based company Havaianas.
6. The Chiso trademark is in the shape of three octagonal *chikiri* wooden pedestals, made by the Nishimura family and used to carry flowers during the Kasuga Shrine festival in Nara. Chiso is actually a branch of Chikiriya, a Kyoto textile wholesaler, who derived their name from the word *chikiri*. See Hiroko T. McDermott, "The Pleasure and Pain of Being the Front-Runner: The Nishimura Sōzaemon House (Chisō) in the Meiji Period," in *Threads of Silk and Gold: Ornamental Textiles from Meiji Japan*, ed. Hiroko T. McDermott and Clare Pollard (Oxford: Ashmolean Museum, 2012), 41.
7. Authors' interview with Isomoto En, July 19, 2019.

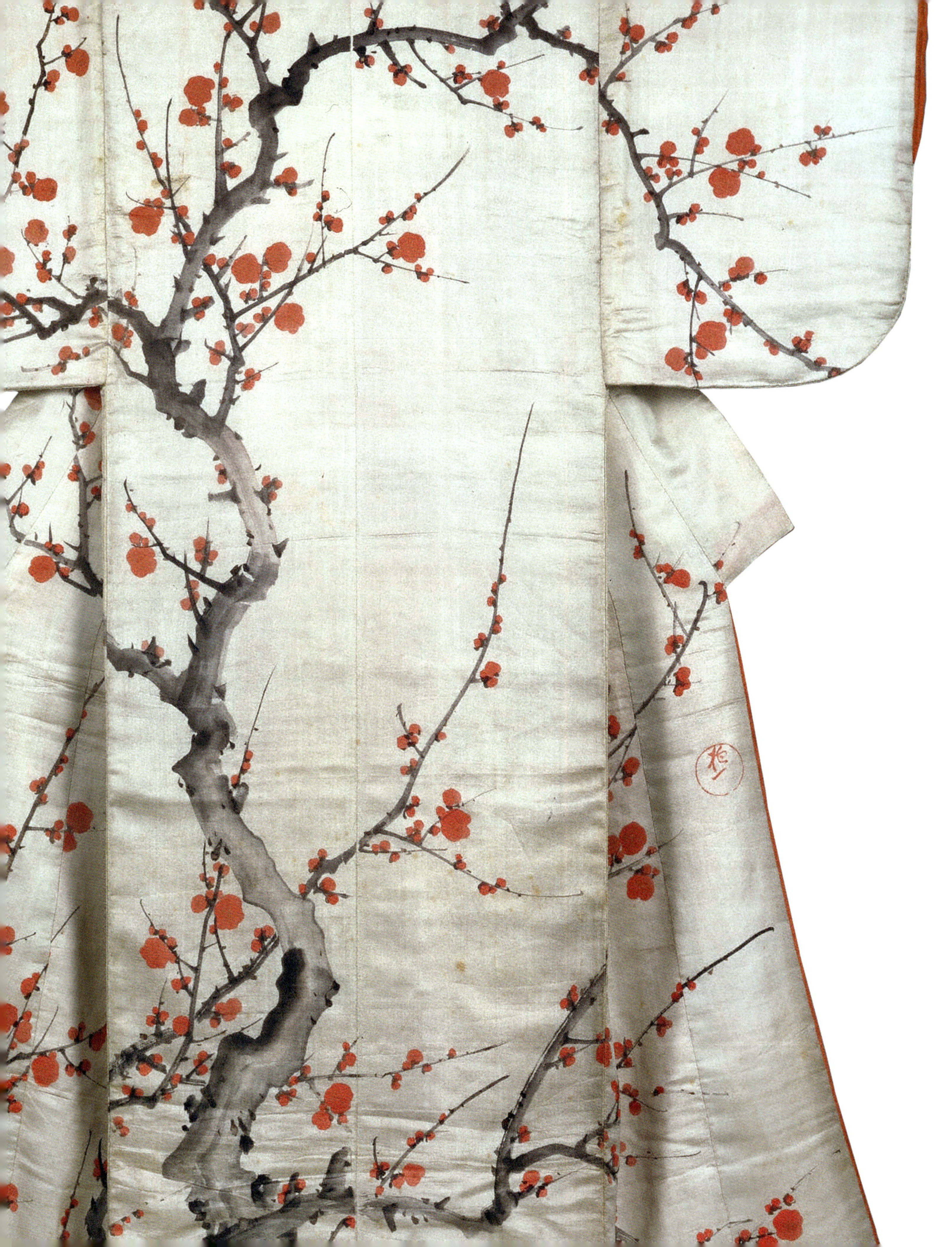

THE KIMONO AS JAPAN'S "CULTURAL PROPERTY"

Kikuchi Riyo

Detail of fig. 1, p. 25

The promulgation of the Japanese Law for the Protection of Cultural Properties (*Bunkazai hogo hō*) in 1950 provided a legal framework that redefined the Japanese kimono as one of the nation's "cultural properties." This law classified the country's cultural patrimony as having "tangible" (*yūkei*), "intangible" (*mukei*), and "folk" (*minzoku*) cultural properties, thereby establishing standards for the categorization of these objects. Certain tangible cultural properties, such as arts and crafts, were judged based on their "value to Japan's art or history," whereas other kinds of tangible cultural properties, such as historical documents, were evaluated in keeping with "their value to scholarship." Folk cultural properties were determined according to "whether or not they are crucial to the understanding of changes in the lifestyles of the Japanese over time."

The kimono, since 1950 a designated cultural property, represents all three of the above classifications—it is tangible (the actual historical kimono), intangible (with techniques such as *yūzen* paste-resist dyeing and embroidery), and folk (regional traditions)—and therefore challenges our understanding of this quintessential form of Japanese dress. In other words, the kimono embraces not only the tangible objects seen in museum exhibitions and collections but also extends to the intangible and the folk.[1] But what was the process by which the kimono came to be regarded as an object of national patrimony? This short essay considers the trajectory that has led to our appreciation of the kimono, a broad term meaning "thing to wear," as one of Japan's cultural properties.

First, however, it might be instructive to reflect on what the term "kimono" actually signifies and how is it used in present-day Japan. The country's most widely consulted dictionary, the *Large Dictionary of the Japanese Language* (*Nihon kokugo daijiten*, 2002), defines it variously as: 1) all clothing of the body, and 2) traditional Japanese clothing (*wafuku*) in contrast to Western-style clothing (*yōfuku*). In her examination of the usage of the word "kimono" in newspapers and magazines from 1874 to 1980, the textile historian Mori Rie discovered that it had divergent meanings and that the definition generally accepted today was only established in the 1970s.[2] Research by Fukai Akiko, also a textile historian, has also shown that in the West the term refers, in the first instance, to traditional Japanese clothing, and secondly to more general types of indoor and informal clothing that are associated with the image of the kimono.[3] As such, its connotation as an object of clothing differs depending on historical era and region.

But how was the term employed around the beginning of the Edo period (1603–1868) when this form of clothing was the daily dress of all Japanese? Interestingly, the *Vocabulário da Língua do Japão* (1603–4), a Japanese-Portuguese dictionary compiled by Jesuit missionaries, includes a range of definitions under the terms *qimono*, *coxiage*, and *qirumono*. These suggest that the word "kimono" was recognized as a general reference to clothing or a type of traditional garment known as *nagagi,* which had the basic shape of a *kosode*, or "small-sleeved" robe.[4] Mori Rie further observed that during the latter half of the nineteenth century, "kimono" still signified clothing more broadly, even as Western-style dress was being adopted as formal wear. This interpretation is underscored in educational publications of the period such as the 1883 *Model Texts for Primary School, Level One* (*Shōgaku sakubun zensho keikobon, kidenbun ikkyū*) and *Completed Texts for Primary School Composition, Level Six, Upper* (*Shōgaku sakubun zensho, roku jō*). After World War II, however, the meaning of the word shifted from the more encompassing connotation of clothing to the narrower definition of traditional Japanese garments in contradistinction to that worn in the West. This change concurred with the rapid acceptance of Western-style dress by the Japanese at this time.

With the advent of the twentieth century, there was a trend to treat the kimono as an object of artistic appreciation. Traditional items of clothing were among the pieces that daimyo families began to sell off at this time, as seen in the now celebrated *kosode* in the National Museum of Japanese History in Sakura, Chiba Prefecture, which has a design of a plum tree and spring grasses on white satin created by Sakai Hōitsu (1761–1828) (fig. 1). An auction catalogue in the collection of the Tokyo National Research Institute for Cultural Properties (Tōkyō Bunkazai Kenkyūjo or Tōbunken) records that the Ikeda daimyo family of Inaba Province (present-day Tottori Prefecture) sold this *kosode* on June 6, 1919 (fig. 2). From the 1910s to the 1930s, similar auction catalogues documented the sale of

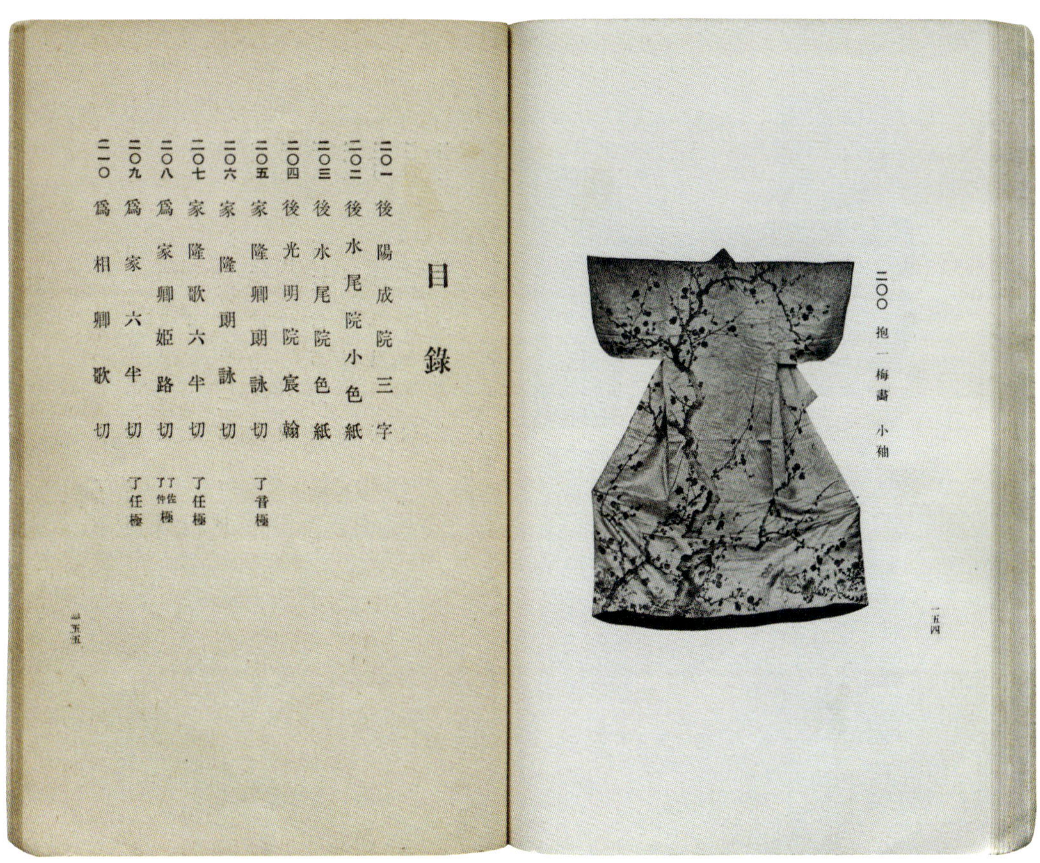

目錄

二〇一 後陽成院三字
二〇二 後水尾院小色紙
二〇三 後水尾院色紙
二〇四 後光明院宸翰
二〇五 家隆卿朗詠切 了音極
二〇六 家隆朗詠切
二〇七 家隆歌六半切 了任極
二〇八 爲家卿姫路切 了佐 了竹極
二〇九 爲家六半切 了任極
二一〇 爲相卿歌切

一五五

二〇〇 抱一梅畫 小袖

一五四

Fig. 2
Auction catalogue of the collection of the Ikeda daimyo family of Inaba Province, June 6, 1919, Tokyo National Research Institute for Cultural Properties (Tōbunken)

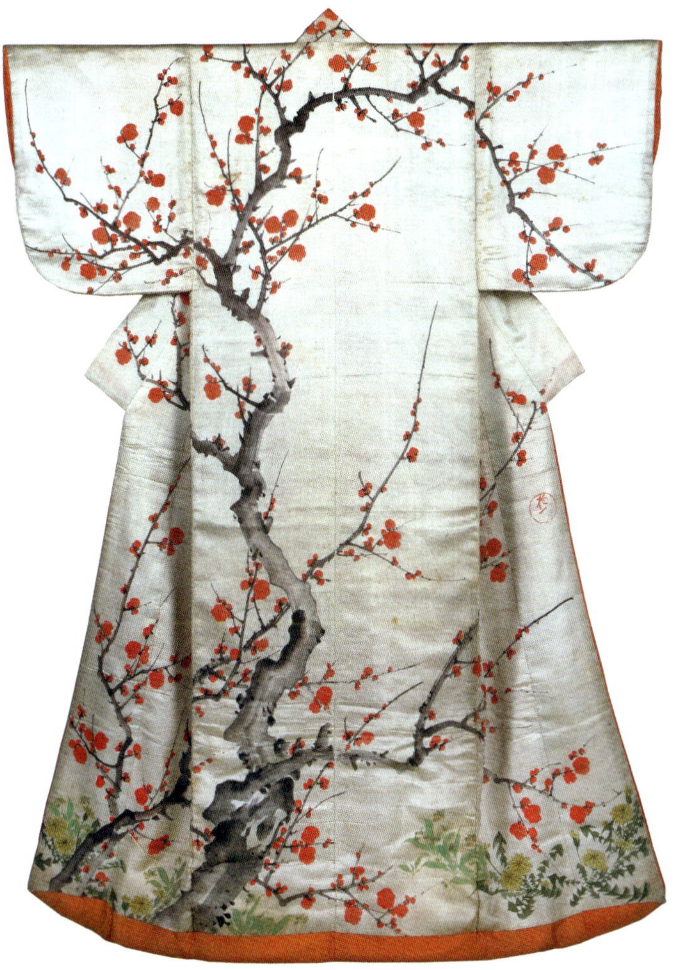

Fig. 1
Kosode with design of plum tree and spring grasses by Sakai Hōitsu, 19th century, Edo period, 1603–1868, white satin, National Museum of Japanese History, Sakura, Chiba Prefecture H-35-182

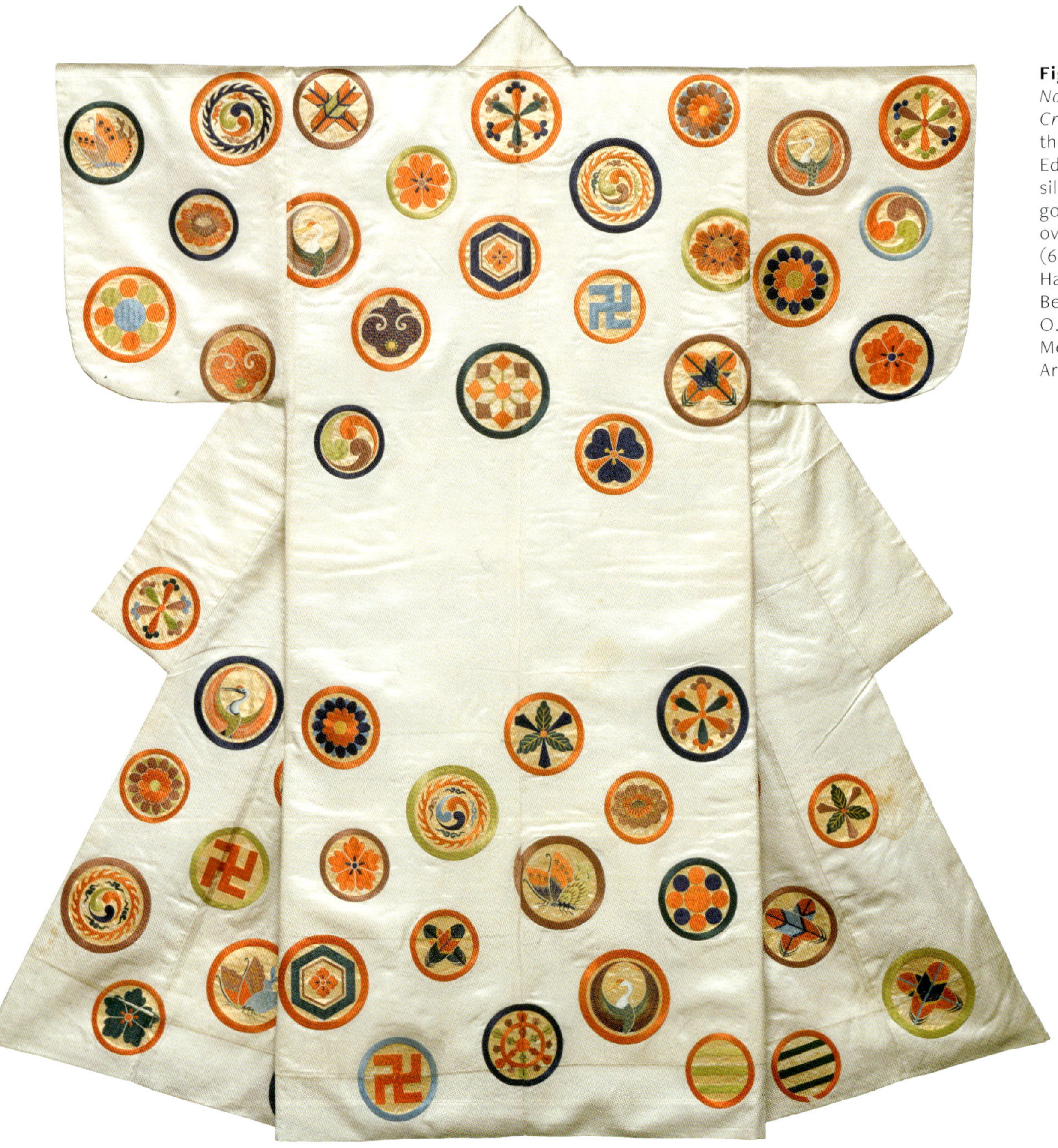

Fig. 3
Noh Costume with Scattered Crests, second half of the 18th to 19th century, Edo period, 1603–1868, silk embroidery and gold leaf on silk satin, overall: 165.1 × 135.9 cm (65 × 53 ½ in.), H. O. Havemeyer Collection, Bequest of Mrs. H. O. Havemeyer, 1929, Metropolitan Museum of Art, 29.100.541

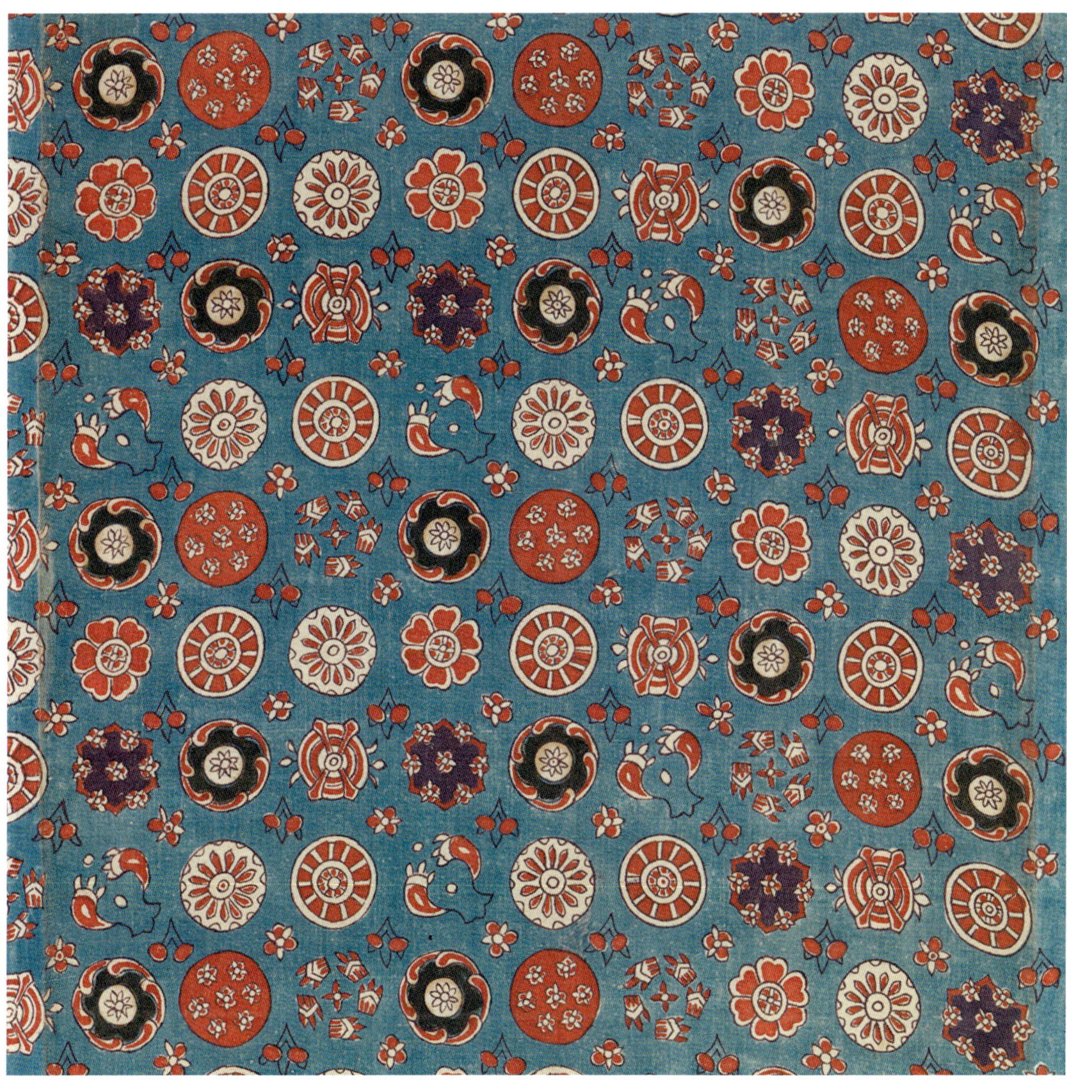

Fig. 4
Sarasa with Small Rosettes, 18th century, Edo period, 1603–1868, India (Coromandel Coast), cotton (painted resist and mordant, dyed), for the Japanese market, overall: 218.8 × 34.9 cm (86 ⅛ × 13 ¾ in.), Purchase, Friends of Asian Art Gifts, 2010, Metropolitan Museum of Art, 2010.57

conventional Japanese clothing listed under the terms *kosode*, *furisode* (long-sleeved robe), *uchikake* (formal overcoat), *katabira* (summer robe), kimono, *bingata* (Okinawan resist-dyed robe), and so forth. These types of Japanese garments were also marketed overseas through antiquities dealers, most notably the firm Yamanaka & Co., which had offices in the United States and Europe.

These auction catalogues elucidate the different ways that particular types of textiles were sold. Certain kinds of robes were dismantled, including examples from the Momoyama period (1573–1603), which utilized the *tsujigahana* technique that combined stitch-resist dyeing with painted ink decoration, or *kosode* of the Keichō era (1596–1615) with their dynamic patterns created through embroidery (*shishū*), foil, and other techniques. They were sold as textile fragments because of their intrinsic aesthetic appeal and used, among other things, as mountings for paintings. Traditional noh theater robes (fig. 3) or female clothing such as *katabira* and *yūzen*-decorated *kosode* were, by contrast, sold intact. Not only do these varied approaches in the sale of kimono textiles reveal how the artistry of traditional clothing was understood, but they also shed light on how kimono, previously viewed as articles of dress, were recast as artworks similar to painting, calligraphy, tea utensils, and noh masks. And textile collectors would now begin to collect these robes.

The art historian Oyama Yuzuruha notes that the collecting patterns of textiles during the premodern era were shifting in the early decades of the modern era corresponding with the Meiji period (1868–1912).[5] Until the later nineteenth century, for instance, the most sought-after textiles included rare foreign fabrics such as Indian chintz (*sarasa*) (fig. 4), fabrics used in the tea ceremony (*chanoyu*) as mounts for paintings and as bags to store tea utensils, as well as unusual examples of Chinese silks employed as wrapping cloths known as *meibutsu-gire* ("famous textile fragments"). In the modern period, however, kimono became reconceptualized from articles of clothing to art objects worthy of collecting. A number of cultural figures from all walks of Japanese society started to acquire kimono and kimono fragments, including the owner of the Daihiko drapery store, Noguchi Hikobei (1848–1925); the Japanese textile historian Nomura Shōjirō (1879–1943); the historian of Japanese dress and *shin-hanga* ("New Print") artist Yoshikawa

Kanpō (1894–1979); the Western-style (*yōga*) oil painter Okada Saburōsuke (1869–1939); the *shin-hanga* artist Itō Shinsui (1898–1972); and the *yūzen* artist Tabata Kihachi III (1877–1956). Business entrepreneurs and industrialists, including the traditional Kyoto draper Chiso—the subject of this publication—the department store Matsuzakaya, the textile company Kanebō, and the trading conglomerate Marubeni also formed kimono collections. Kimono in both private and corporate collections were thereafter regularly exhibited in museums.

The Tōbunken is an invaluable source for early auction catalogues, and since its opening in 1930 the institute has also collected domestic exhibition (and auction) catalogues that are available on its online database.[6] A search there of the words kimono, *kosode*, *senshoku* (textiles), *fukushoku* (clothing accessories), and *ishō* (performance robes) uncovers some 150 exhibition catalogues to demonstrate that from the 1920s to the 1950s textile-related exhibitions were being organized at the Kyoto and Tokyo imperial (now national) museums and at department stores, including the Mitsukoshi and Matsuya, located respectively in Tokyo's Nihonbashi and Ginza districts. What sorts of objects would have been on display? The *Catalogue for the Exhibition of Ancient Textiles* held at the Imperial Museum of Kyoto from October 12 to October 26, 1924, for instance, lists private, temple, and shrine holdings, such as noh robes, Buddhist vestments (*kesa*), ritual altar textiles (*uchishiki*), Indian chintz, and *meibutsu-gire*, together with kimono in general. The Imperial Museum of Kyoto also mounted shows of the Nomura Shōjirō textile collection that principally comprises kimono. The number of kimono exhibitions has gradually increased since the 1960s, a period that also coincided with shows concentrating on cotton folk textiles and items such as *futon* bedding influenced by the folk-art (*mingei*) movement. The ongoing popularity of kimono exhibitions in the 2010s, both in Japan and at institutions internationally, is testimony to the transitioning of kimono as objects of dress to objects distinguished as cultural properties and precious works of art.

There are many kimono preserved as cultural properties and works of art for which no records of their creators or wearers exist. Rare exceptions are robes with designs by artists such as the Rinpa artists Sakai Hōitsu (see fig. 1) and Ogata Kōrin (1658–1716), and examples in the Mitsui family collection in the Mitsui Memorial Museum in Tokyo with designs by Maruyama-school artists. These anonymous pieces are prized, not because of the "artist" but because they offer an idea about the standing of the "wearer" (and cultural/societal milieu) based on the style of the kimono and the techniques employed to make it.

During the Edo period, sumptuary laws were also enacted that affected the techniques and materials used to adorn kimono. The 1683 sumptuary regulation known as the Tenna-era Sumptuary Law (*Tenna no kinrei*), for instance, forbade the sale of robes decorated with embroidery or the labor-intensive technique of tie-resist dyeing (*shibori*) required to produce the elaborate *kanoko* (literally "fawn spots") pattern (cat. 4). In order to circumvent these laws new techniques were developed such as stenciled imitation tie-dyeing (*surihitta* or *kata-kanoko*) that resembled the visual effects of tie-resist dyeing (cat. 11). The combination of the desire to wear beautiful, refined clothing plus the extraordinary skill of artisans raised the level of textile artistry and resulted in the creation of diverse patterns and effects. Robes of the Momoyama and Edo periods that no longer function as items of dress are now found in museum collections, kept in storage facilities, and will therefore be transmitted to future generations as one of Japan's cultural properties.

A survey of the Tōbunken site also discloses that there were exhibitions from the 1930s featuring the work by contemporary textile artists, an indication of an emerging trend to recognize these individuals. Nakamura Katsuma (1894–1982), designated an "Artist of Important Intangible Cultural Property" (*Jūyō mukei bunkazai hojisha*) in 1955 for his work in *yūzen*-dyeing, began to sign his kimono in the same way that artists sign paintings, ceramics, or lacquerware.[7] This practice was continued by artists engaged in *yūzen* and stencil-dyeing techniques. Also, during the Meiji period Chiso was the first firm to engage artists, including the *nihonga* (Japanese-style painting) artists Sakakibara Bunsui (1825–1909), Kishi Chikudō (1826–97), Imao Keinen (1845–1924), Kubota Beisen (1852–1906), and Fujii Gyokushū (ca. 1860–1910) (cats. 14–21) to produce underdrawings for kimono designs. The inscription on the storage box of the pair of 1890 textile hanging scrolls designed by Kishi Chikudō, *Apprentice Maiko and Cherry Tree* and *Skull in the Moonlight*, also names the *yūzen* dyer Murakami Kahei and the embroiderer Kobayashi Kyūjirō (both dates unknown) (cat. 16). These advancements would further influence the process by which kimono came to be treasured not only as clothing but equally as art. This transition is also linked to the fact that in the modern era the techniques used to create kimono have themselves come to be valued as "art."

The history of the kimono also embraces its place as a form of folk cultural property, and this is grounded in the rich regional traditions of the Japanese archipelago that spans some 3,000 km from north to south. The dramatic variations in climate led to the development of myriad clothing materials and types to meet these conditions, and these would come to be designated as tangible folk cultural properties. During the mid-seventeenth century, for instance, dress, particularly that worn by farmers in the warmer regions, was primarily made from cotton, whereas in the colder climate of the northeastern Tōhoku region, bast-fiber clothing such as hemp or ramie (linen was then unknown) with stitched patterns (*sashiko*) in cotton thread predominated. Although hemp is well ventilated, the addition of stitched cotton adds layers that protect the wearer against the cold.

As noted above, the techniques used to create kimono are currently protected as intangible cultural properties. And while robes can be protected in storage facilities, the same cannot be said for the techniques employed in their fabrication—it is for this reason they are acknowledged as cultural properties. The money spent on kimono production in the 2010s has dropped to one-sixth of what it was during the 1970s.[8] So too, the environment within which the materials and tools previously adopted to create kimono has changed. For example, hemp fiber (*taima*), a conventional kimono material, is now difficult to produce because of the enforcement of the Cannabis Control Law (*Taima torishimari hō*). With the passage of time and shifting values, more and more traditional techniques are not being transmitted and are at risk of being lost.

The kimono identified today as cultural properties thus are not just objects kept in museums. How the intangible skills related to kimono production are passed on during Japan's Reiwa era, which began in 2019, should concern us. As Japanese sartorial culture is now centered around Western-style clothing, the kimono, once the standard form of dress, is now protected as a cultural property. How the kimono continues to be preserved, collected, and appreciated abroad as works of art, rather than as contemporary clothing, is of great consequence when considering the transmission and knowledge of Japanese tradition.

Translated by Yukio Lippit

Notes

1. It should be noted that the standards employed to categorize tangible and intangible cultural properties are the same.
2. Mori Rie, "Kindai ni okeru 'kimono' no hyōkihō to sono imi no hensen—1874 nen–1980 nen no shinbun kiji o chūshin ni—," *Nihon kasei gakkaishi* 66 (2015): 197–212.
3. Fukai Akiko, "Kimono no chikara—seiyō no deai to eikyō," in *Kimono Beauty—shikku de modan na yosōi no bi Edo kara Shōwa*, ed. Nagasaki Iwao (Tokyo: Tōkyō Bijutsu, 2013), 35–39.
4. I consulted the Japanese translation of this text; see Dōi Tadao et al., eds., *Hōyaku Nippo jisho* (Tokyo: Iwanami Shoten, 1980). The *Vocabulário da Língua do Japão* was published in the port city of Nagasaki and includes Portuguese definitions of some 32,000 Japanese words.
5. Oyama Yuzuruha, "Senshoku korekushon no rekishi," in "Senshoku korekushon no keifu," special issue, *Me no me* 505 (2018): 22–34.
6. See www.tobunken.go.jp/archives.
7. Todate Kazuko, *Nakamura Katsuma to Tōkyō yūzen no keifu* (Tokyo: Senshoku to Seikatsusha, 2007).
8. A discussion of prices can be found in the publication Wasō Shinkō Kenkyūkai, ed., *Wasō Shinkō Kenkyūkai hōkokusho* (Tokyo: Keizai Sangyōshō Seizō Sangyōkyoku Sen'i-ka, 2015).

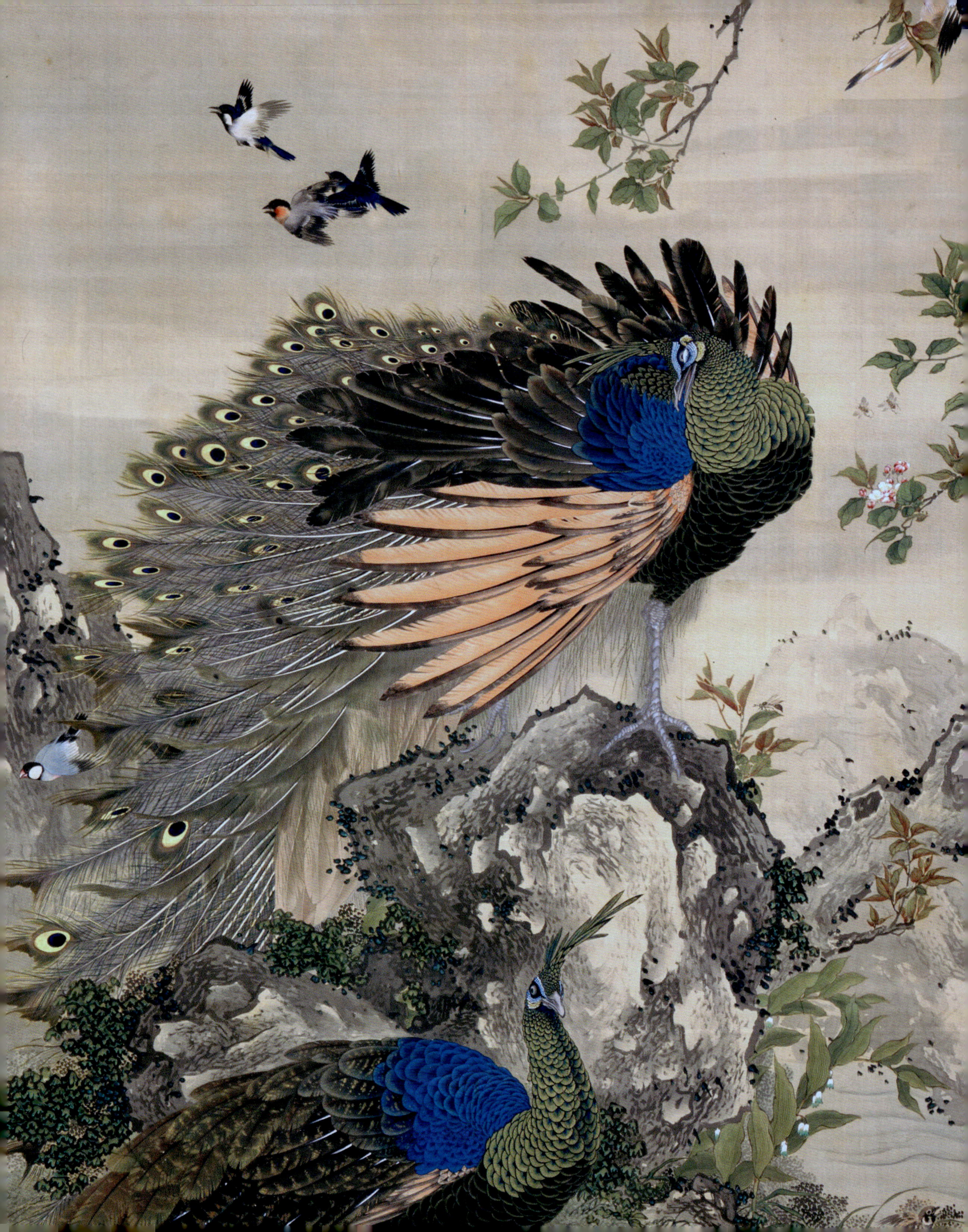

THE TURNING POINT

Kishi Chikudō's *Ōtsu and Karasaki* Screens

Yukio Lippit

Detail of fig. 4, p. 34

Among the many notable artworks in the collection of the traditional Kyoto draper Chiso, the pair of eight-panel folding screens by Kishi Chikudō (1826–97) entitled *Ōtsu and Karasaki* (fig. 1) is perhaps the most impressive. Its expansive, laterally unfolding surface—each screen measures over 4 m from side to side—offers a panoramic view of two sites on the shores of Lake Biwa, Japan's largest freshwater lake situated northeast of Kyoto. The right screen portrays Ōtsu, a bustling port city that served as the lake's main entrepot for trade and travel during the premodern era, while the left screen depicts an ancient pine tree that stood as a famous natural landmark at Karasaki, a small cape along Biwa's shoreline.

Ōtsu and Karasaki was completed in the year 1876, and in its own time would have been understood as radically innovative and closely associated with Western pictorialism. Firstly, although its choice of subject matter pairs two well-known sites linked to Lake Biwa, this pairing deviates from the conventional theme of the "Eight Views of Ōmi Province" (*Ōmi hakkei*), which was the traditional framework within which the scenery of Lake Biwa was imagined in cultural representation (see cat. 9).[1] Although the "Pine at Karasaki" was one of these "Eight Views," rarely was it offered as the sole subject of a large folding screen in this manner; a straightforward rendering of the merchant warehouses of Ōtsu, meanwhile, is unknown in earlier Japanese painting. Secondly, *Ōtsu and Karasaki* effectively conveys its vistas through the setting of a low horizon line, a technique derived from European linear perspective and only widely embraced in Japan with the advent of landscape prints by the *ukiyo-e* artists Katsushika Hokusai (1760–1849) and Utagawa Hiroshige (1797–1858) from the 1830s onward. Until *Ōtsu and Karasaki*, no large-scale work had featured the dropped horizon so dramatically to generate such a powerful sense of thereness on the part of the viewer. Thirdly, both screens are characterized by a specificity of time. The right screen portrays the port at the break of dawn on a winter morning, with frosty mist hovering in the air and a thin layer of snow dusting the warehouse rooftops. Aurora is countered with twilight in the left screen, where the venerable pine is set against a landscape of advancing nightfall and a full moon visible low on the horizon. In both scenes, black *sumi* ink, vegetal dyes, an abundance of gold and silver paint, and shell white pigment (*gofun*) are mobilized to create subtle atmospheric effects resonant of the transitional moments of sunrise and sundown. In one, the air fills with the accumulating radiance of the rising sun, in the other the aqueous surface bruises over as it reflects the slowly dimming light of nightfall (figs. 2–3). Materiality and temporality are evocatively conjoined. It should come as little surprise that *Ōtsu and Karasaki* is universally considered to be Chikudō's masterpiece.

The creation of *Ōtsu and Karasaki* came at a crucial turning point for its artist. Indeed, the life of Kishi Chikudō can be understood as spanning two disparate careers; the first as the fourth-generation head of the traditional Kishi painting lineage, and the second as a key figure in Kyoto's emerging modern art world.

Born in 1826 in the castle town of Hikone, along the shores of Lake Biwa, Chikudō was the son of a low-ranking samurai named Terai Magojirō Shigenobu (dates unknown). Because he was the third son, Chikudō was destined for a career outside of domainal administration like his father, and a life in painting appears to have been chosen for him early on. In 1842, at the age of sixteen, he entered the atelier of Kano Eigaku (1790–1867), an established painter who was part of a prestigious lineage of painters-in-attendance to the elite status groups going back centuries.[2] Apparently Chikudō did not take to the Kano method, however, and he eventually found his way to the studio of Kishi Renzan (1805–59). Renzan was the third-generation head of the Kishi lineage of painting, which traced its origins back to Renzan's teacher, the dynamic Ganku (1749/56–1838) (fig. 4).[3] During the 1780s Ganku moved to Kyoto and joined the studio of Maruyama Ōkyo (1733–95), the most successful Kyoto painter of the era. Through his teacher Ganku gained entrée to imperial circles, in particular, the aristocratic Arisugawa family, and became the rare Edo-period painter to achieve his own court rank. Chikudō entered Renzan's studio only several years after Ganku's demise, but the stature of the Kishi school had been firmly secured. As an apprentice under Renzan, Chikudō played a role in the refurbishment of mural decor for important sites such as Nijō Castle and even the Imperial Palace during the 1850s. Chikudō rose to become

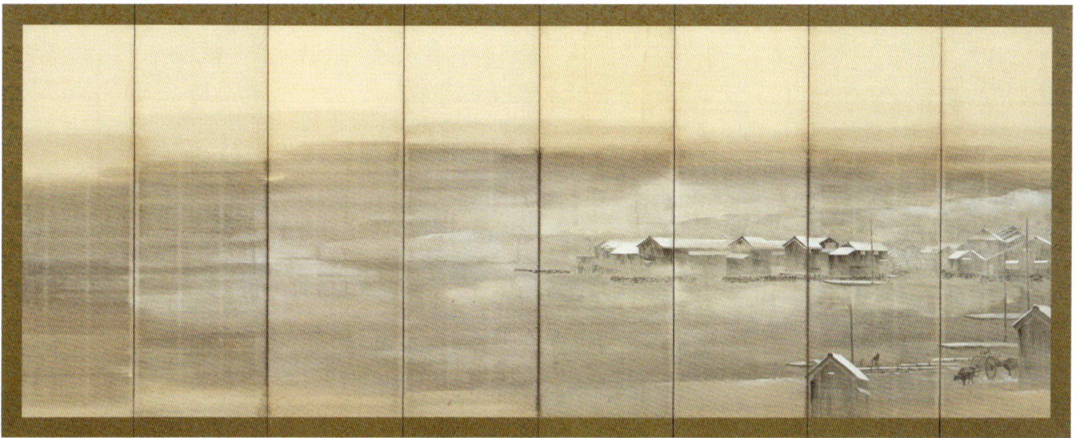

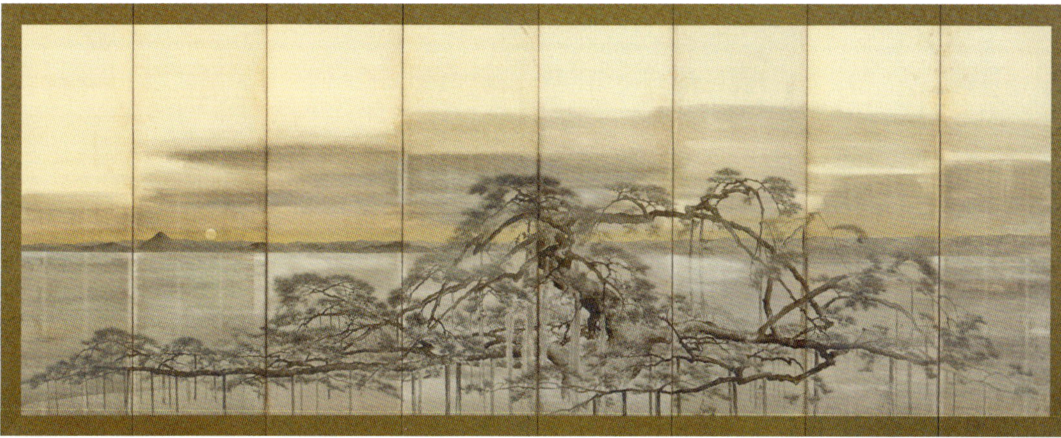

Fig. 1
Kishi Chikudō, *Ōtsu and Karasaki* (bottom and top), dated ca. 1876, pair of eight-panel folding screens; ink, colors, gold and silver on paper, 158 × 422 cm (62 3/16 × 166 1/8 in.), Chiso Collection, Kyoto

Figs. 2–3
Kishi Chikudō, *Ōtsu and Karasaki*, details of the pair of eight-panel folding screens; ink, colors, gold and silver on paper

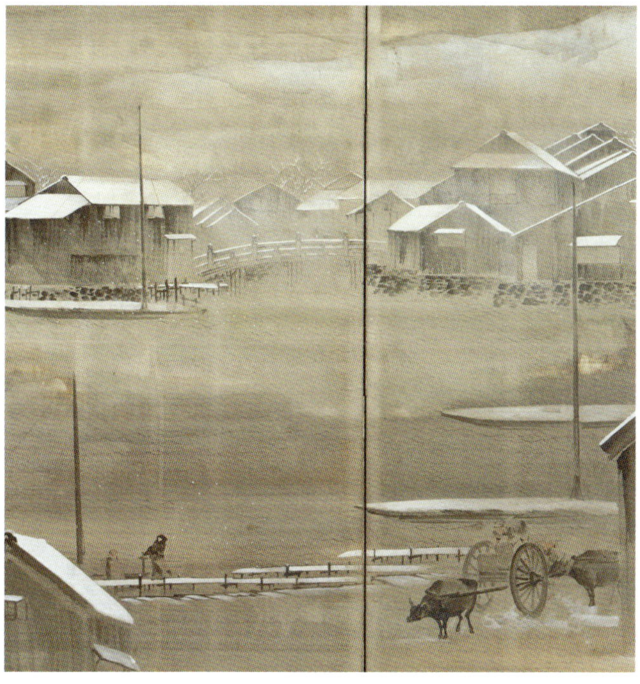

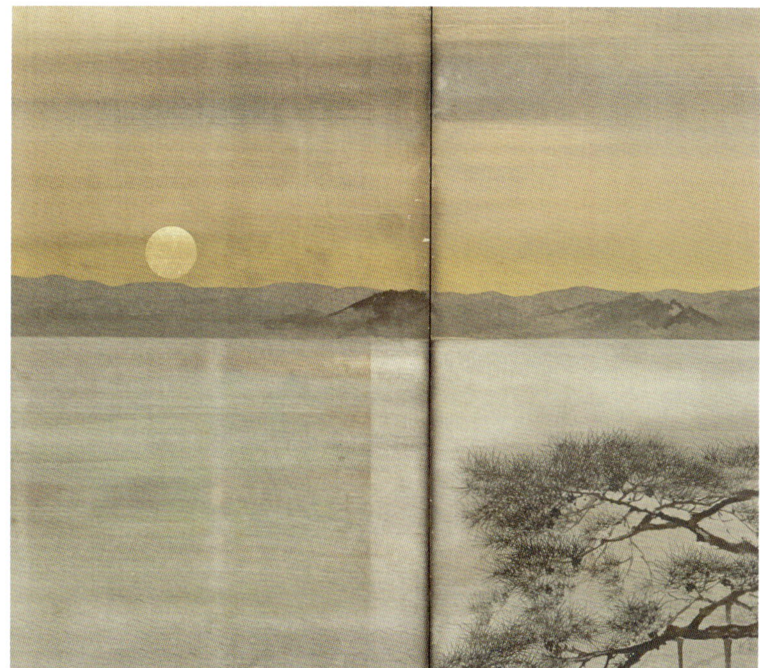

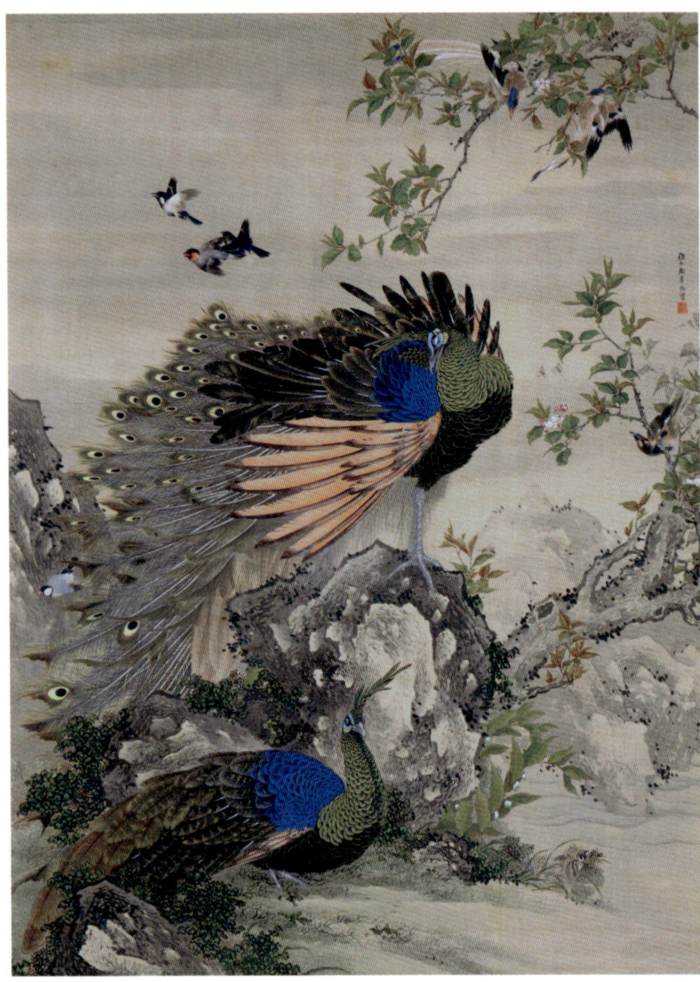

Fig. 4
Ganku, *Peacock*, late 18th or early 19th century, hanging scroll; ink and colors on silk, 191.7 × 144.2 cm (75 ½ × 56 13/16 in.), Chiso Collection, Kyoto

Renzan's foremost disciple, and in 1857 he was appointed painter-in-attendance to the Arisugawa. He was so favorably looked upon by his teacher that Renzan named him his successor in 1859 over his own son.

Chikudō thus assumed headship of one of the most prestigious schools of painting in Kyoto at the time. As was the case with the majority of painters for the elite, however, Chikudō's fortunes took a turn for the worse during the years before and after the Meiji Restoration of 1868, when the Tokugawa shogunate was overthrown and a new government established in the name of the Japanese emperor. The tumult leading up to regime change proved disastrous for Chikudō. His teacher Renzan died in 1860, and four years later, Chikudō's home was destroyed by fire in the Forbidden Gate Incident (Kinmon no hen), in which a group of imperial loyalists sought to topple the shogunate. Chikudō lost his entire cache of model paintings and sketchbooks, materials that were crucial to his practice and studio pedagogy. Further tribulations ensued after the Restoration. Having lost his patronage base, Chikudō attempted to support himself through a number of failed endeavors, including the management of an inn, the founding of a candle shop, and the sale of mosquito nets.[4]

It was at this moment, the nadir of Chikudō's career, that the painter encountered the textile wholesale dealer Nishimura Sōzaemon XII (1855–1935) in 1873. The year before, at the age of seventeen, Nishimura had become the twelfth-generation head of the Chiso merchant house with roots extending back to the sixteenth century, although then in the midst of reform.[5] Initially Chikudō served as Nishimura's art teacher, but in 1874 was persuaded to make designs for his fabrics that were transposed into patterns of embroidery (*shishū*) and the traditional *yūzen*-dyeing technique.

Chikudō's collaboration with Chiso catalyzed his career. In 1880, he was appointed to the faculty of the newly established Kyoto Prefectural School of Painting (Kyōto-fu Gagakkō), the forerunner of today's Kyoto City University of the Arts (Kyōto Shiritsu Geijutsu Daigaku). At around this time, Chikudō also began to design images for the textiles of Iida Shinshichi III (d. 1909) and his Takashimaya department store (cats. 1–2).[6] Meanwhile, the artist regularly exhibited at both domestic and international expositions, including the second Domestic Competitive Painting Exhibition (Naikoku Kaiga Kyōshinkai) of 1884 and the third Domestic Industrial Exposition (Naikoku Kangyō Hakurankai) of 1890, where he garnered critical acclaim. These public acknowledgments would culminate in Chikudō winning a Bronze Medal at the World's Columbian Exposition at Chicago in 1893. In 1896, a year before his death, Chikudō was appointed an Imperial Household Artist (Teishitsu Gigei-in). He would go on to be remembered as a key figure in the transition to modernity of the Kyoto painting world.[7]

Ōtsu and Karasaki, then, can be positioned at the pivot between Chikudō's two careers, the first as a head of the Kishi lineage during the Edo period (1603–1868), and the second as a painter, designer, and instructor in the Meiji period (1868–1912). Although the circumstances surrounding its commission are unclear, the approximate time line of its creation can be determined thanks to the archive of Chikudō's sketches preserved in the Kyoto Institute of Technology (Kyōto Kōgei Sen'i Daigaku). Among these are four preparatory sketches (*shita-e*) for *Ōtsu and Karasaki* (figs. 5–8). Not only do they provide insight into the

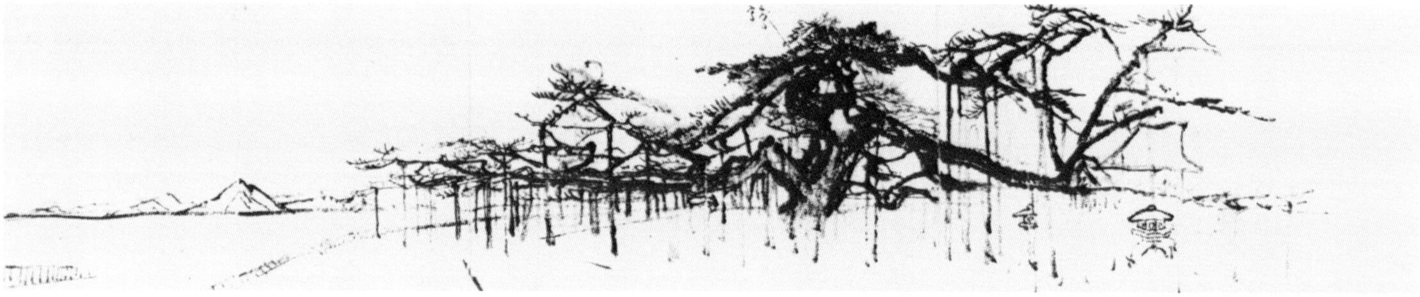

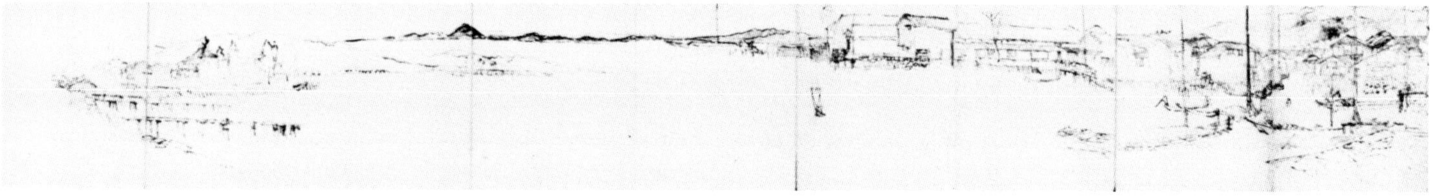

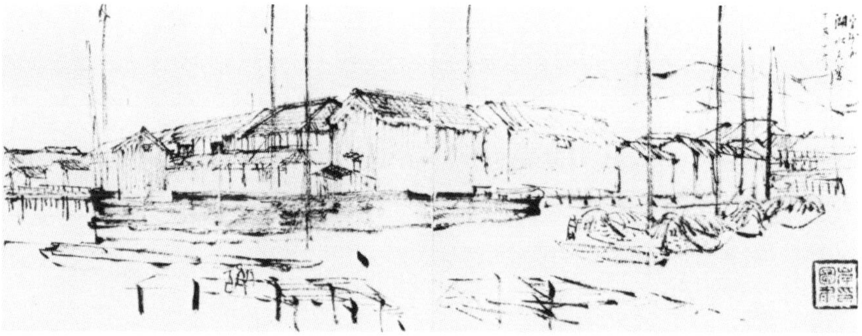

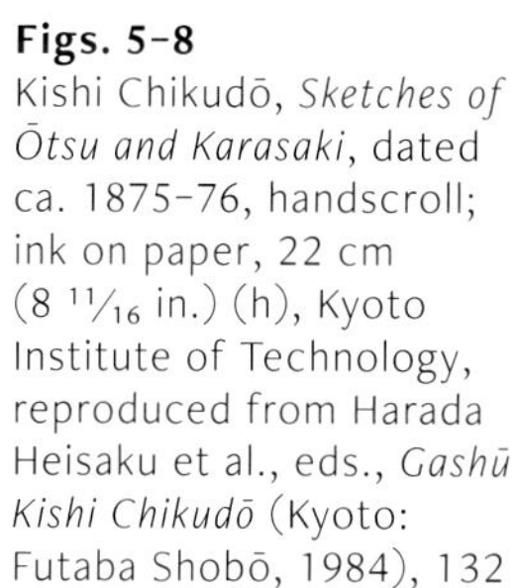

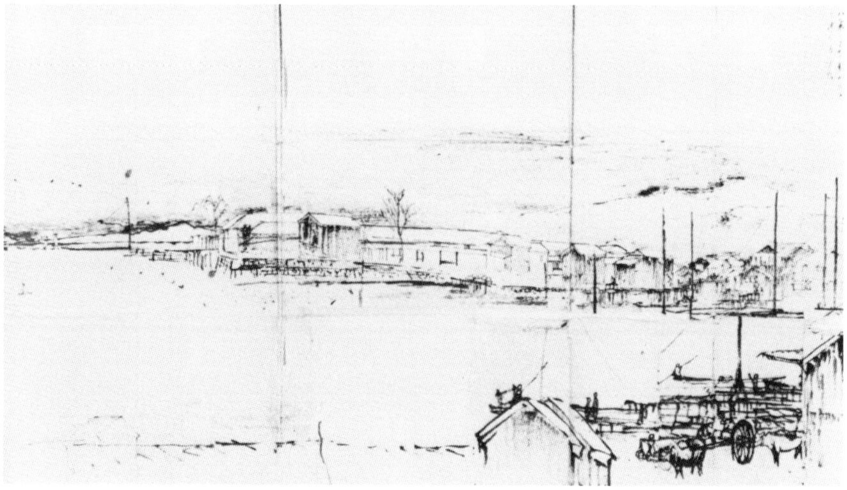

Figs. 5–8
Kishi Chikudō, *Sketches of Ōtsu and Karasaki*, dated ca. 1875–76, handscroll; ink on paper, 22 cm (8 $^{11}/_{16}$ in.) (h), Kyoto Institute of Technology, reproduced from Harada Heisaku et al., eds., *Gashū Kishi Chikudō* (Kyoto: Futaba Shobō, 1984), 132

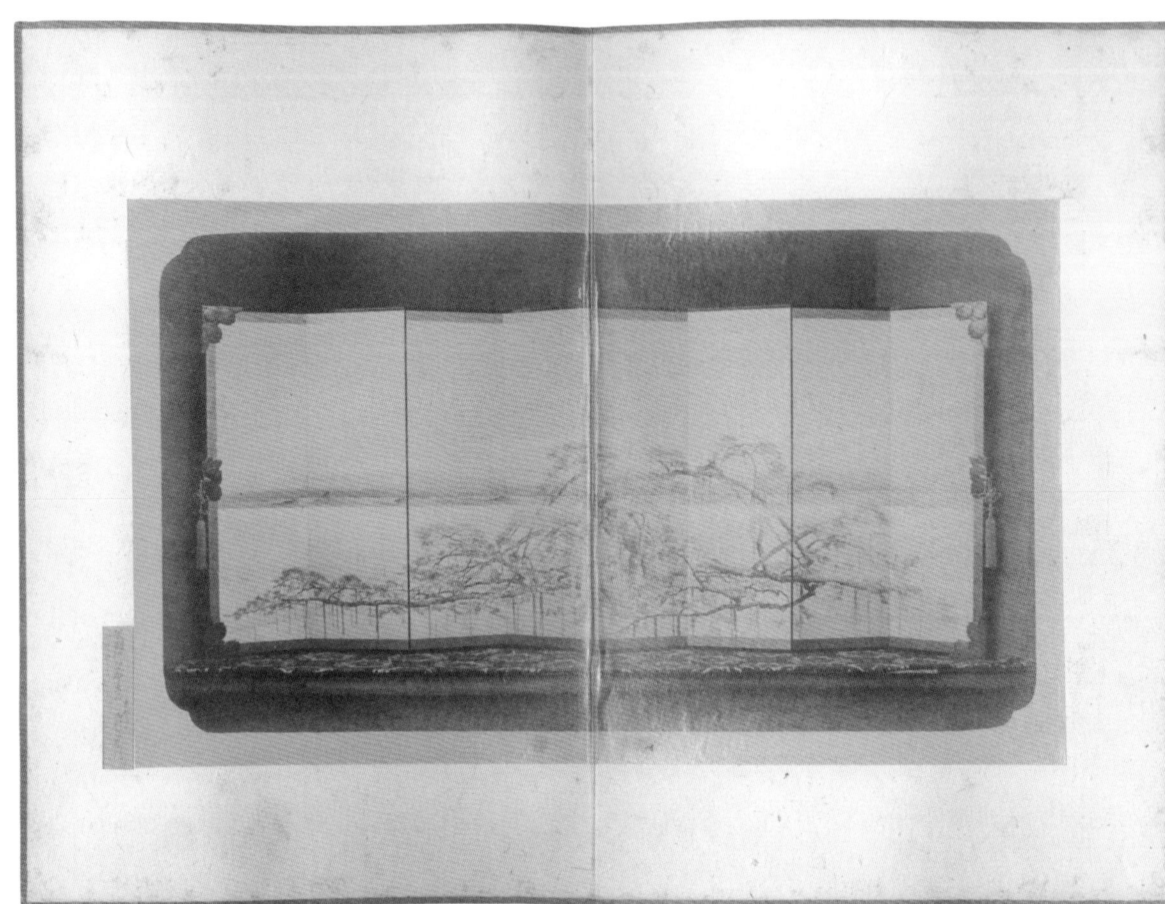

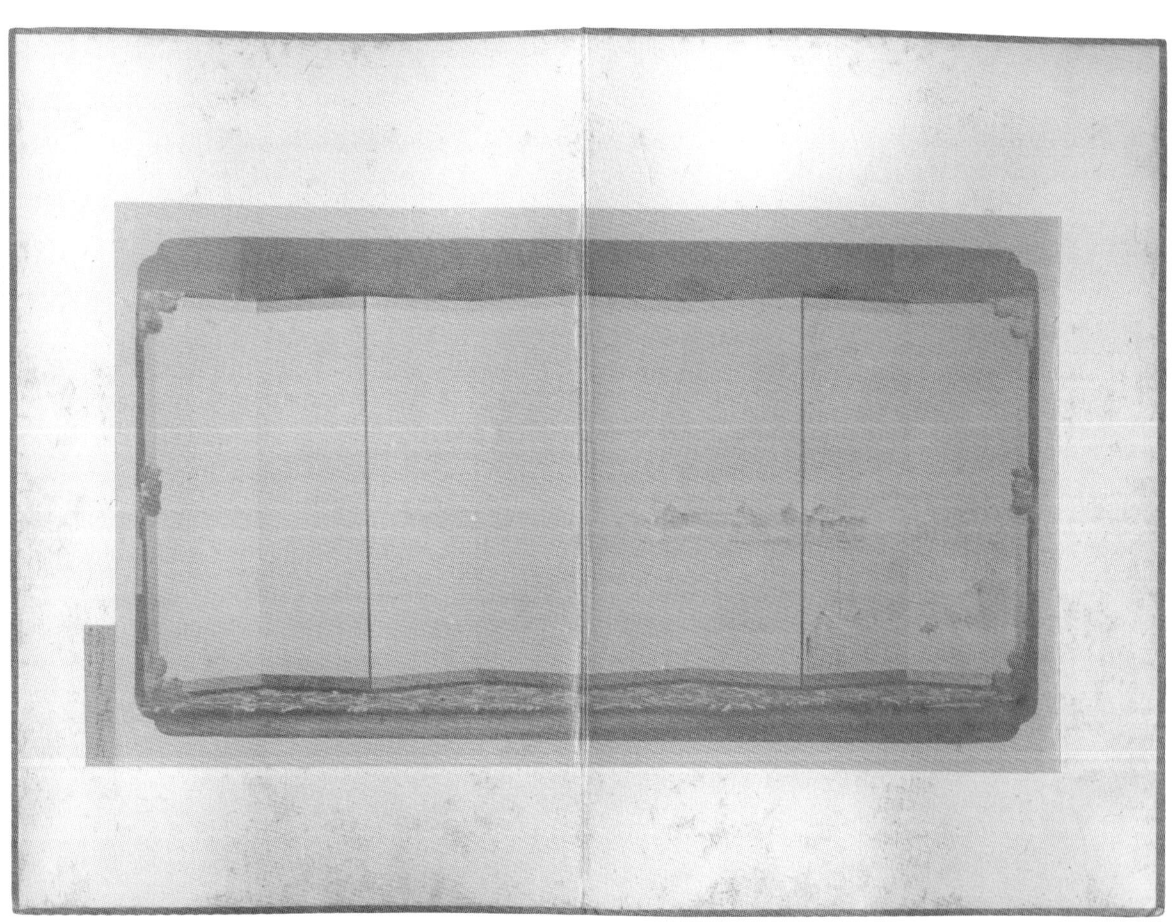

Figs. 9–10
Photographs of *Ōtsu and Karasaki* by Kishi Chikudō, from an unpublished album with a cover label reading "Meiji 8 [1875], Works for Display at the American Government Exposition," Chiso Collection, Kyoto

artist's preparation and engineering of the pictorial composition, but one of them is inscribed with the words "[Meiji] 8th year, winter, 11th month, 26th day, snowy dawn at the Great Bridge of Ōtsu," indicating that the sketch was done late in the year 1875 (Meiji 8).[8] The inscription suggests that Chikudō was making sketches in the Lake Biwa region during the winter of 1875 and that the screen must have been completed soon thereafter.

Ōtsu and Karasaki was one of the rare Japanese screen paintings to be included in the Philadelphia Centennial International Exhibition of May 10–November 10, 1876. Although the piece is not listed in the official catalogue to the exhibition, its display can be confirmed in a photo album of Nishimura's works sent to Philadelphia that is today in the Chiso collection (figs. 9–10).[9] It is likely that Nishimura commissioned the screens precisely for this purpose, as he is known to have been an active participant in the exhibition, sending over two hundred fabrics that showcased embroidered and *yūzen*-dyed designs, many of which must have been based on Chikudō's underdrawings. Of the items Nishimura sent to Philadelphia were several folding screens that included textile fragments composed of different types of historical weaving and dyeing techniques.[10] *Ōtsu and Karasaki* was apparently intended to augment and ornament the virtuosity of Japanese artisans overseas.

As an ambassador of Japanese painting in Philadelphia, *Ōtsu and Karasaki* can once again be said to mark a key turning point in Chikudō's career. Not only was it created in the wake of Chikudō's work as a designer for Nishimura and Chiso but it also embodies a number of revealing shifts taking place in Japanese painting as a whole during the heady early years of the Meiji period. Its manifestation of these changes can be summarized in the following observations. The unusual scale of *Ōtsu and Karasaki*—most large folding screens in premodern Japan spanned six, as opposed to eight, panels—presupposes a culture of public exhibition. Such exhibitions were virtually unknown in premodern Japan, when paintings were typically displayed in semiprivate spaces or intimate settings for specific occasions such as the visit of a guest, the *chanoyu* tea ceremony, a religious ritual, or temple airing.[11] From the mid-nineteenth century onward, however, as Japan participated with increasing frequency in international expositions and organized their domestic equivalents, painting would gradually internalize modern exhibition culture and adjust its dimensions, materiality, and compositional profile accordingly. *Ōtsu and Karasaki* stands as an early example of a Japanese painting that anticipates viewership by larger audiences in more capacious institutional spaces.

Ōtsu and Karasaki also manifests a new modality of landscape in the context of Japanese painting. While natural scenery was of course not unknown before the Meiji period, its frameworks of meaning and compositional schema differed, ranging from blue-green landscape screens that served as a backdrop for poetic composition to panoramic views of shrine precincts for ritual use, literati landscapes (*sansui*, or "mountain-land," paintings) that expressed an eremitic ideal, and "famous-place" (*meisho*) pictures that pictorialized the cultural and historical narratives associated with a given site. Slowly over the course of the Edo period, with the influence of European pictorialism, aspects of the Western genre of landscape were integrated into these visual systems of meaning. This integration was invariably linked to the embrace of single-point perspective and its presupposition of a single viewing position with a fixed relationship to the scene, as in the landscape prints of Hiroshige. One might say that *Ōtsu and Karasaki* scales up and dramatizes this relationship under the newly emerging display conditions of modern Japan. Indeed, the English word "landscape" is an inadequate translation for many of the pictorial genres of natural scenery practiced in premodern Japan, and the philosopher Karatani Kōjin has noted the epistemological quandary of having to define retroactively these genres after the shift in perception engendered by the domestication of the Western idea of landscape.[12] In this regard, Chikudō's screens, in their rejection of the traditional "famous-place" rubric such as the "Eight Views of Ōmi Province" for the rendering of Lake Biwa imagery, represent an early and notable instance of what Karatani refers to as Japan's "discovery of landscape."

And finally, *Ōtsu and Karasaki* showcases the newly prominent role of *plein-air* sketches in the preparation of a Japanese painting. Upon first glance this should come as little surprise, as the direct observation of nature has been associated with Japanese painting practice for many centuries.

The degree to which nature sketches were reflected in the final product, however, could vary and was generally minimal. The shogunal painter Kano Tan'yū (1602–74), for instance, left numerous drawings of rare plants and vegetables, as well as sketches of Mt. Fuji made while traveling between Kyoto and Edo, but these studies left little imprint on his pictorial production.[13] Similarly, while Maruyama Ōkyo has conventionally been understood as basing much of his approach to picture-making around the study of nature, the fruits of his preparation were typically applied to traditional subject matter and combined with highly decorative pictorial schemes. In contrast to these examples, *Ōtsu and Karasaki* projects a direct relationship to the artist's on-site experiences of its scenery.

With its less mediated relationship to its *plein-air* origins, the Chiso screens mark an important shift in the status of the direct observation of nature in Japanese painting. The establishment of European-style art schools during the late nineteenth century, most notably at the Technical Fine Arts School (Kōbu Bijutsu Gakkō, est. 1876), the Kyoto Prefectural School of Painting (est. 1880), and Tokyo School of Fine Arts (Tōkyō Bijutsu Gakkō, est. 1889), introduced a formalized curriculum of Western art education and ensured that sketching from life would be equated with advanced art-making. It came to be designated in Japanese by the word *shasei*, engendering a shift in the meaning of this term. *Shasei* had been a mainstay of the traditional lexicon of East Asian painting theory for centuries, and traditionally could refer to a wide range of practices through which a painter attempted to convey the vitality of her or his subject.[14] The term was used in contrast to *sha-i*, which suggested the transmission of the concept or (literary) idea of a subject in pictorial terms.[15] During the Meiji period, amid the influx of new modes of reproduction with a higher reality index and the increasing presence of Western art pedagogy, *shasei* came to be associated almost exclusively with the practice of sketching from life or outdoors.

This new conceptualization of progressive art practices inflected narratives of Japanese art history that were being authored during the late nineteenth and early twentieth centuries. Sketching from life was framed as an indigenous practice whose greatest advocate was Ōkyo. As Julia Sapin writes, Ōkyo was "recast as an artistic revolutionary in the nineteenth century, offered to both domestic Japanese audiences and foreign audiences as a symbol of an indigenous Japanese naturalism emblematic of cultural and artistic ingenuity, a form of artistic modernism."[16] This framing of Ōkyo enabled Meiji art critics to understand the new artistic practices of the era as being just as much native as foreign and to conceive of advanced painting of the era in a continuum with Edo art-making.[17]

The meteoric rise during the Meiji period of *shasei* as a valorized indigenous practice, along with the overattention paid to Tokyo's art schools, has obscured the importance of "transitional" Kyoto painters such as Kishi Chikudō, who from the 1870s onward demonstrated a willingness to experiment with and intensify traditional approaches. At the same time, however, his innovations were catalyzed by a unique partnership with Nishimura Sōzaemon XII and Chiso, and can be situated at the convergence of a number of historical and cultural factors, including the demise of Edo-period painting lineages and their patrons, the dawning culture of public exhibition, and the inexorable pull of foreign markets for Japanese crafts. These factors are all apparent in the visual profile of *Ōtsu and Karasaki*: the abandonment of traditional, poetry-based frameworks for the visualization of Lake Biwa; the intensive use of metallic pigments to convey atmosphere; and the unmediated influence of on-site sketches to its final appearance. And these qualities reflect an early and compelling way of reimagining Japanese painting as it began to attract new types of viewers, in distant lands, with unknown sensibilities.

Notes

1. Much has been written on the theme of the "Eight Views of Ōmi Province." For a survey of paintings on this subject, see the exhibition catalogue: Ōtsu City Museum of History, ed., *Ōmi hakkei—kokoku no fūkō, Nihon no shokei—* (Ōtsu: Ōtsu-shi Rekishi Hakubutsukan, 2004).
2. By age eleven Chikudō was already studying the fundamentals of Japanese painting with the Hikone domainal painter-in-attendance Nakashima Antai (dates unknown). On the Kano house of painting, see Yukio Lippit, "The Painter-in-Attendance," in *The Artist in Edo*, ed. Yukio Lippit (Washington, DC: Center for Advanced Study in the Visual Arts, 2018), 23–46.
3. Two exhibition catalogues offer useful introductions to the Kishi lineage: *Kishi-ha to sono keifu—Ganku kara Kishi Chikudō e*—(Rittō: Rittō Rekishi Minzoku Hakubutsukan, 2006) and *Kyōto gadan Kishi-ha no tenkai* (Tsuruga: Tsuruga Shiritsu Hakubutsukan, 2015).
4. For an earlier thorough overview of Chikudō's life, see Ōhashi Tsuneyasu, "Kishi Chikudō," in *Gashū Kishi Chikudō*, ed. Harada Heisaku et al. (Kyoto: Futaba Shobō, 1984), 169–85.
5. See Hiroko T. McDermott, "The Pleasure and Pain of Being the Front-Runner: The Nishimura Sōzaemon House (Chisō) in the Meiji Period," in *Threads of Silk and Gold: Ornamental Textiles from Meiji Japan*, ed. Hiroko T. McDermott and Clare Pollard (Oxford: Ashmolean Museum, 2012), 41–52.
6. The precise date of their collaboration is unclear. See Hiroko T. McDermott, "The Way of the Newcomer: A History of the Iida Shinshichi House (Takashimaya)," in McDermott and Pollard, eds., *Threads of Silk and Gold*, 55–65.
7. The most recent survey of Chikudō's career and oeuvre is Museum of Modern Art Shiga, ed., *Kishi Chikudō—kindai Kyōto gadan no yo-ake* (Ōtsu: Shiga Kenritsu Kindai Bijutsukan, 1987).
8. Chikudō's sketches in the context of his painting are examined by Ōhashi Tsuneyasu, "Kishi Chikudō no shita-e ni tsuite," *Kyōto Kōgei Sen'i Daigaku Kōgei Gakubu kenkyū hōkoku jinbun* 28 (1979): 37–65.
9. Although the label lists the year 1875, it is assumed that this refers to the compilation of the catalogue before the works were sent abroad.
10. For a list of Nishimura's display items, see Tōkyō Kokuritsu Bunkazai Kenkyūjo, ed., *Meiji-ki Bankoku Hakurankai bijutsuhin shuppin mokuroku* (Tokyo: Chūō Kōron Bijutsu Shuppan, 1997), 213.
11. An exception can be made for the semipublic exhibitions in the Higashiyama mountains of Kyoto during the 1790s, or the viewings of paintings and calligraphy known as *shogakai* among literati of the early to the middle nineteenth century.
12. Karatani Kōjin, *Origins of Modern Japanese Literature* (Durham and London: Duke University Press, 1993), 17–22.
13. See illustrations of Tan'yū's sketches of flowers and plants in Nakamura Tanio, ed., *Kano Tan'yū sōbokuka shasei* (Kyoto: Shikōsha, 1977). Tan'yū's Mt. Fuji sketches are discussed in Yukio Lippit, *Painting of the Realm: The Kano House of Painters in 17th-Century Japan* (Seattle: University of Washington Press, 2012).
14. Kōno Motoaki, "Edo jidai shasei kō," in *Nihon kaigashi no kenkyū*, ed. Yamane Yūzō-sensei Koki Kinenkai (Tokyo: Yoshikawa Kōbunkan, 1989), 387–428, and Kōno Motoaki, "Shasei no gensen—Chūgoku," in *Akiyama Terukazu-hakase koki kinen bijutsushi ronbunshū*, ed. Akiyama Terukazu-hakase Koki Kinen Ronbunshū Kankōkai (Kyoto: Benridō, 1991), 479–514.
15. For a study of the modern transformation of the Chinese term *xieyi*, the equivalent to *sha-i*, see Eugene Wang, "Sketch Conceptualism as Modernist Contingency," in *Chinese Art: Modern Expressions*, ed. Maxwell Hearn and Judith Smith (New York: The Metropolitan Museum of Art, 2001), 102–61.
16. Julia Sapin, "Naturalism Fusing Past and Present: The Reconfiguration of the Kyoto School of Painting and the Revival of the Textile Industry," in *Kyoto Visual Culture in the Early Edo and Meiji Periods: The Arts of Reinvention*, ed. Morgan Pitelka and Alice Y. Tseng (London and New York: Routledge, 2016), 138–60. A clear example of this rhetoric concerning Ōkyo and *shasei* is found in the inaugural issue of the art journal *Kokka*, which features an essay on Ōkyo by Okakura Kakuzō (Okakura Tenshin, 1862–1913).
17. This traditional view of Ōkyo as the founder of the "Naturalism School" (Shasei-ha) in Edo painting has been increasingly questioned by specialists. See, for example, Nezu Art Museum, ed., *Maruyama Ōkyo—shasei o koete* (Tokyo: Nezu Bijutsukan, 2016), and Reizei Tamehito, *Maruyama Ōkyo ron* (Kyoto: Shibunkaku Shuppan, 2017).

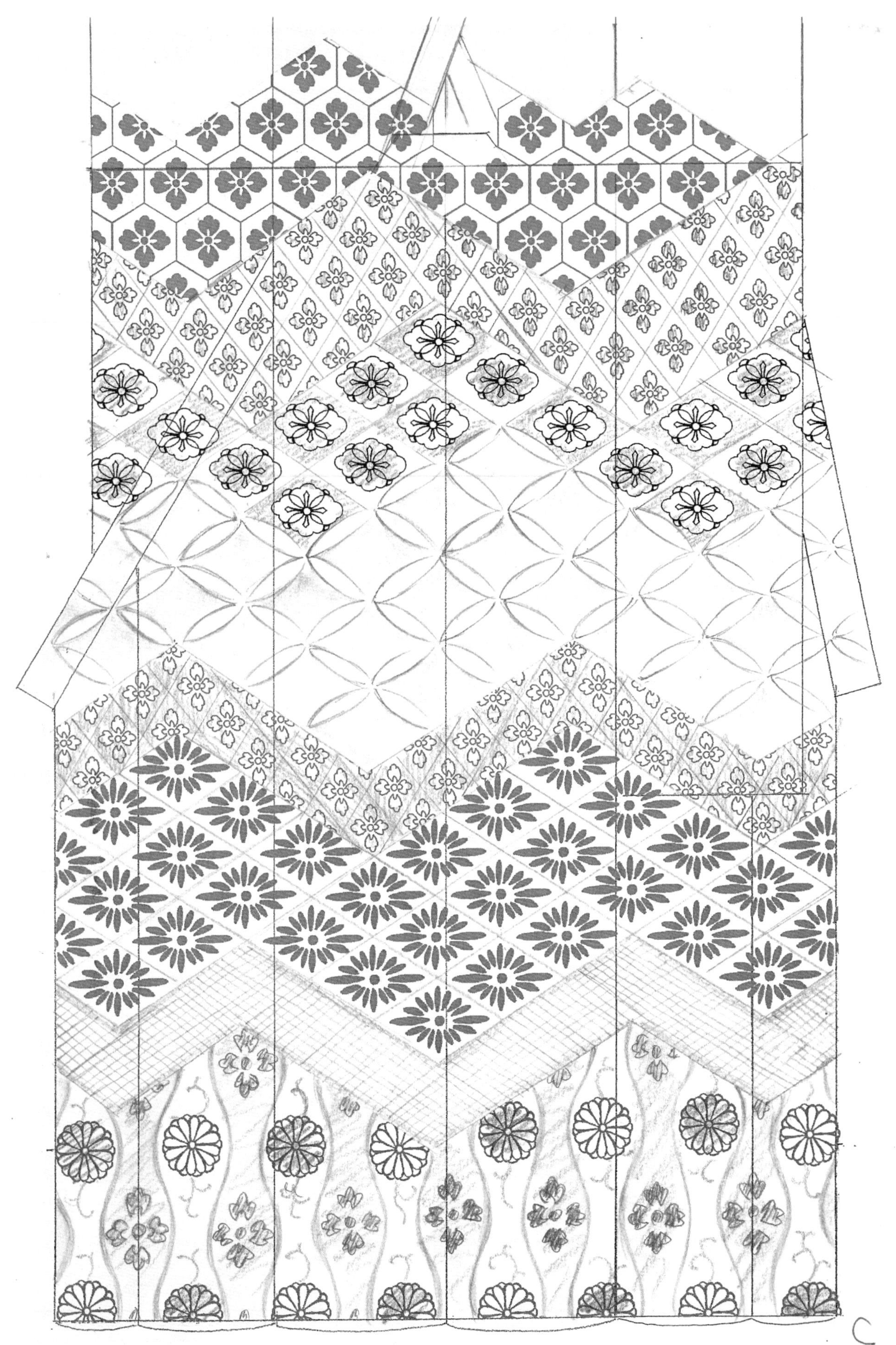

INSIDE CHISO

A Conversation with Kimono Designer Imai Atsuhiro

Monica Bethe, Vivian Li, and Christine D. Starkman

Page 40 & fig. 1
Nine proposed designs by Chiso designer Imai Atsuhiro

Li: We would first like to talk about your training as a designer. What was your training, how did you arrive at Chiso, and how did you adapt to becoming a designer of kimono?

Imai: I became interested in art in high school. I was always good at painting, but until then I did a lot of sports. When I went to high school, though, my art teacher there praised me, telling me I was good at painting, and that encouraged me. So, when I was thinking about where to go to college, my art teacher suggested, "How about applying to art school?" I took the university entrance exam and was accepted into Osaka University of Arts [Ōsaka Geijutsu Daigaku]. This was the starting point.

Osaka University of Arts had a textile course of study called *senshoku*, which focused on dyeing, and I took that as a major. The professor who happened to become my advisor was knowledgeable about Japanese traditional crafts and culture. He really inspired me. At the time, there were two kinds of students: those who were quite up-to-date using computers to do modern design and those who did analogue design. Partly under the influence of my professor, and my own personal preference, I continued along the path of working with my hands, pursuing analogue design.

Bethe: Who was the teacher?

Imai: The teacher was Hiragane Yūichi.

Bethe: I don't know a great deal about the Osaka University of Arts but weren't there many teachers there interested in traditional art and dyeing?

Imai: Yes, there were around three, but Hiragane-sensei was also new at the school when I started. His first year of teaching corresponded to my freshman year. So we had a very close relationship and spent a lot of time together. The conversations I had with him and the information he gave me influenced my own creative stance, and I often sought guidance from him. When I came to think about my work or what sort of artwork I should make, he frequently gave me advice.

When I began to reflect on the type of job I should look for—what with having studied traditional Japanese culture with a focus on textiles—I felt that the closest area would be the kimono. But I did not know how to approach looking for work related to kimono because it was very difficult to understand what was going on within the kimono industry from the outside. Let's say that the doors are not very open. So I asked Hiragane-sensei what to do about getting a job in the kimono industry.

By chance, Hiragane-sensei had worked at a department store before coming to the university, and for that reason he had connections and knew a lot about Chiso. He told me about this traditional kimono company in Kyoto and advised me to look into it.

Bethe: So you graduated from university and went directly to Chiso?

Imai: Yes, I went there directly [after university]. At that time, it seemed a bit like my destiny. Chiso was holding a design competition open to the general public. I heard about it from my professor, and he thought it would be a good idea for me to participate. As a result, my work caught the eye of Chiso's production department and the company's owner. And that led to me joining the firm.

Li: So the introduction of your professor, as well as the design competition, had a huge impact. What year was this?

Imai: I joined the company in 1998. I didn't actually learn about kimono at university as I was more focused on my own artwork. I had tried to take in a lot about traditional Japanese art and culture during my studies, but when I joined Chiso that world was completely different. There was much to absorb, and there was much hands-on learning in Chiso's design department.

Bethe: In art school they do modern "Western" things; they don't do "Japanese" things.

Li: So where do kimono designers usually come from, if not from art schools?

Imai: Before my time at Chiso, those who had a certain level of education and who had painting skills apprenticed as assistants under a respected designer.

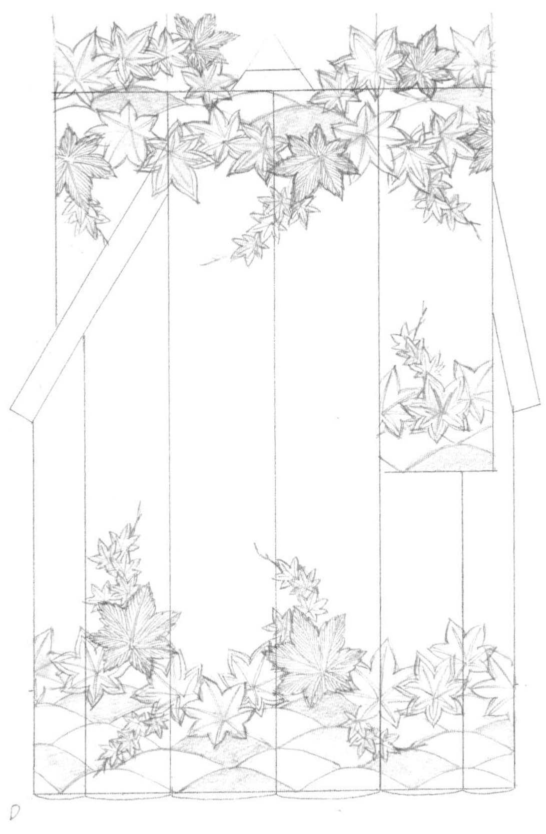

D

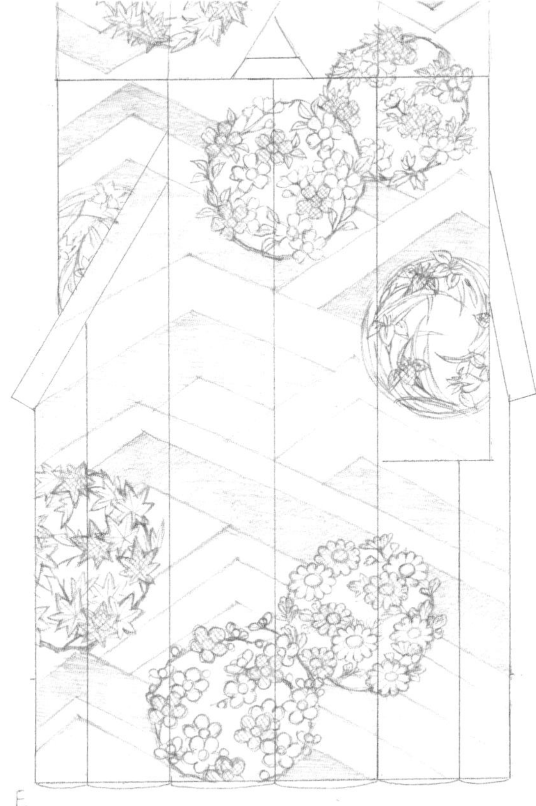

E

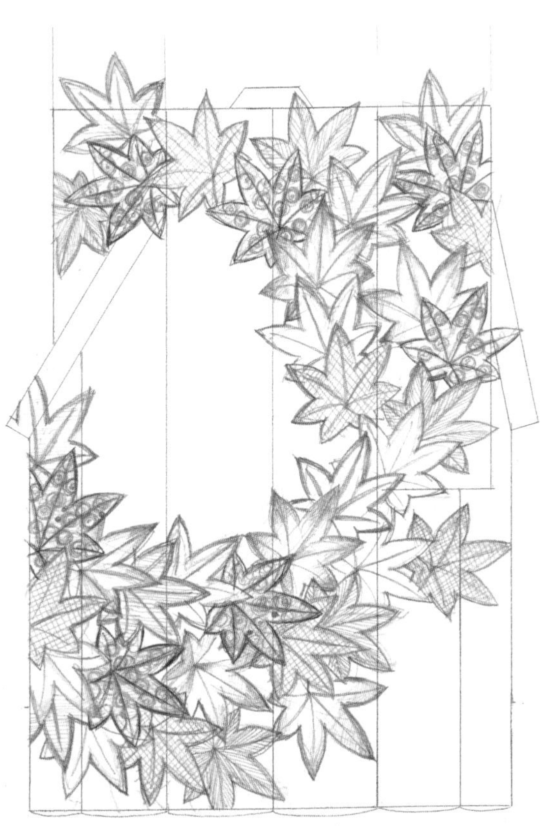

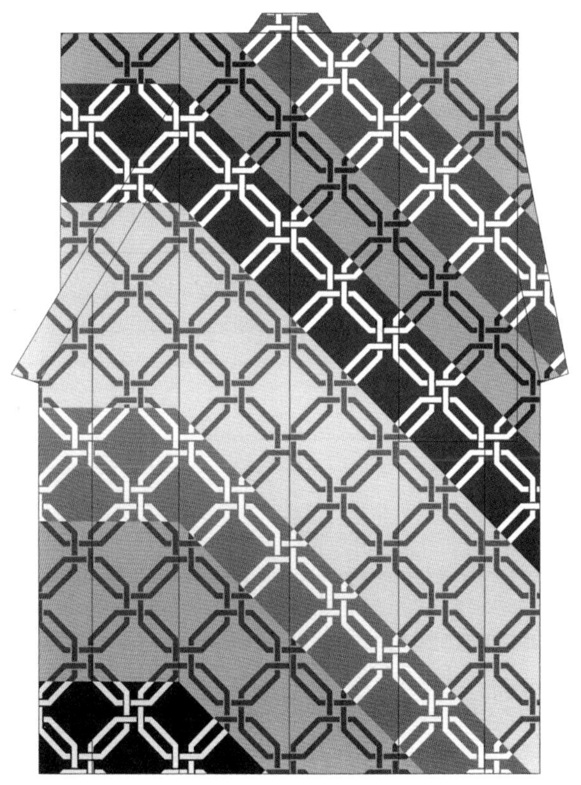

B

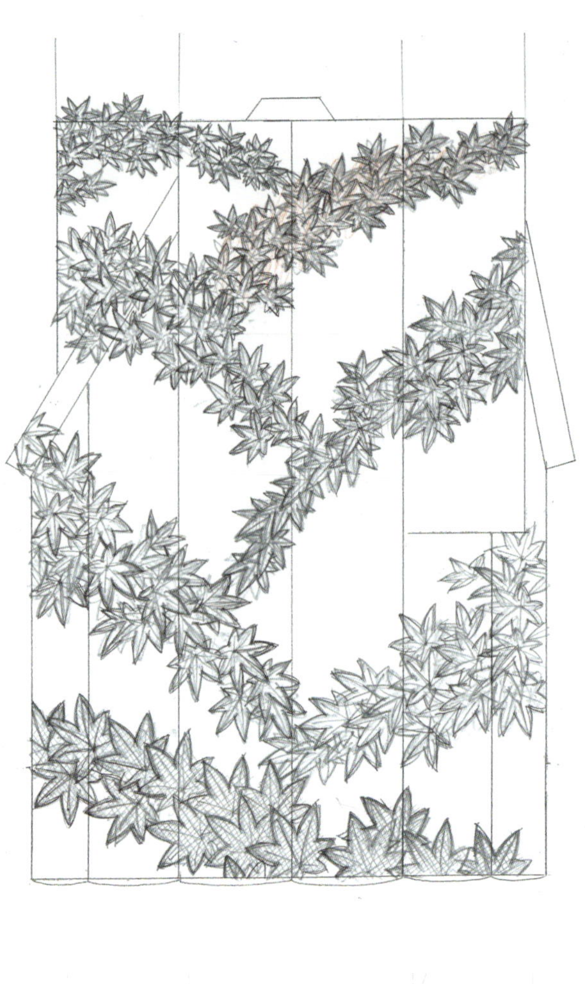

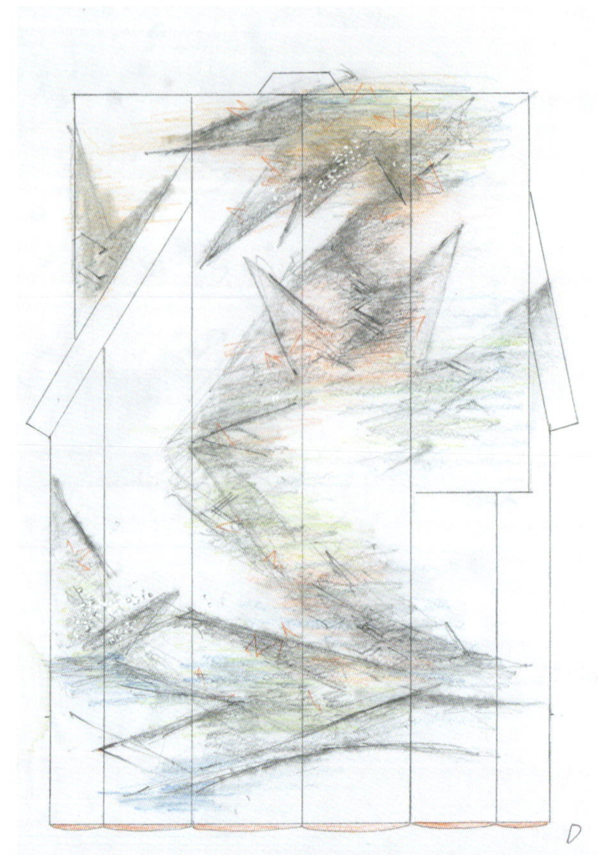
D

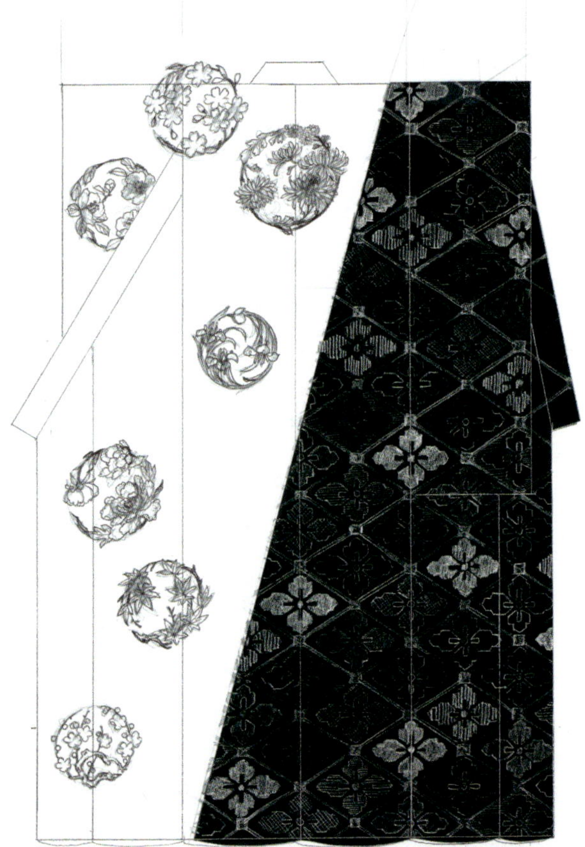

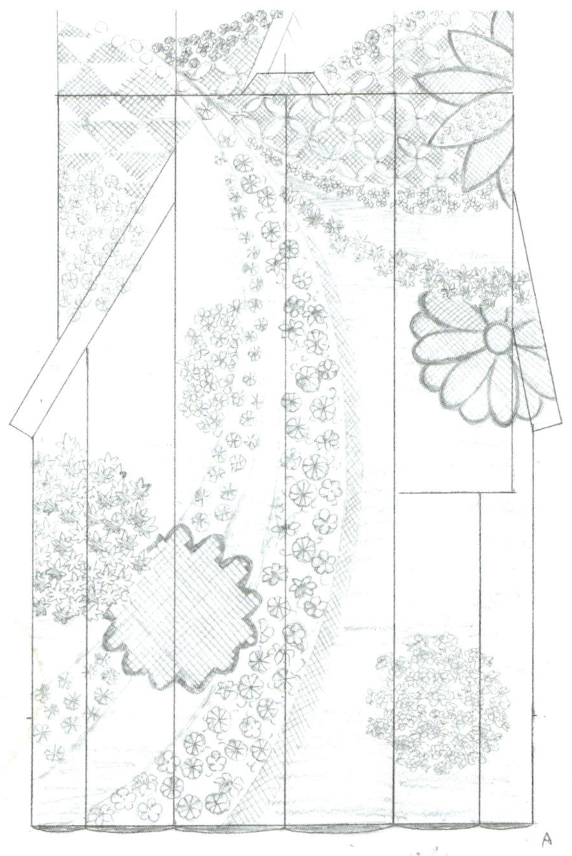
A

They trained in pictorial design and built up their skills until they became independent artisans.

Bethe: So the traditional system is to be connected with a particular teacher, not a university teacher, and with someone who is a practitioner. That person would take you on as an apprentice and then you would learn by doing.

Imai: It was the same at Chiso. I was the first one there who had a university background.

Bethe: So all the other people have come up through the apprenticeship system. Does the master-apprentice system continue even today?

Imai: Today, that system is no longer the main one; we have many students from art schools.

Bethe: Was it difficult going there [Chiso]? Did you need to rethink a number of things or did you have to learn new things regardless of what you had done until that point? Did you have to change your mindset?

Imai: In the beginning, I didn't even have a foundation to rethink anything. There were nine respected designers when I joined the company, and I was treated like a rookie. I wanted to catch up with those people as soon as possible, so I listened to what they said and absorbed it. That was the only way to develop my skills and refine my design, and to catch up with them.

Bethe: I think at art school, the basis for design is drawing. But here, what is interesting is the process of designing a kimono that incorporates diverse techniques. When designing a kimono, don't you have to keep in mind the techniques you want to use and how they affect the outcome? How did you study that?

Imai: We acquire drawing skills from the people in the design department. Because there is a production department, we can look at the actual kimono being made there and also at the beautiful old kimono in the company's collection. In this way, it is possible to learn and assimilate the technical aspects related to the designs. Additionally, in talking with the craftspeople and getting information from them, one learns which techniques are used to express which design elements. You then consider which techniques would be right for your own personal expression.

There are two approaches to creating a kimono at Chiso. One is to design based on the techniques, and the other is to select the most appropriate techniques for the design. There are various roles and features of each technique, so I place more emphasis on how they can best bring out a given design.

Starkman: This seems to be a negotiation: once you decide on one technique, it affects the visual impact of another, which in turn will impact another.

Imai: You can say that. When I visited Worcester earlier this year, I proposed ten designs for the kimono commission to the [Worcester Art] Museum's director [and curators] (the first nine on p. 40 & fig. 1). The design selected was the most distinctive among them, and in a sense, it had the most possibilities in the use of different techniques (fig. 2). The other designs had a specific method in mind from the beginning. The design chosen was more experimental and had more flexibility in how it might be expressed.

Li: Is this why it was your favorite design?

Imai: I guess so. After all, it was the most distinctive, and it incorporates various ideas. I feel like both ideas and beauty coalesce [in this piece].

Starkman: Your ninth design (p. 44, upper right-hand design) proposal had many Western elements.

Imai: Ah, the [Gustav] Klimt.

Starkman: Your presentation of the ten design proposals was interesting because in a way, numbers one to eight went through the history of kimono design. And it was quite surprising when you got to nine, you were almost there and [we were] thinking, "Maybe that's possible." But then we had reservations that it was still traditional.

Bethe: You didn't want something traditional?

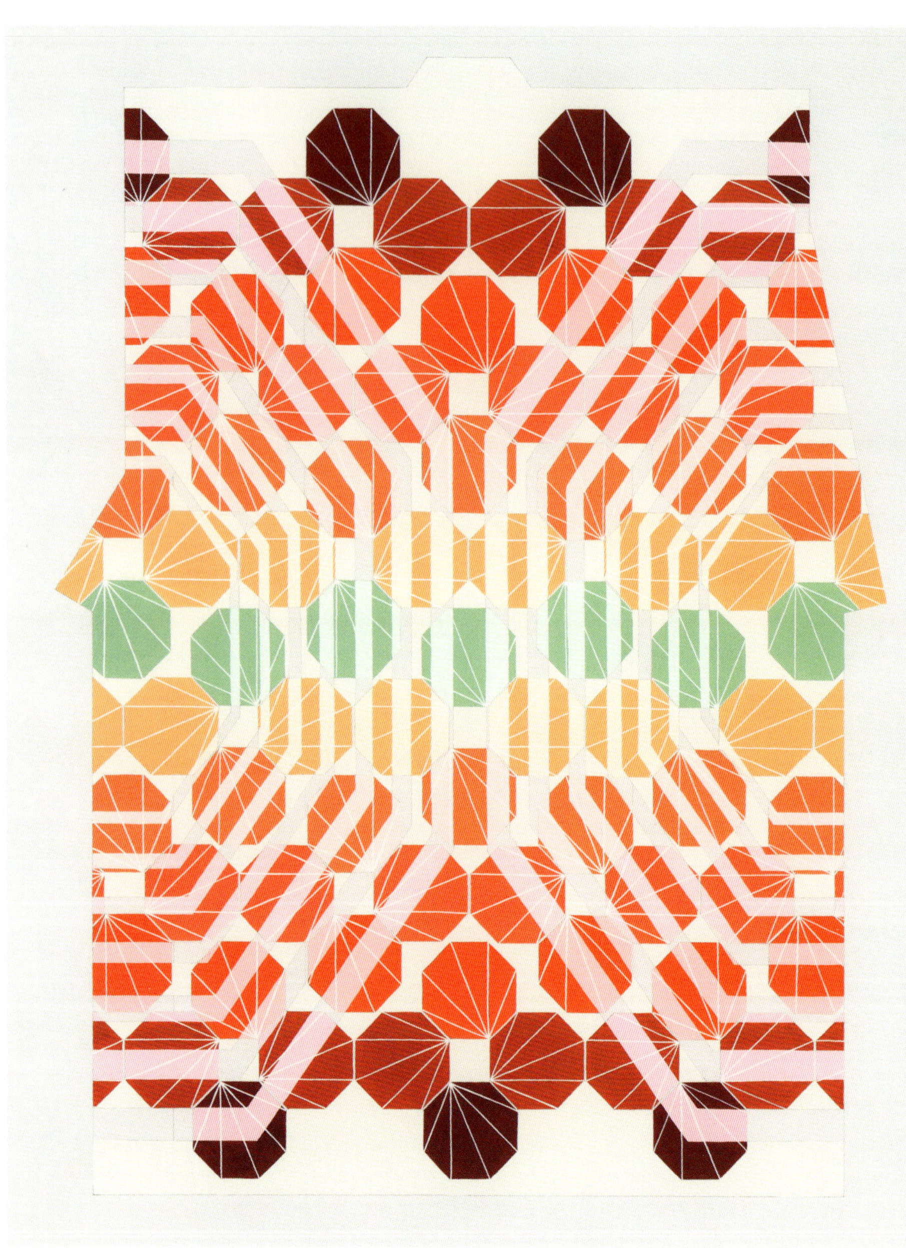

Fig. 2
Selected design for Worcester Art Museum commission

Li: Also Western. We didn't want any that were too Western.

Starkman: We were looking for this [*points to the commissioned kimono design, which was the tenth design*].

Li: This is the perfect balance between the two.

Starkman: It seems that you had to pause. You had to think of a new one. It was like you needed to leave tradition. I don't think you left tradition, but it seemed like you had to drop everything to create.

Li: And you have to know the history to make something new. So, then, is that part of the process that formed your approach to this project?

Starkman: Because this was completely outside of the box.

Bethe: It seems as if you passed through time periods and arriving at the modern, embracing the Western, finally came to one that is neither Japanese nor Western: it is Imai-san.

Imai: Yes. I laid the presentation out so that it had that kind of flow. Of course, for this design to be born I put a lot of work into it, and I received a lot of advice from various people, including Mr. Shiba Daisuke [Chiso's Communications Director]. Not only did we want to show the possibilities of Chiso but also the future of the

Fig. 3
View of Fruitlands Museum in Worcester County during the site visit of Imai Atsuhiro

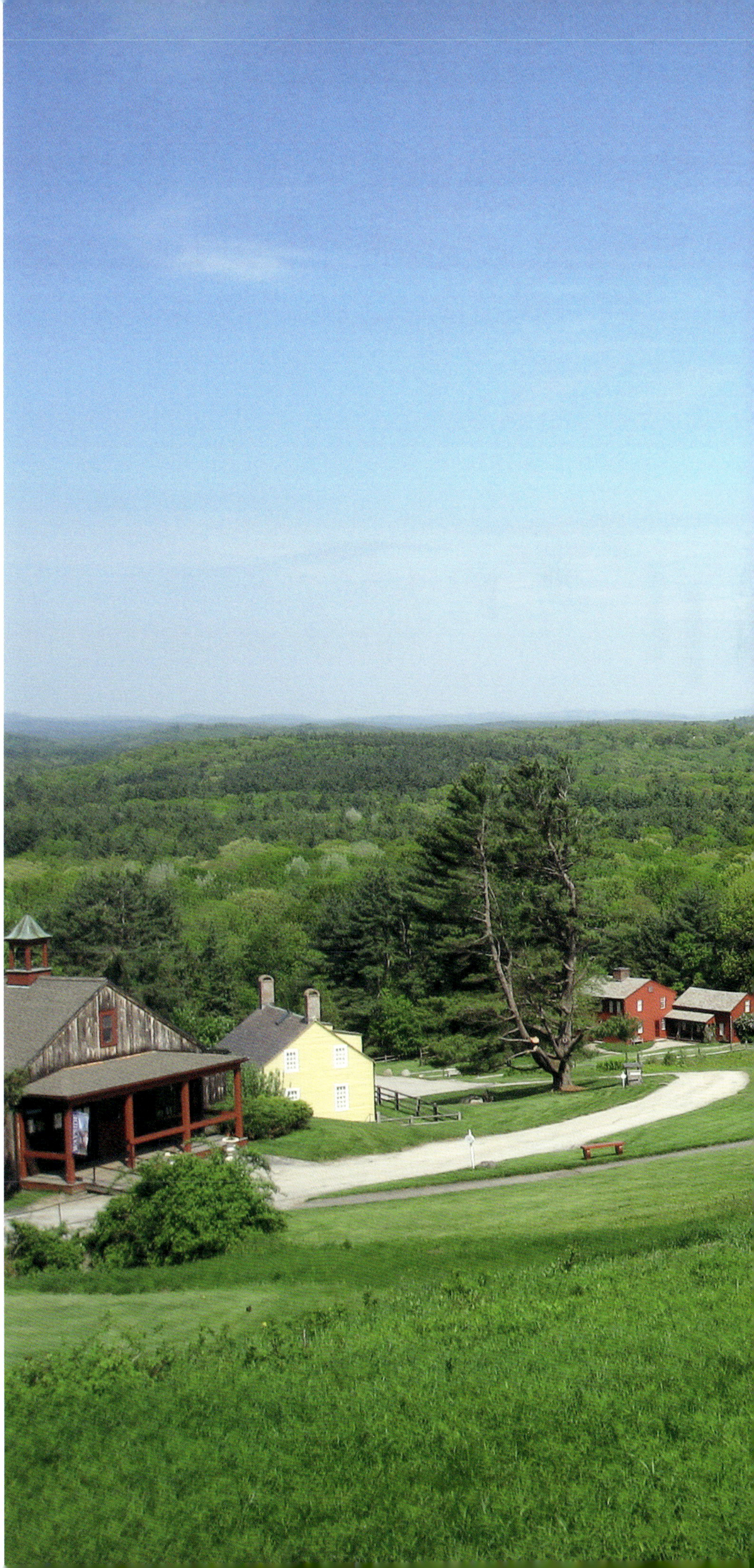

kimono, so we felt that we needed to have a design like this.

Shiba [*also present, interjects*]: As Mr. Imai mentioned, when we discussed design proposal numbers one to nine, our discussions were more about the traditional. Then we just realized, “Oh, just forget about ‘What is Western?’ ‘What is traditional?’ Just think about something new.” Ultimately, it’s about beauty.

Li: During the presentation you talked a little bit about how this also represents the marriage between Japan and Japanese culture and art with Worcester and the art and culture of New England. Can you talk about how you arrived at this idea and how you translated it into the kimono design?

Imai: A theme suggested by the Worcester Art Museum was the celebrated “Seven Hills” of Worcester, so we wanted to focus on the number seven. Worcester and Japan both have an abundance of natural beauty (fig. 3). The rich nature surrounding us became an inspiration for the designs, motifs, colors, and so forth. People have always looked to nature for inspiration, and that is no different with kimono design. The Japanese have always regarded nature very closely in design, and I felt we needed to include that element here.

I decided that the kimono type should be an *uchikake*, a type of overcoat that is worn in Japan for the most formal celebrations. Traditionally *uchikake* are worn at wedding ceremonies.

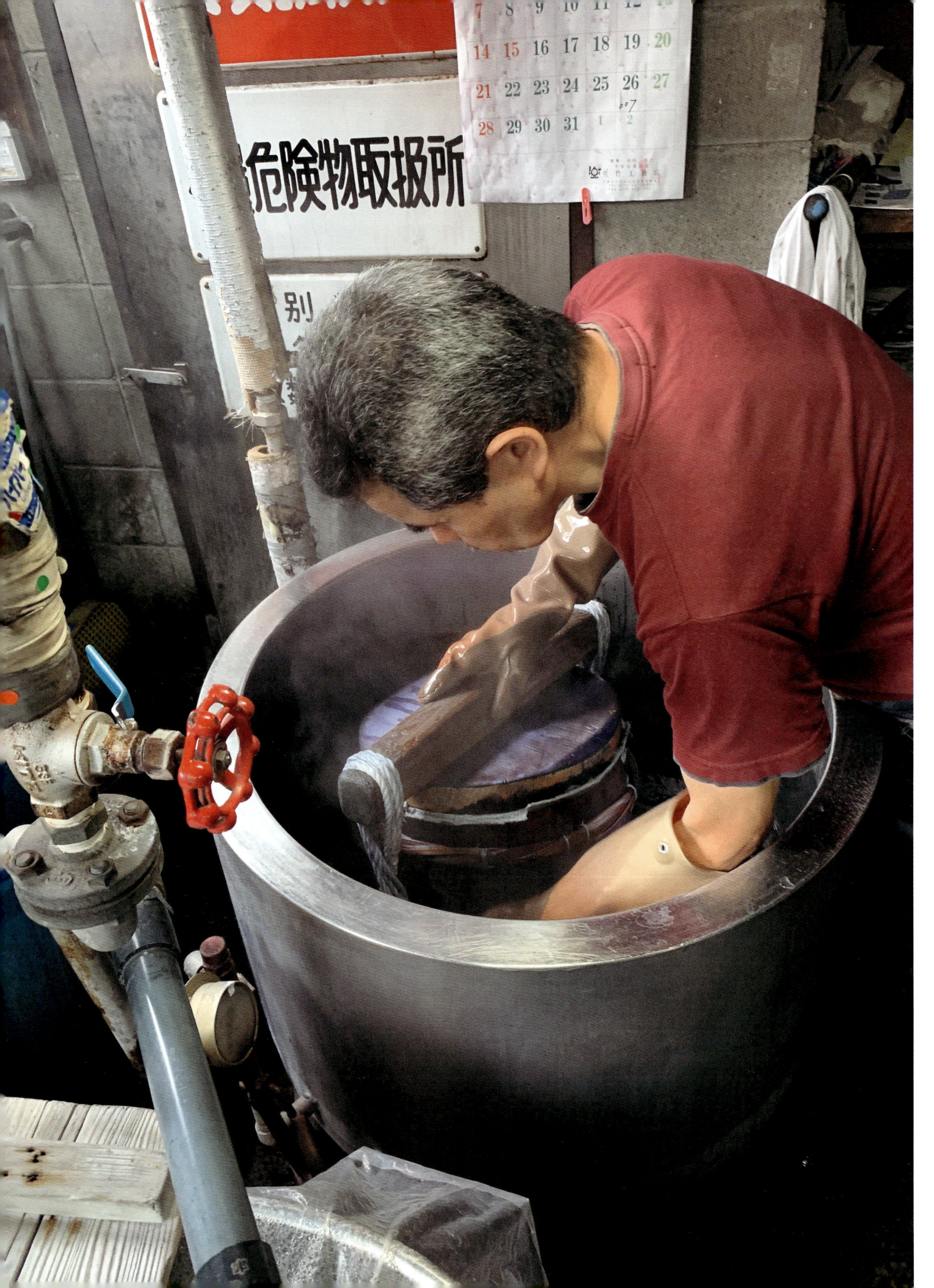

危険物取扱所
14 15 16 17 18 19 20
21 22 23 24 25 26 27
28 29 30 31 1 2

Fig. 4
Dyer immersing barrel in dye vat for barrel tie-dying (*okedashi shibori*)

Talking about the number seven, we incorporated seven special techniques: barrel tie-dyeing (*okedashi shibori*) (fig. 4), paste-resist dyeing (*yūzen*), colored flour paste-resist dyeing (*iro utsushi itchin yūzen*), threadline paste-resist dyeing (*itome-yūzen*), "snowstorm" wax-resist dyeing (*fubuki rōketsuzome*), gold leaf, and embroidery on woven silk. The design also has seven gradations of color to represent the changing seasons. In addition, I included the octagon, which is the Chiso trademark (see fig. 6, p. 18), and this also is reflected in seven concentric octagons that frame the design. From the perspective of nature, this is obviously a graphic design, but it is characteristic of Japanese design to abstract nature and transform it into a pattern. So here, I have rendered the maple leaf as an octagon, making it into a pattern. This is then placed such that it offers a sense of beauty throughout the design.

The kimono is sumptuous when it is spread out; it has a different beauty when it's worn. In this kimono the two halves of an octagon come together to form one octagon at the front. One half represents Chiso, while the other half represents Worcester—it expresses a bond between the two places. The octagon formed by the overlapping front panels, which only appears when the kimono is worn, was one of the most crucial concepts of this design.

Ever since I joined Chiso there is one thing I've always been aware of when designing kimono. People tend to think that the ultimate splendor of a kimono is when it is displayed. Yet the true beauty of a kimono and its most important function is to make the wearer look wonderful. I always have two aspects in mind: the kimono's beauty as an art piece and the beauty born when worn by women.

Bethe: With this design, would you go, for example, to an embroiderer and ask them to work on specific sections? How do you give instructions to your craftspeople?

Imai: I usually meet with the craftspeople and explain my ideas with graphics or a drawing by hand, referencing back to the original design and the actual piece. From this point onward, it's somewhat out of my hands, so I try to be careful to be as clear as possible and make it understandable to them. The key thing is to be able to share the same image. If the craftsperson is struggling to form a visual image, I might write on top of the design or give instructions by a more graphic approach, and sometimes might draw it.

Bethe: Do artisans A and B know what the other is going to do? Or do you always stand in the middle, so there is no communication between the artisans?

Imai: There is a certain amount of communication between the artisans. In many cases, the artisans will consider the next process and will work with some assumptions about what will follow. With the Worcester kimono the artisans needed to work with some understanding of the whole process. But my role as a producer does not change, so I will always be at the center giving instructions.

Bethe: So communication is always from you to each of the individual craftspeople. Because a great many of the techniques are cumulative, however, it would be like saying "you do the tie-dye first, and then on top of that you do the embroidery." There's an order to it, so that the person who is doing the tie-dye base should be aware that this area will have gold leaf or embroidery or something on top. In other words, you should be aware of what's coming on top of it in the process and in that sense, you make them aware of the entire process, but still the communication focuses on what each individual has to do.

Starkman: Is there a general Chiso set of values that you also have to keep in mind when designing?

Imai: Well, I think that is an aspect that is always changing. But designs are made by people here at Chiso and realized by artisans who work with Chiso, so I think that will naturally lead to designs that embody "Chiso-ness" and have a unique style that no other company has.

Our approach is two-fold. One is that there is no "You know you have to fit into this frame." But Chiso is constantly evolving and changing with the times. The firm is also working with specific artisans, and those artisans have their own approaches. There is a give-and-take that creates a kind of Chiso style.

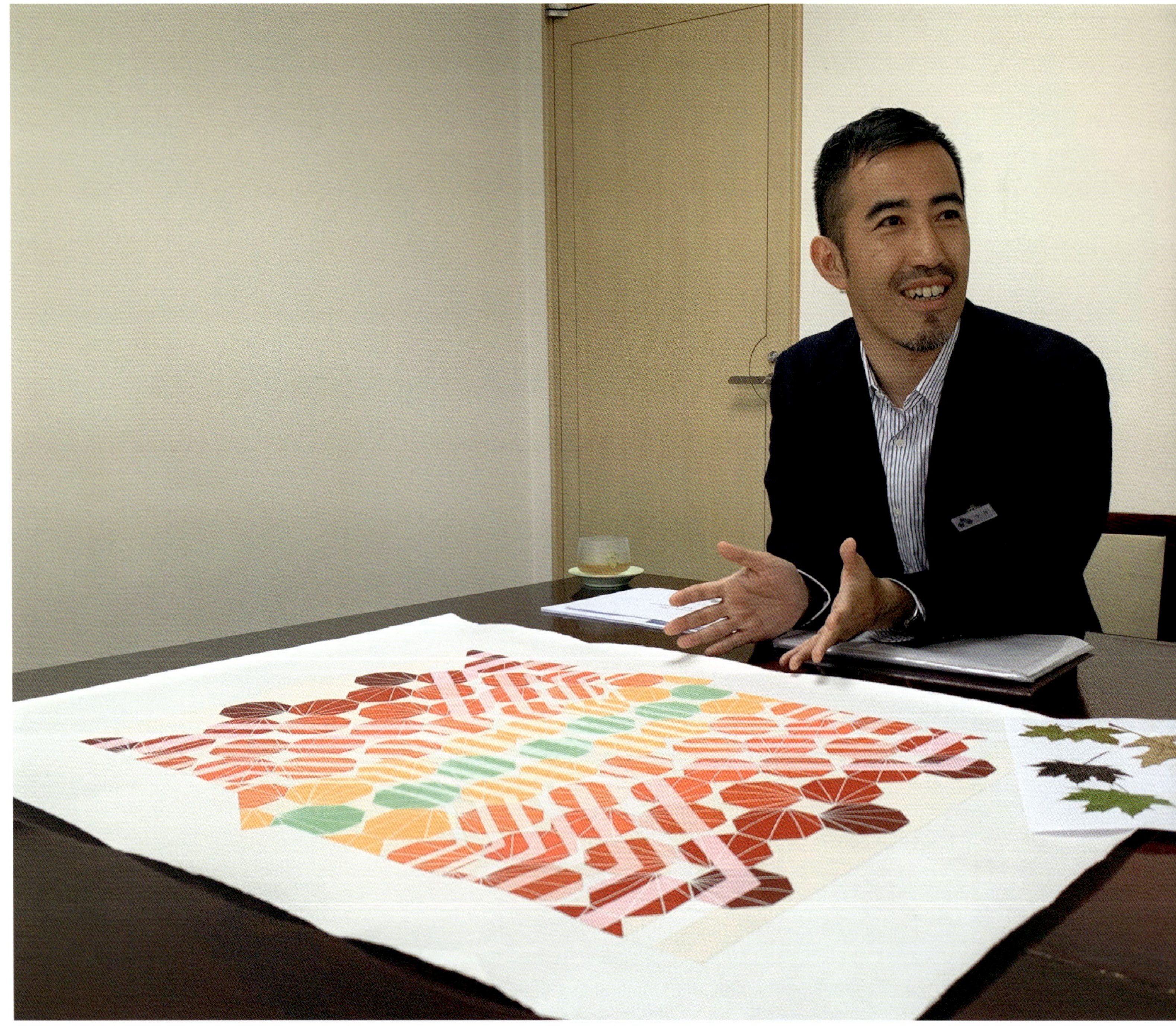

Li: What is the relationship you hope this commissioned kimono will have with the US public even after the exhibition is over?

Imai: I don't know how much an American audience will understand about kimono but the shape is obviously a kimono, and it will be a unique garment. We are presenting something that we believe is beautiful. It is something sent from Japan, from Kyoto, yet there is always a different viewpoint regarding Japan and its art when seen by foreigners. I think there are many ways to look at the work; however, many people have a slightly old-fashioned image when it comes to kimono. I am confident that this design can be appreciated by an American audience—the people in Worcester—and the world as a contemporary kimono. I hope it will be received as [an emblem of] the beauty of Chiso and the beauty of Japan (fig. 5 & cat. 24).

Translated by Miyo Sugimoto

Fig. 5
Imai Atsuhiro with design on paper of Worcester Art Museum commission and samples of maple leaves he collected during his site visit to Worcester

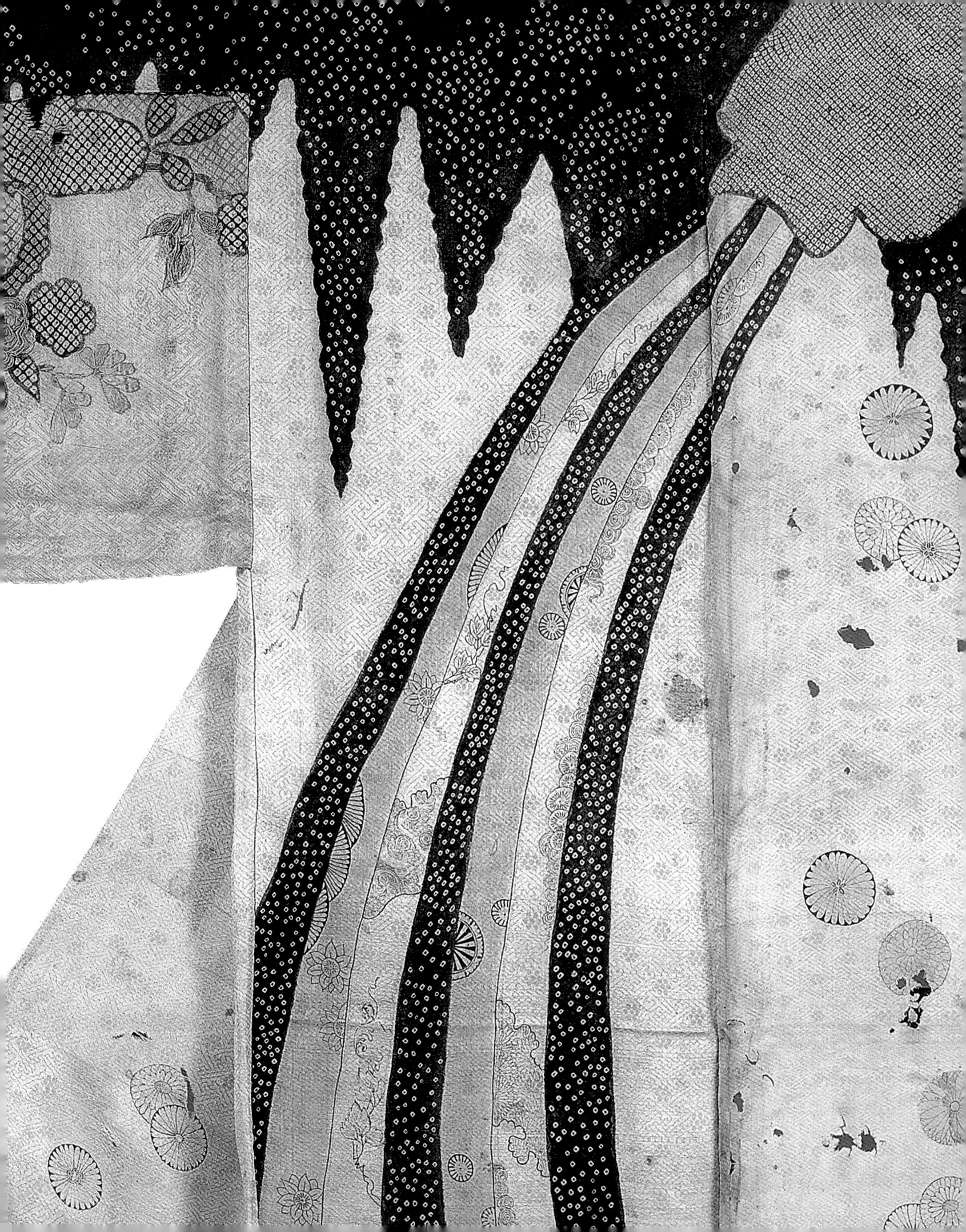

PLATES

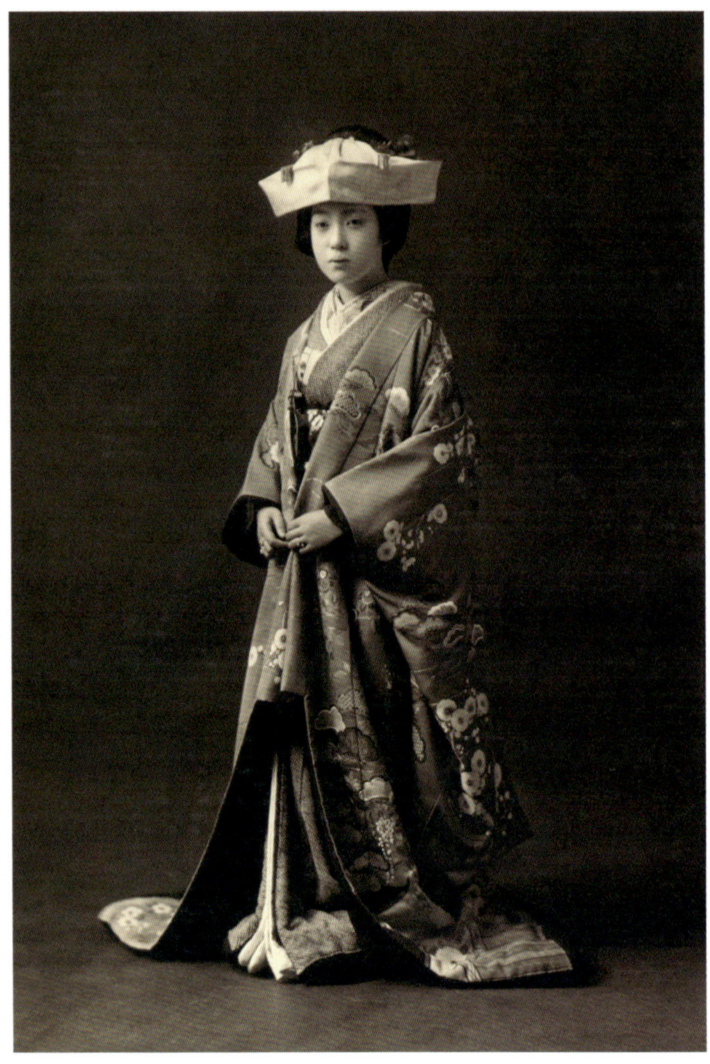

1

Chiso Co., Ltd.
Uchikake with Palace Garden Design
Made for Iida Taka, the thirteenth Madame Nishimura (pictured)
1913, *yūzen*-dyeing and embroidery on woven silk
175 × 125 cm (68 7/8 × 49 3/16 in.)

The Chiso firm created this wedding kimono (*uchikake*; see also cats. 2 & 5) for Iida Taka, who became the thirteenth Madame Nishimura. Already in the early twentieth century, the kimono had become less a marker of class status and more a symbol of national dress, but the quality of the materials, the choice of patterns, and the colors continued to convey the rank, age, and gender of the wearer. In this work there are numerous visual allusions to the classical literature of the Heian period (794–1185), such as the bridge, Yatsuhashi, from the *Tales of Ise* (*Ise monogatari*) and the courtly palanquins from the *Tale of Genji* (*Genji monogatari*). These motifs express the literary prowess and refinement of the bride, whose family established the prominent dry goods dealer, later department store, Takashimaya in 1831.

The Nishimura family, in welcoming their future daughter-in-law with the gift of this *uchikake*, is referenced in the repeated round *tachibana* (mandarin orange) pattern—the Nishimura family crest—in the lower section to the right of the bridge and peony. Chiso is most celebrated for the *yūzen*-dyeing technique lavishly employed here. The remarkable graduated colors, seen in the peony flowers and layers of mists in the lower back panel, lends the scene a sumptuous painterly feel. **VL**

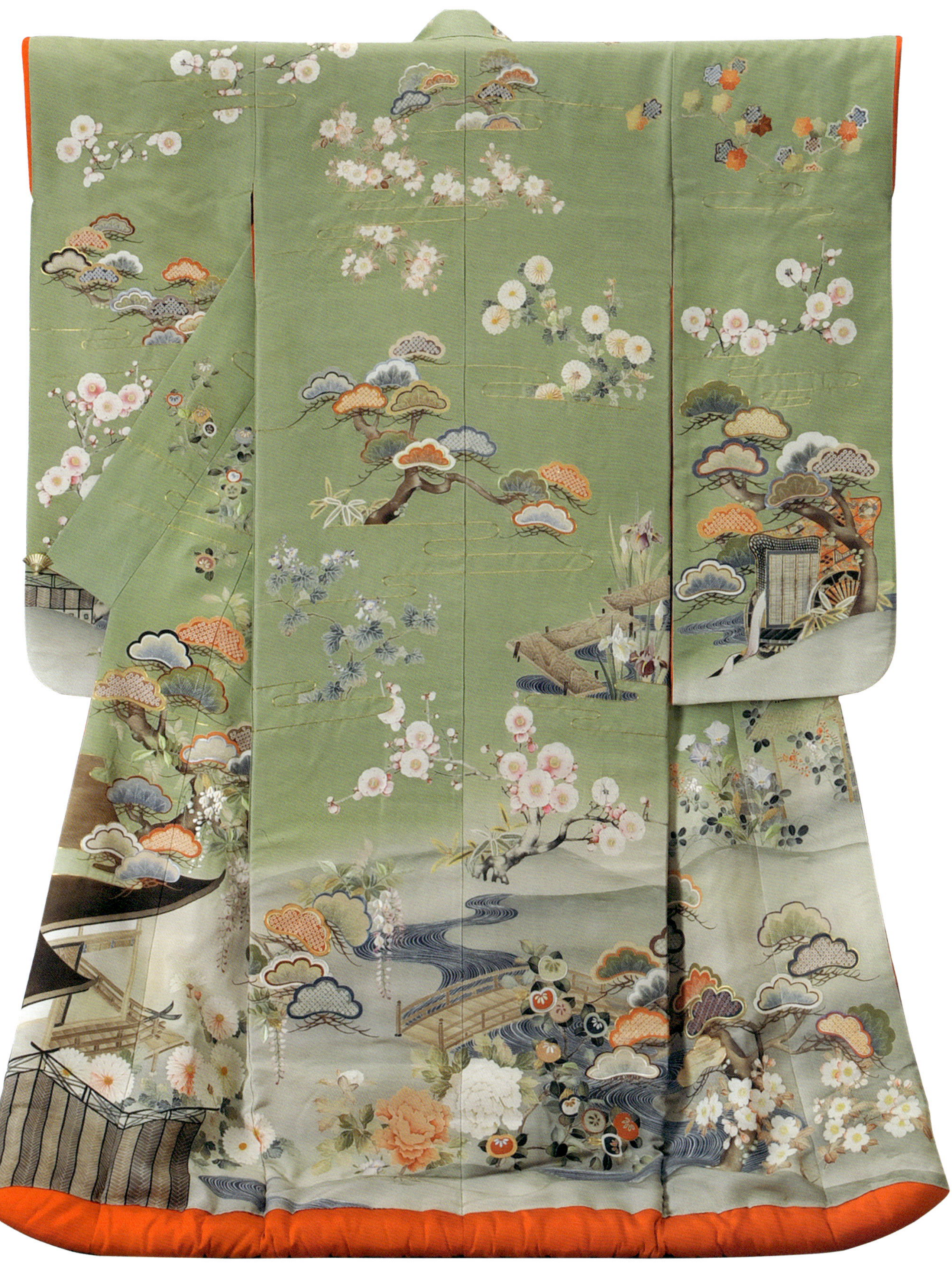

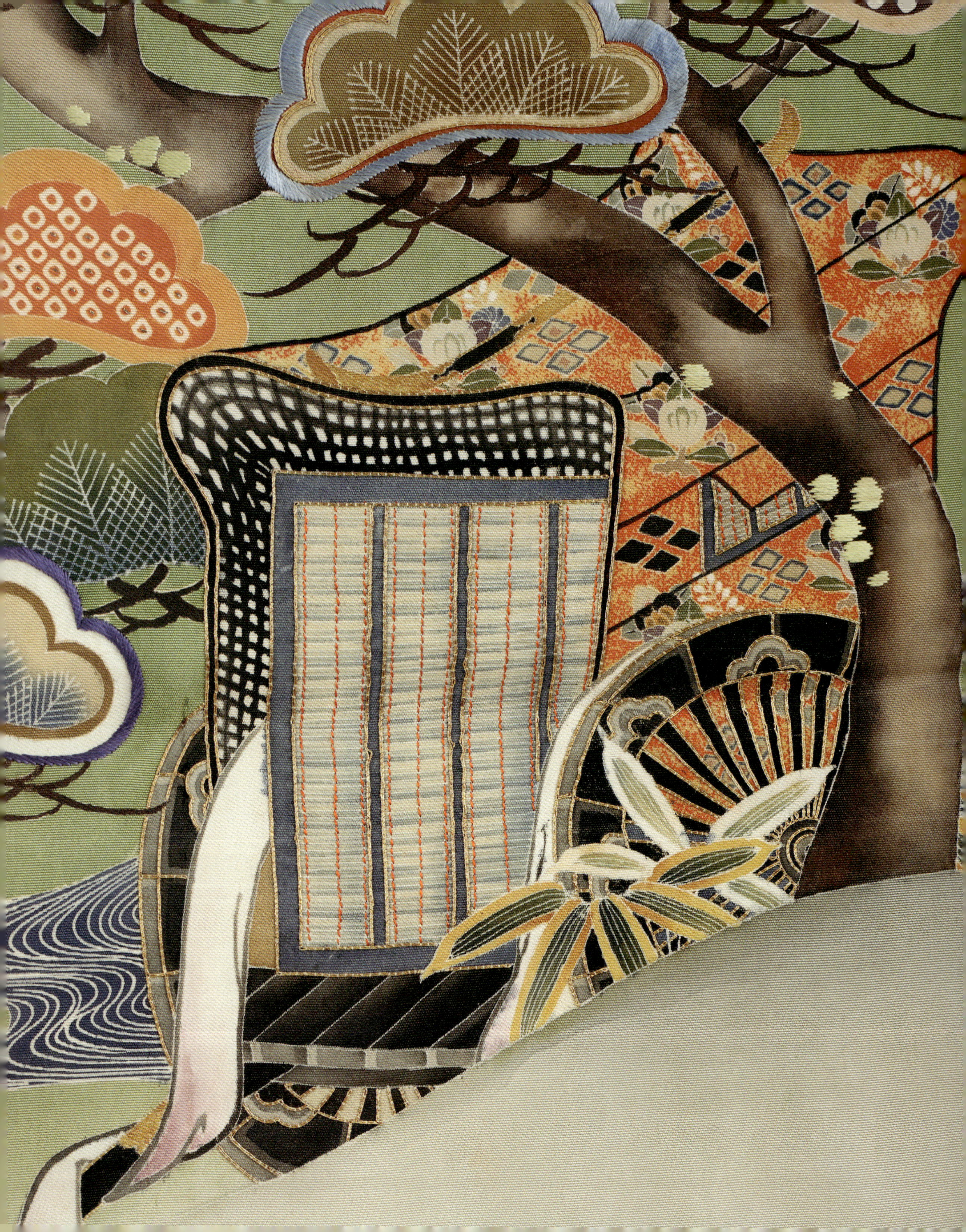

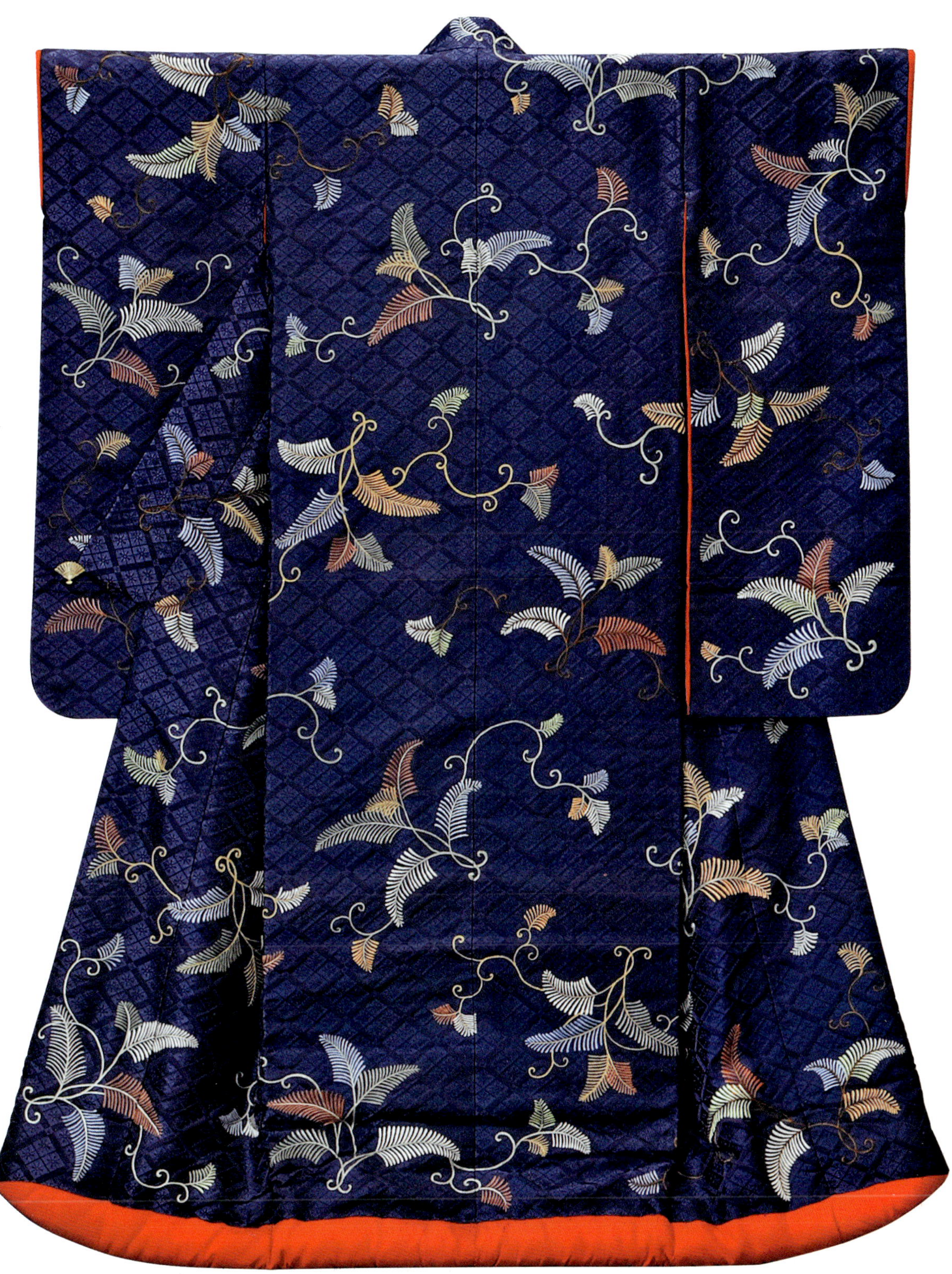

2

Chiso Co., Ltd.

Uchikake with Pine Leaf Design

Made for Iida Taka, the thirteenth Madame Nishimura

1913, embroidery on woven silk

168 × 126 cm (66 ⅛ × 49 ⅝ in.)

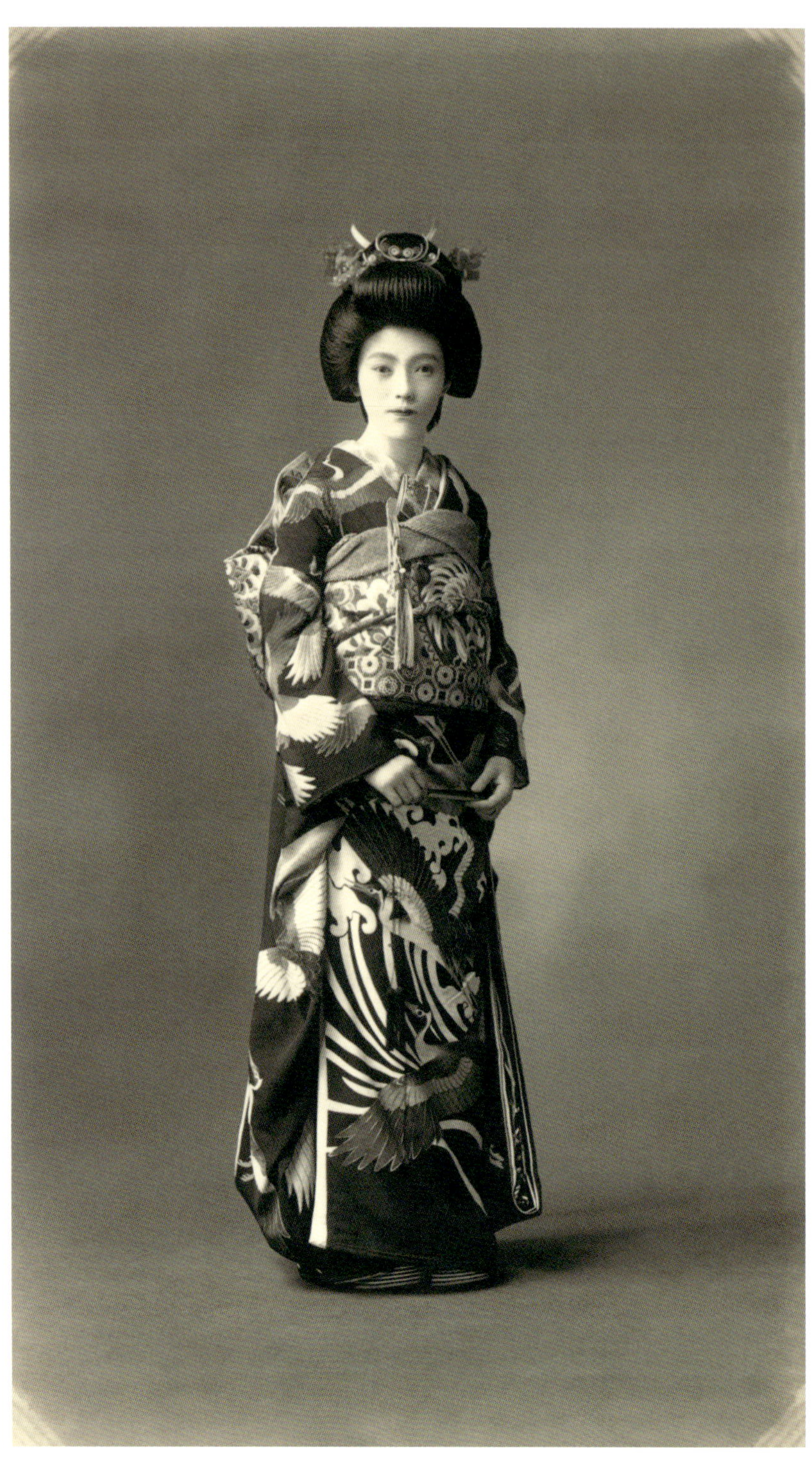

3

Chiso Co., Ltd.
Furisode with Wave and Crane Design
Made for Nishimura Tokuko, the fourteenth Madame Nishimura (pictured)
1938, *yūzen*-dyeing and embroidery on woven silk
171 × 128 cm (67 $^{5}/_{16}$ × 50 $^{3}/_{8}$ in.)

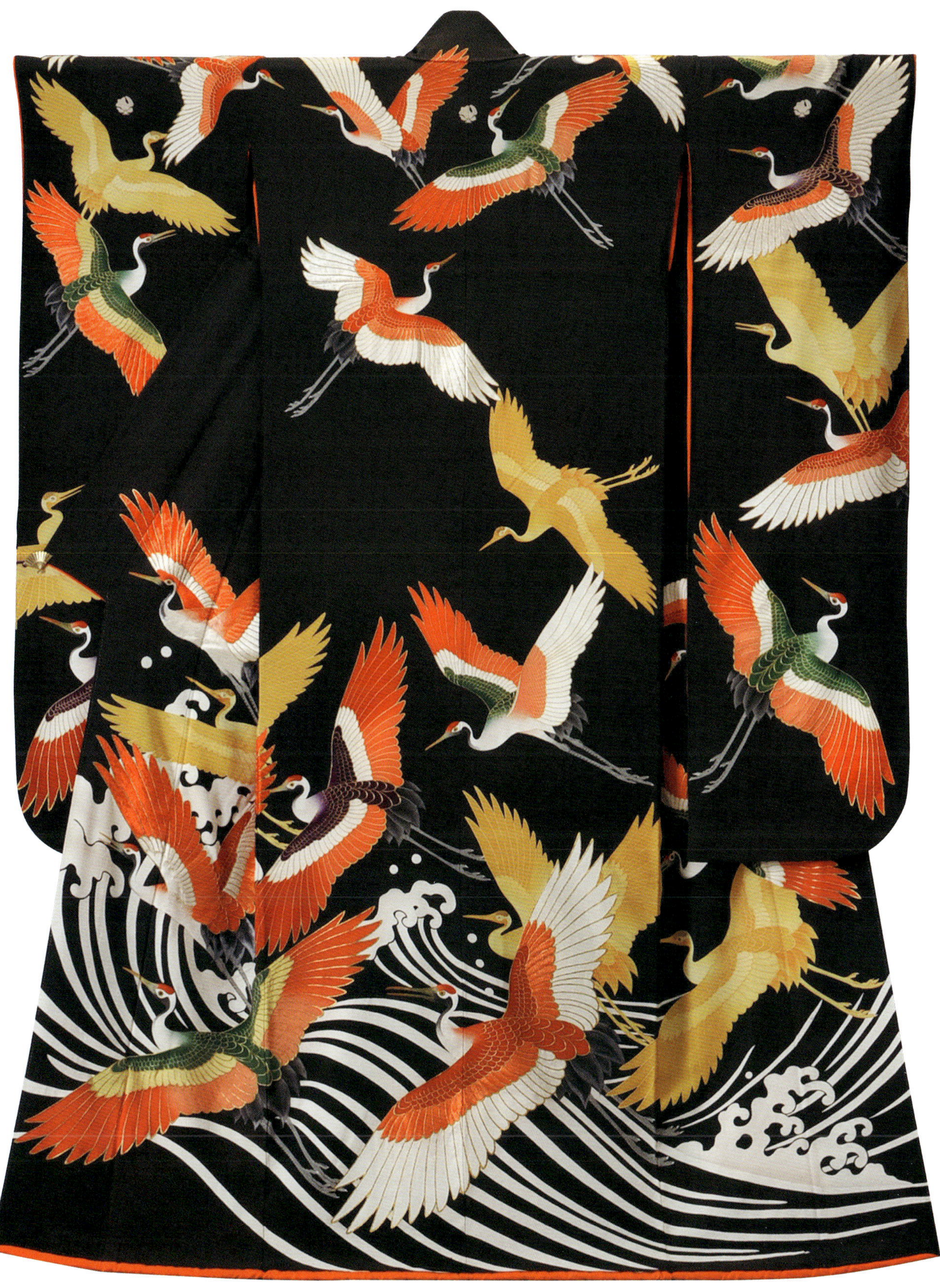

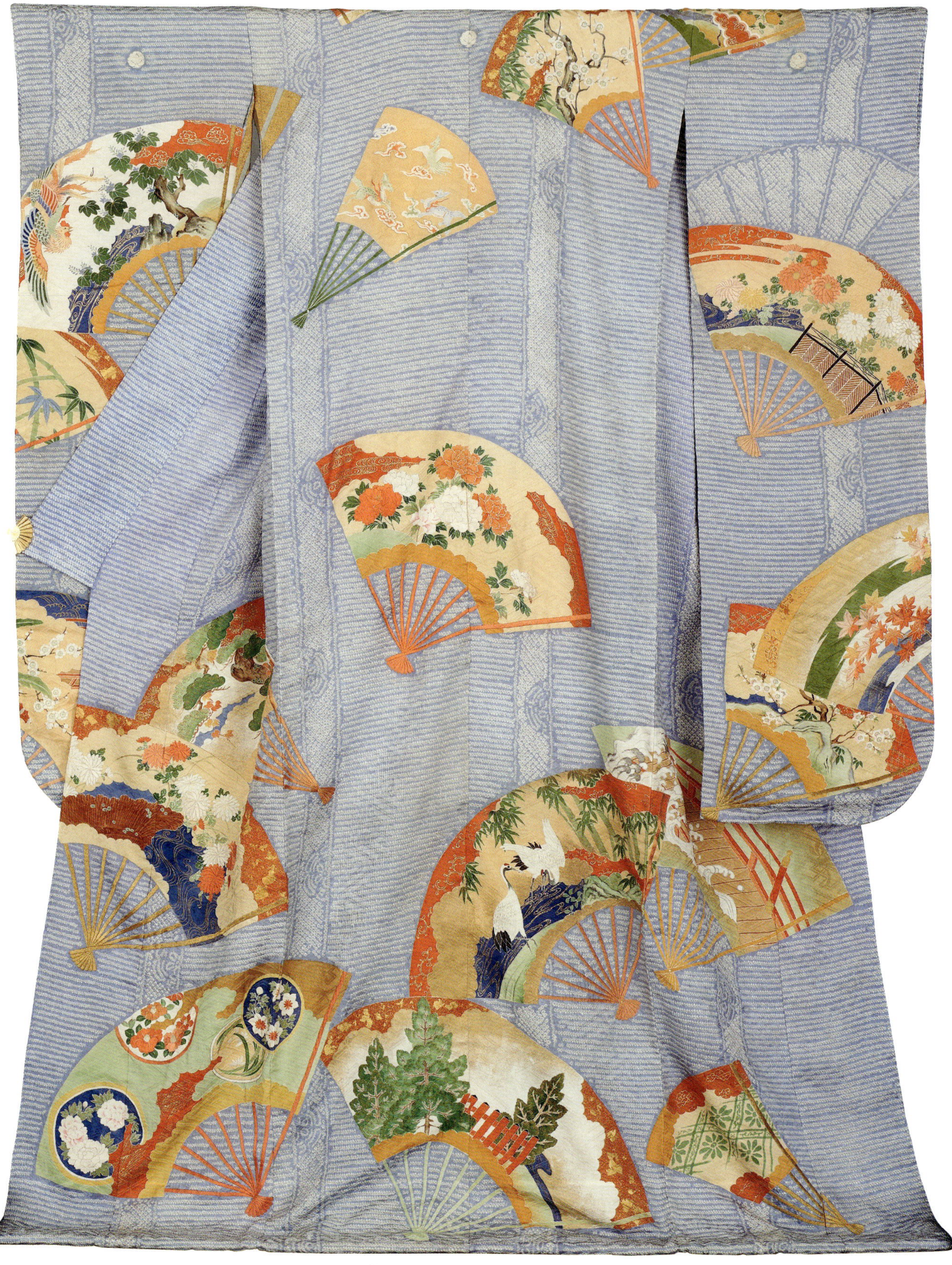

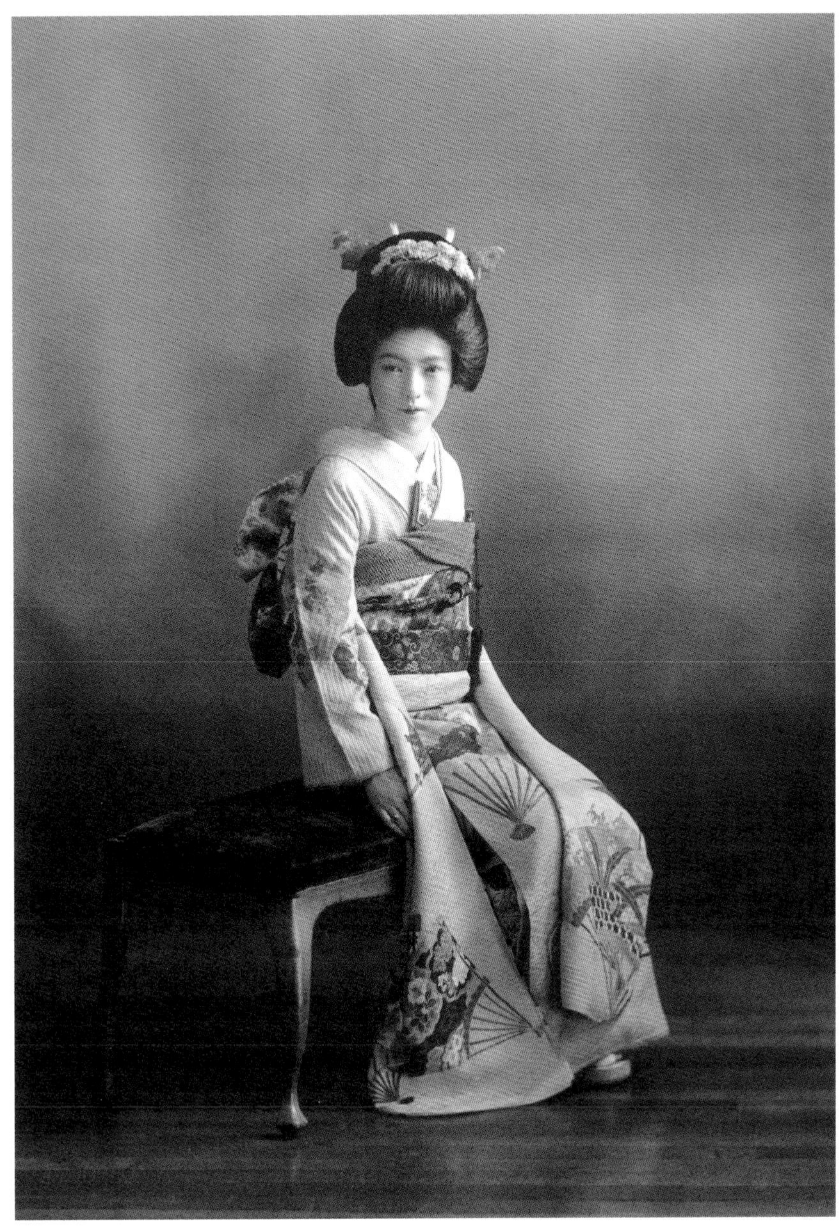

4

Chiso Co., Ltd.

Furisode with Fan and Bamboo Blinds Design

Made for Nishimura Tokuko, the fourteenth Madame Nishimura (pictured)

1938, *yūzen*-dyeing, *kanoko shibori* tie-dyeing, embroidery, and gold leaf on woven silk

170 × 128 cm (66 15⁄16 × 50 3⁄8 in.)

This long-sleeved kimono, or *furisode* (literally "swinging sleeves"), is decorated with fan motifs set against a background depicting a light-blue pattern of bamboo blinds created through the technique of *kanoko* (literally "fawn spots") *shibori*, a type of small circular tie-dyeing. The result is a work that is a tour de force in manual tie-resist dyeing. The dozens of fans ornamenting this *furisode* illustrate auspicious pairings of flora and fauna such as the foxglove and phoenix on the verso of the left sleeve (see image details p. 62). It was a custom within elite Japanese families to plant a foxglove tree (also known as paulownia, *kiri*) when a girl was born into the family. Years later, the wood of the tree would be carved into boxes and accessories for her marriage dowry. The phoenix represents female virtue and grace. **CS**

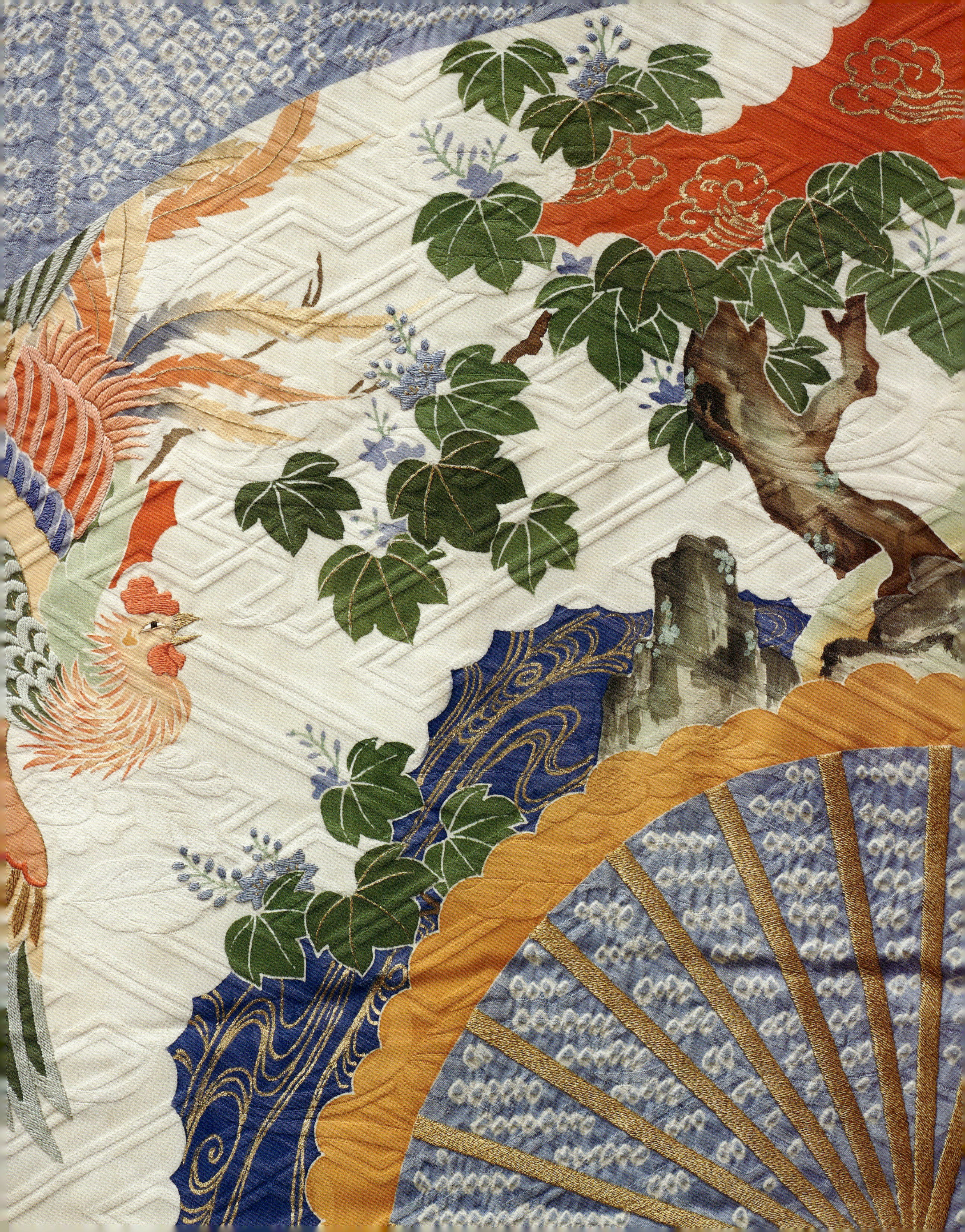

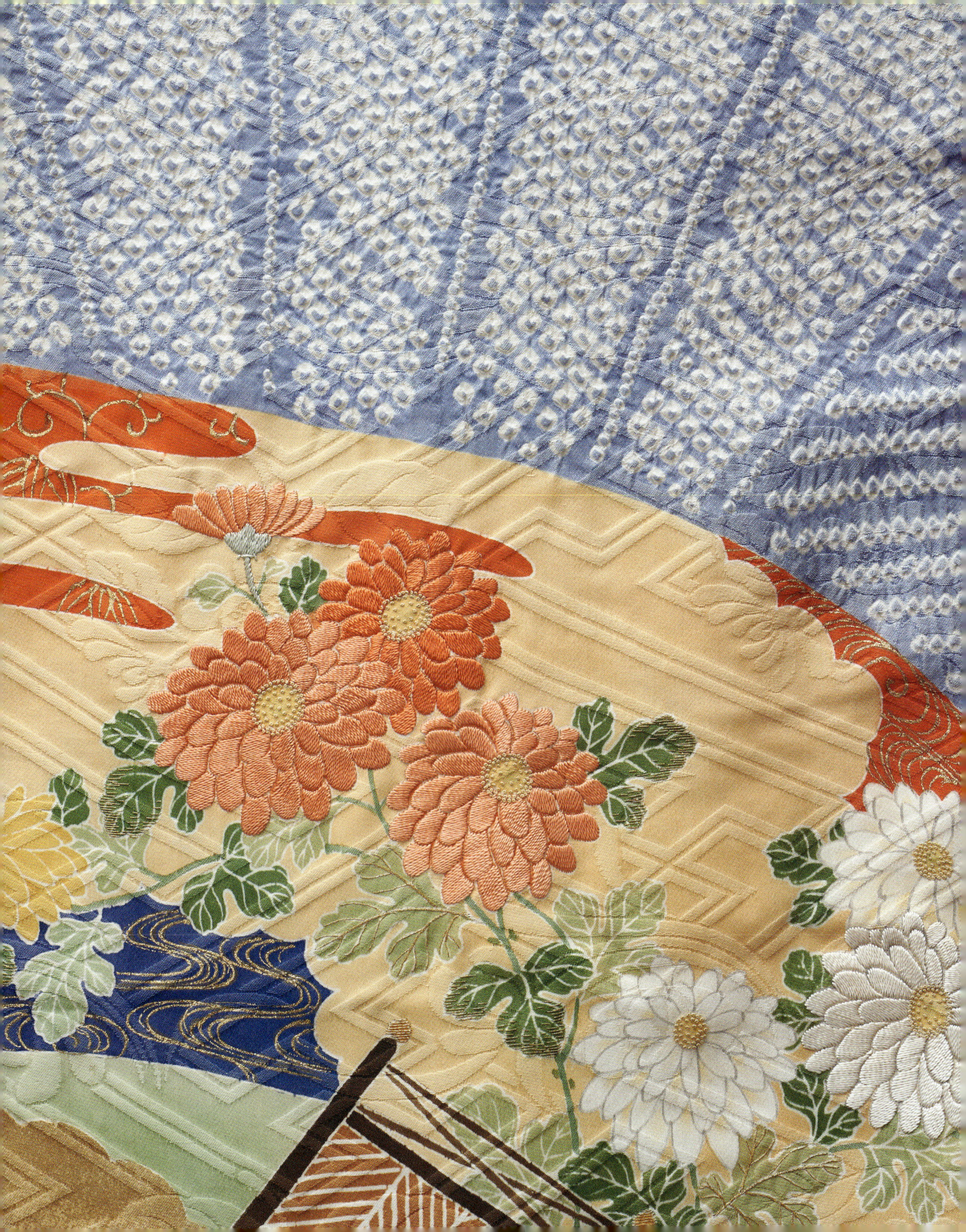

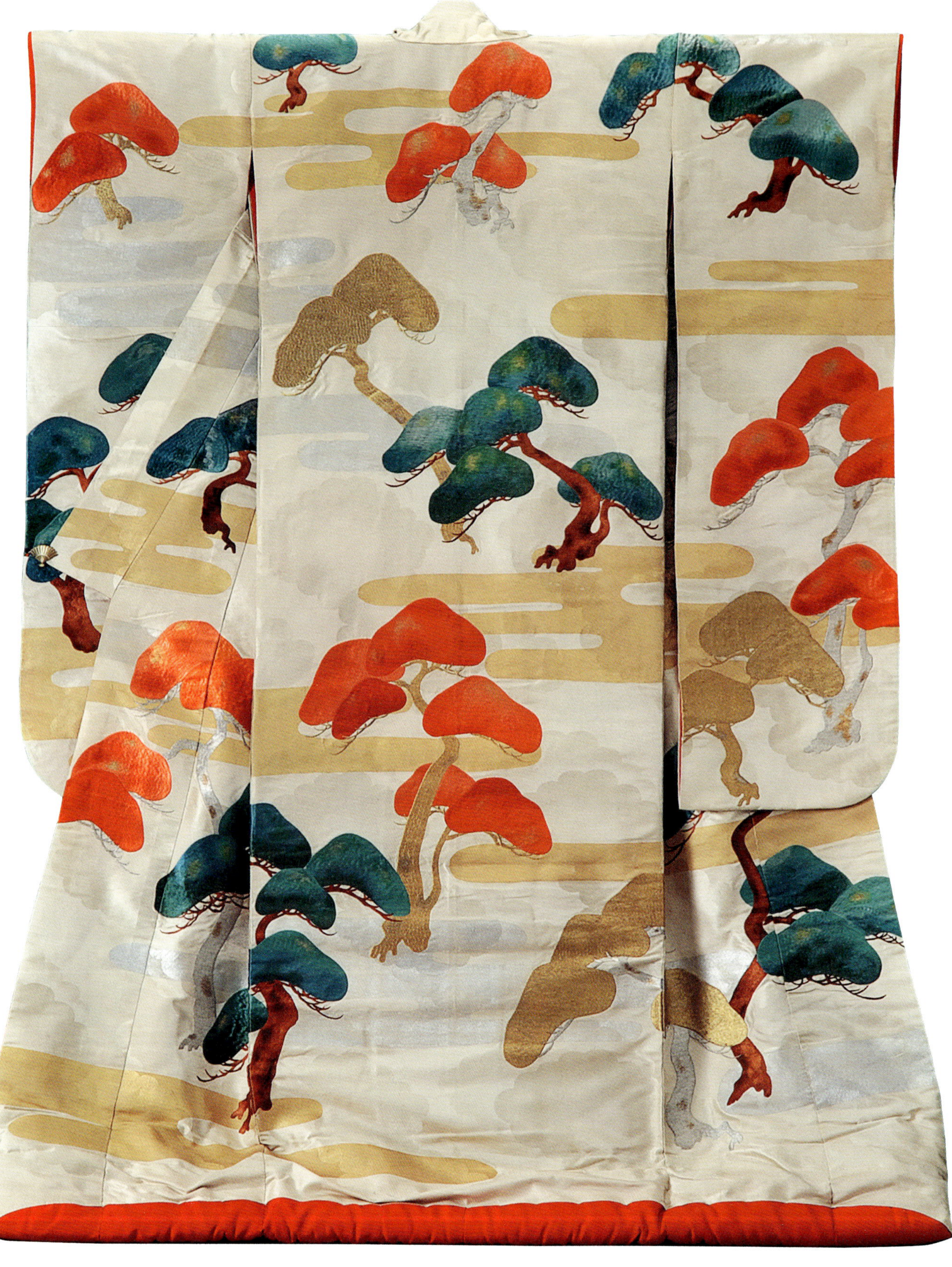

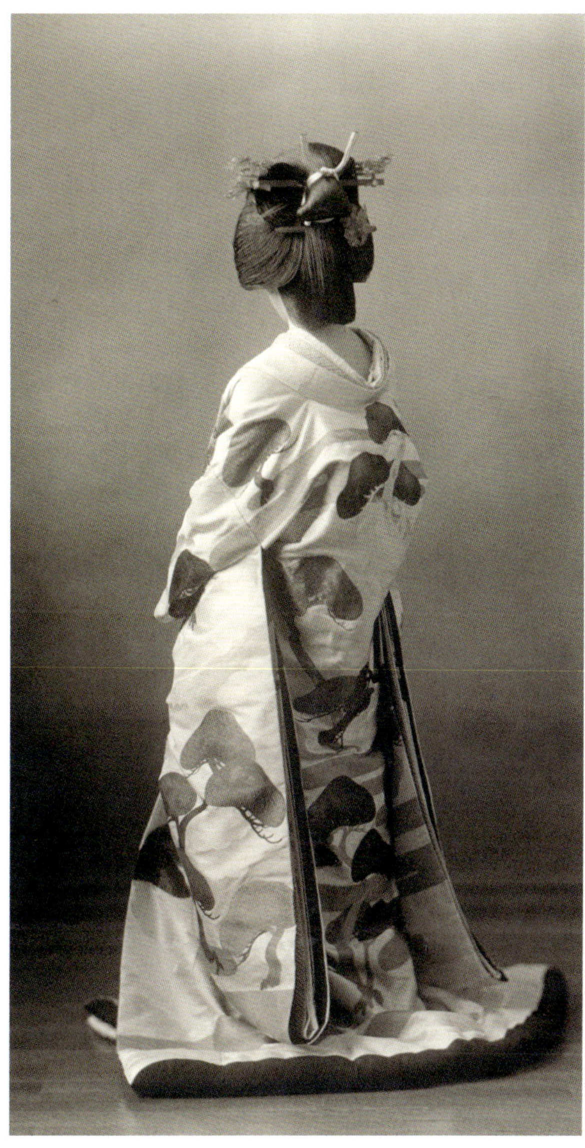

5

Chiso Co., Ltd.
Uchikake with Clouds and Pine Trees Design
Made for Nishimura Tokuko, the fourteenth Madame Nishimura (pictured)
1938, embroidery on woven silk
180 × 127 cm (70 ⅞ × 50 in.)

This extraordinary wedding kimono is one of three such kimono made for Nishimura Tokuko, the fourteenth Madame Nishimura and the daughter of Taka (see cat. 1). While the *furisode* is customarily worn by unmarried women, as seen in the women's photographs that would have been exchanged between families during the matchmaking (*omiai*) process (cats. 3, 4, 6 & 7), the *uchikake* is reserved for the formal wedding ceremony or the reception festivities (cats. 1–2). It is worn over a white silk kimono (*shiromuku*), unbelted like an overcoat, and usually with a silk lining (*fuki*) sewn on the hem to add elegance.

The cloud and pine tree design on this *uchikake*, embroidered in red, green, and bluish-green with gold and silver-wrapped threads, evokes one of the "Kōrin patterns" (*Kōrin moyō* or *Kōrin mon'yō*) by the Rinpa artist Ogata Kōrin (1658–1716) featured in textile pattern books (*hinagatabon*). These *hinagatabon* served as reference catalogues for the public and for textile makers. CS

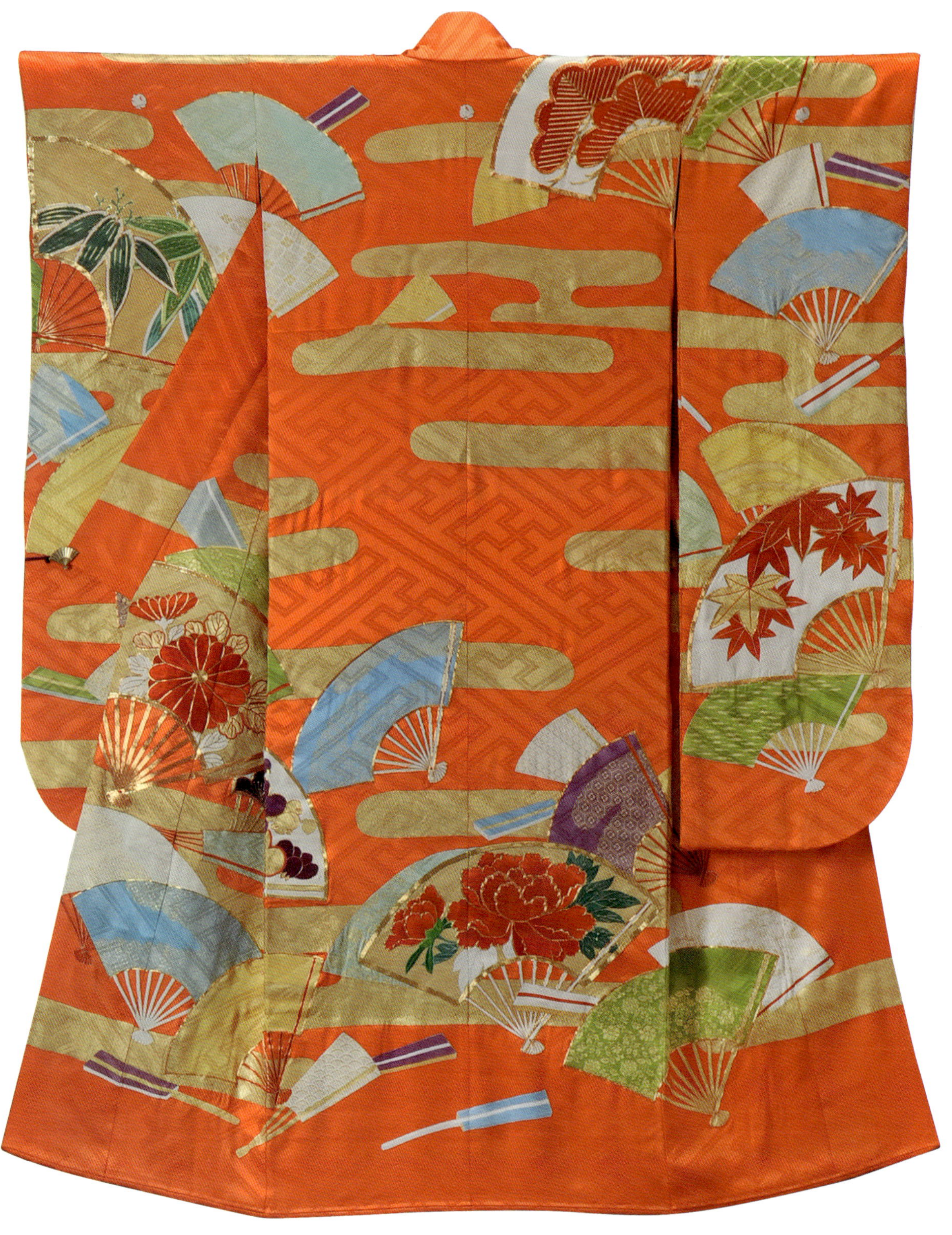

6

Chiso Co., Ltd.
Furisode with Mist and Fan Design
Made for Kawakami Masako, the fifteenth Madame Nishimura
1971, embroidery and gold leaf on woven silk
163 × 126 cm (64 $^{3}/_{16}$ × 49 $^{5}/_{8}$ in.)

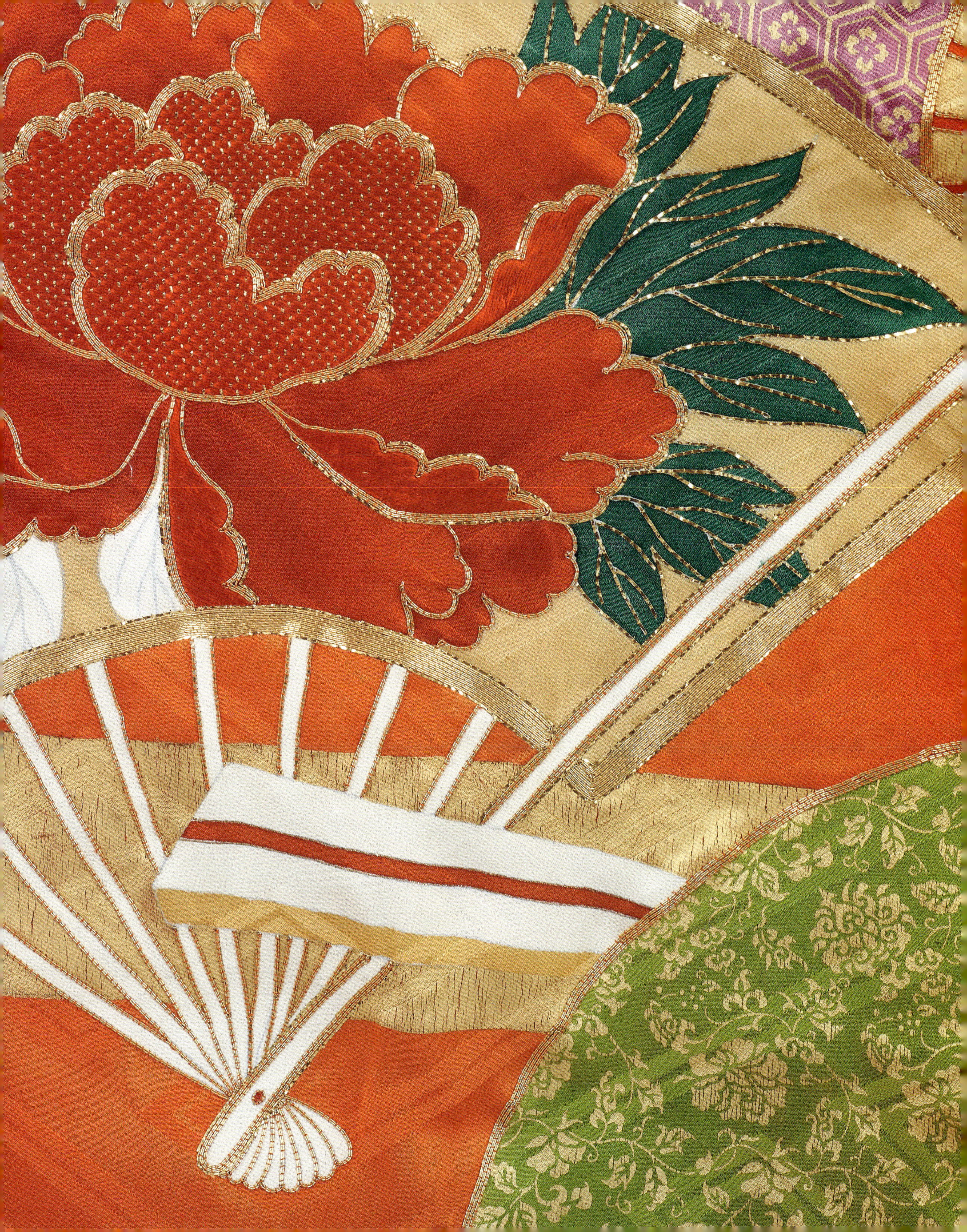

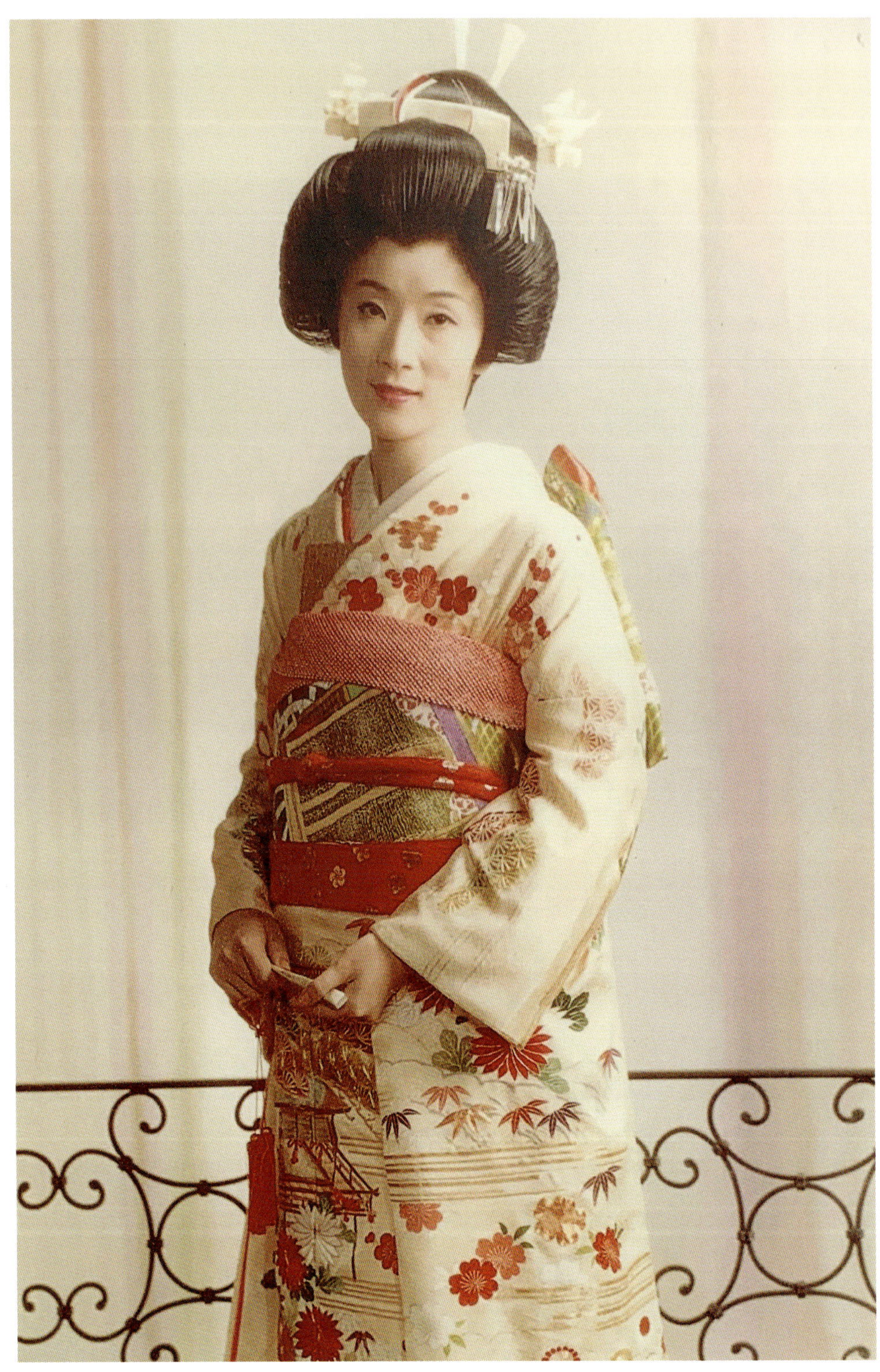

7

Chiso Co., Ltd.
Furisode with Palace Garden Design
Made for Kawakami Masako, the fifteenth Madame Nishimura (pictured)
1971, *yūzen*-dyeing, embroidery, and gold leaf on woven silk
165 × 138 cm (64 $^{15}/_{16}$ × 54 $^{5}/_{16}$ in.)

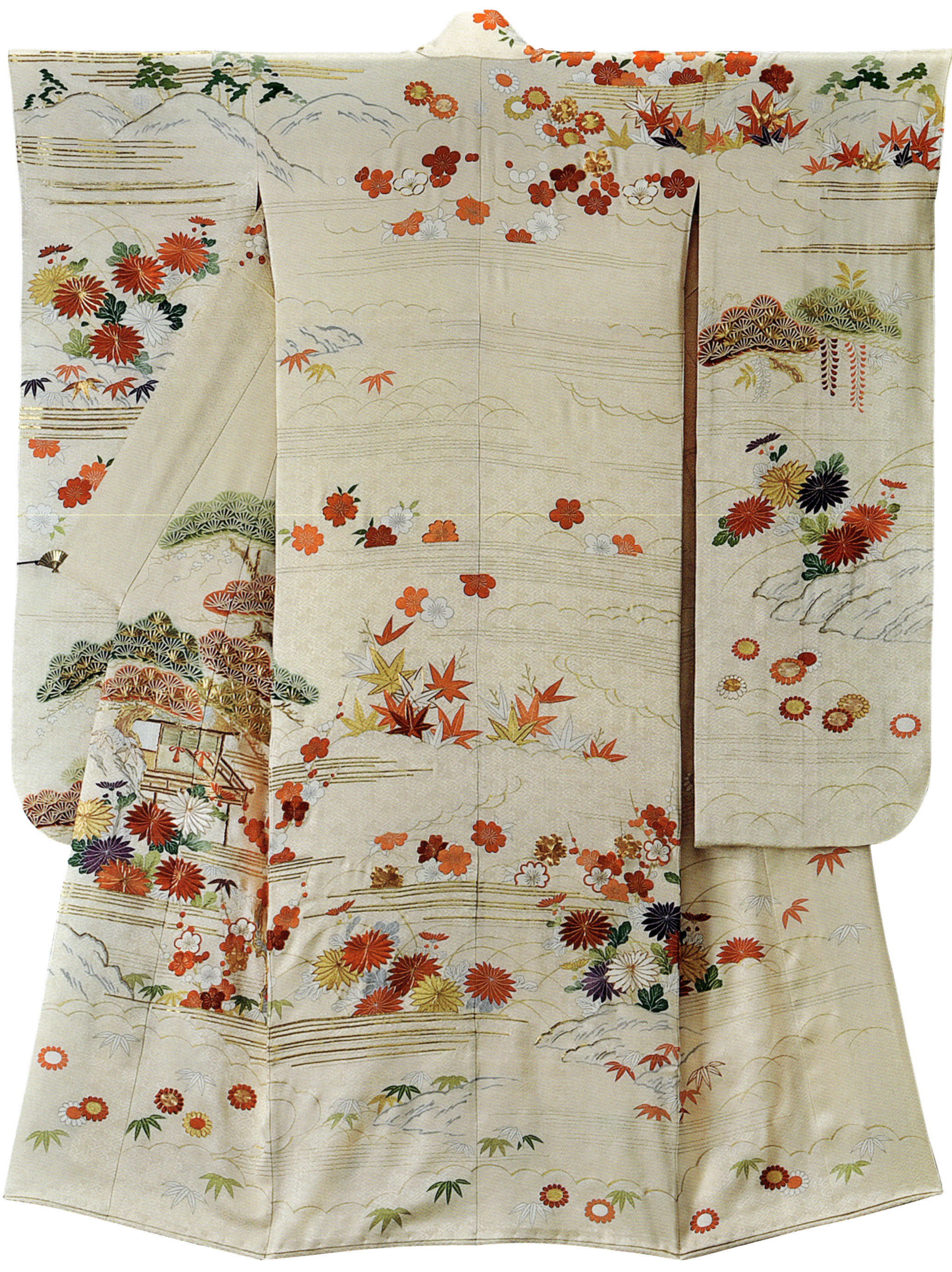

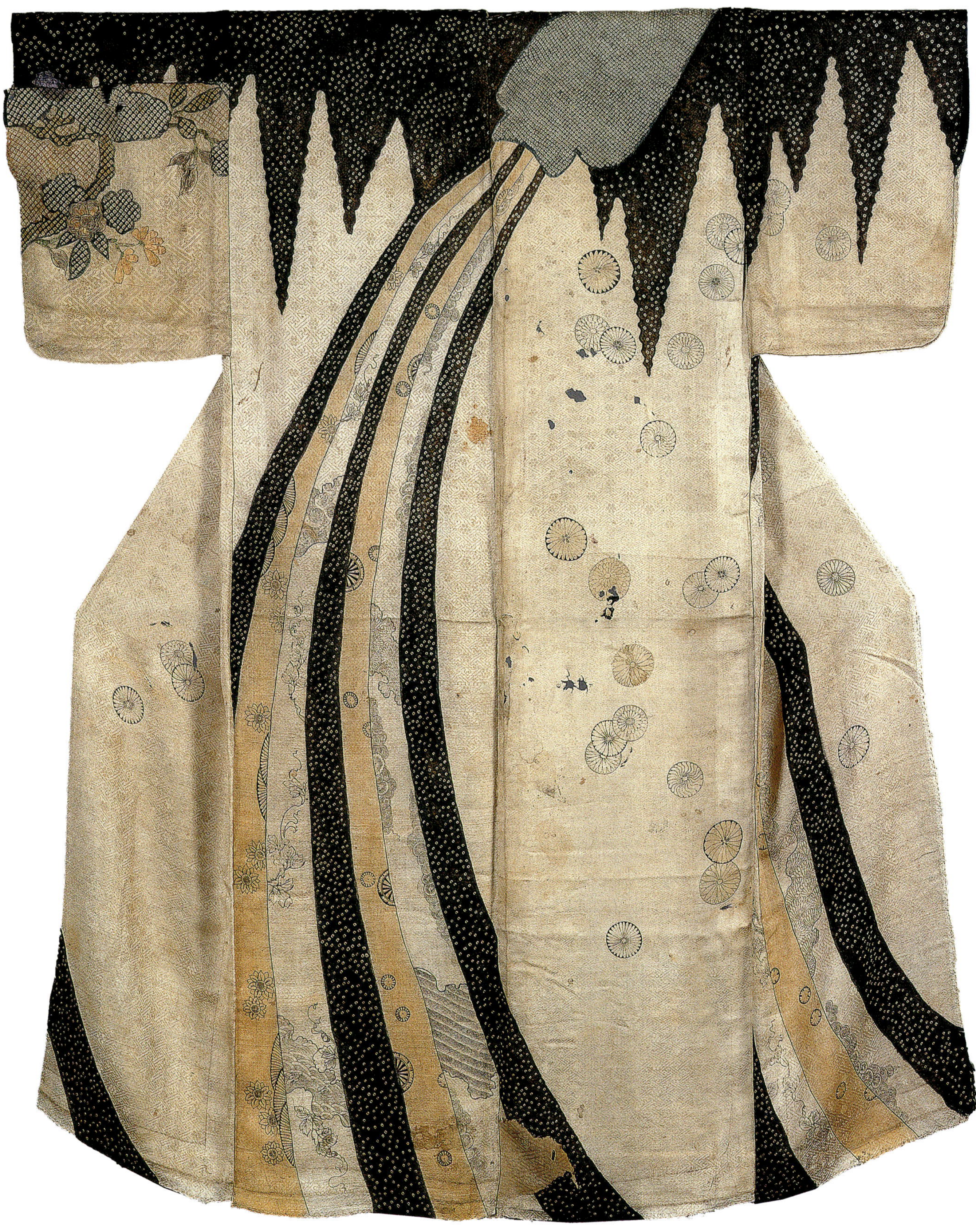

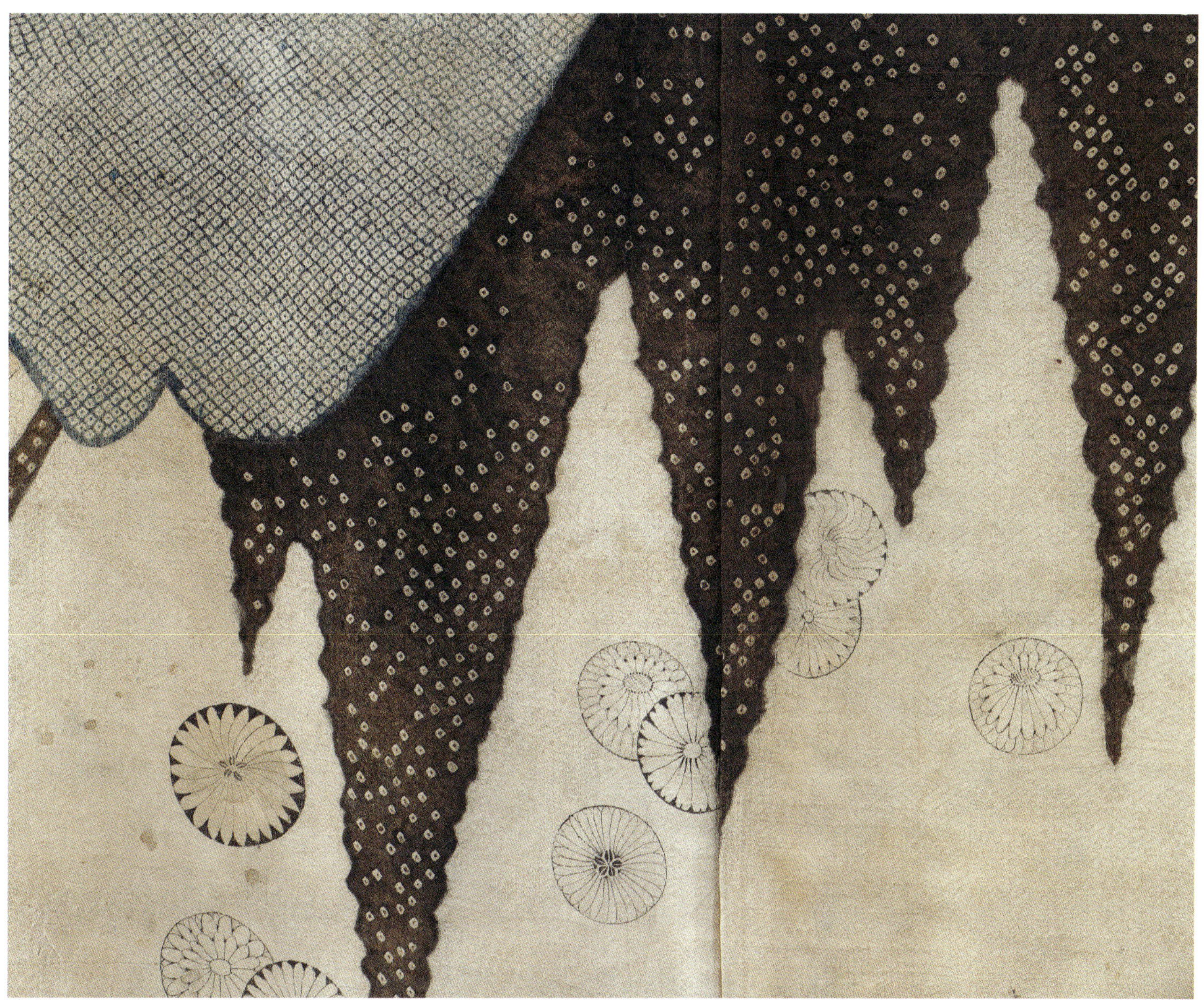

8

Artist unknown
Kosode with Overturned Flask Design
Mid to late 17th century, Edo period, 1603–1868
Kanoko shibori tie-dyeing and ink on white figured satin
157 × 128 cm (61 13⁄16 × 50 3⁄8 in.)

The early style of *kosode*, or small-sleeved robe, from the Kanbun era (1661–73) during Japan's Edo period (1603–1868) was noted for its dramatic, asymmetrical designs that swept diagonally across the garment from the upper back shoulder to the hem. This *kosode* showcases the motif of an overturned flask—created with the *kanoko shibori* technique (see detail p. 73)—along the shoulder that spills forth a multicolored stream of alternating dotted *shibori* and painted abstract cloud, wave, and floral patterns.

Kosode of the early Edo period, such as this example, were wider than in later eras because women were permitted to sit cross-legged. In the late seventeenth and early eighteenth centuries, however, people began to sit in what was considered the more formal kneeling position known as *seiza* with legs folded underneath and the thighs and knees together. Moreover, the bold kimono designs that characterized the Kanbun and the subsequent Genroku era (1688–1704) were eventually replaced in the second half of the 1700s with a preference for an understated sophistication and small repetitive patterns (*komon*). **VL**

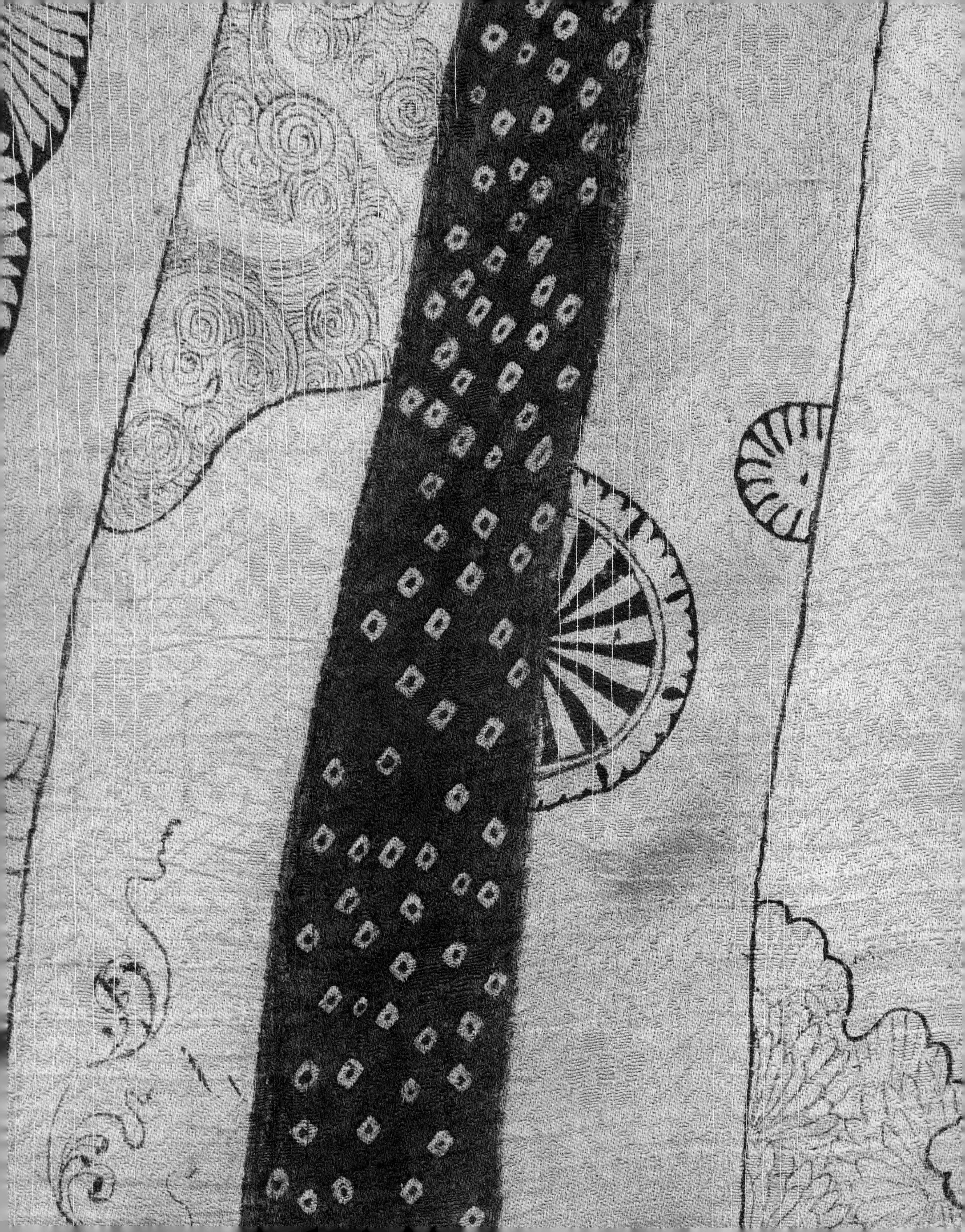

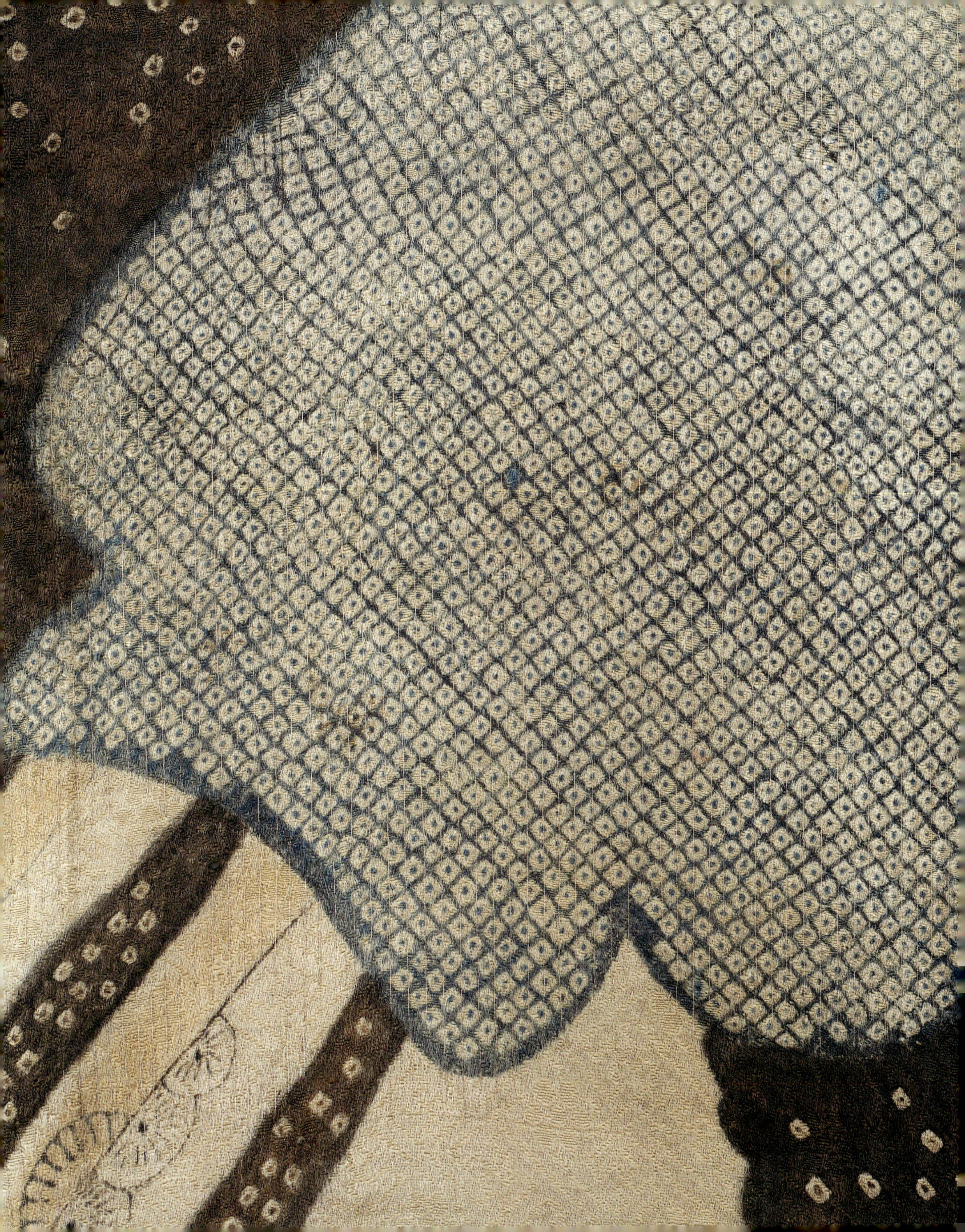

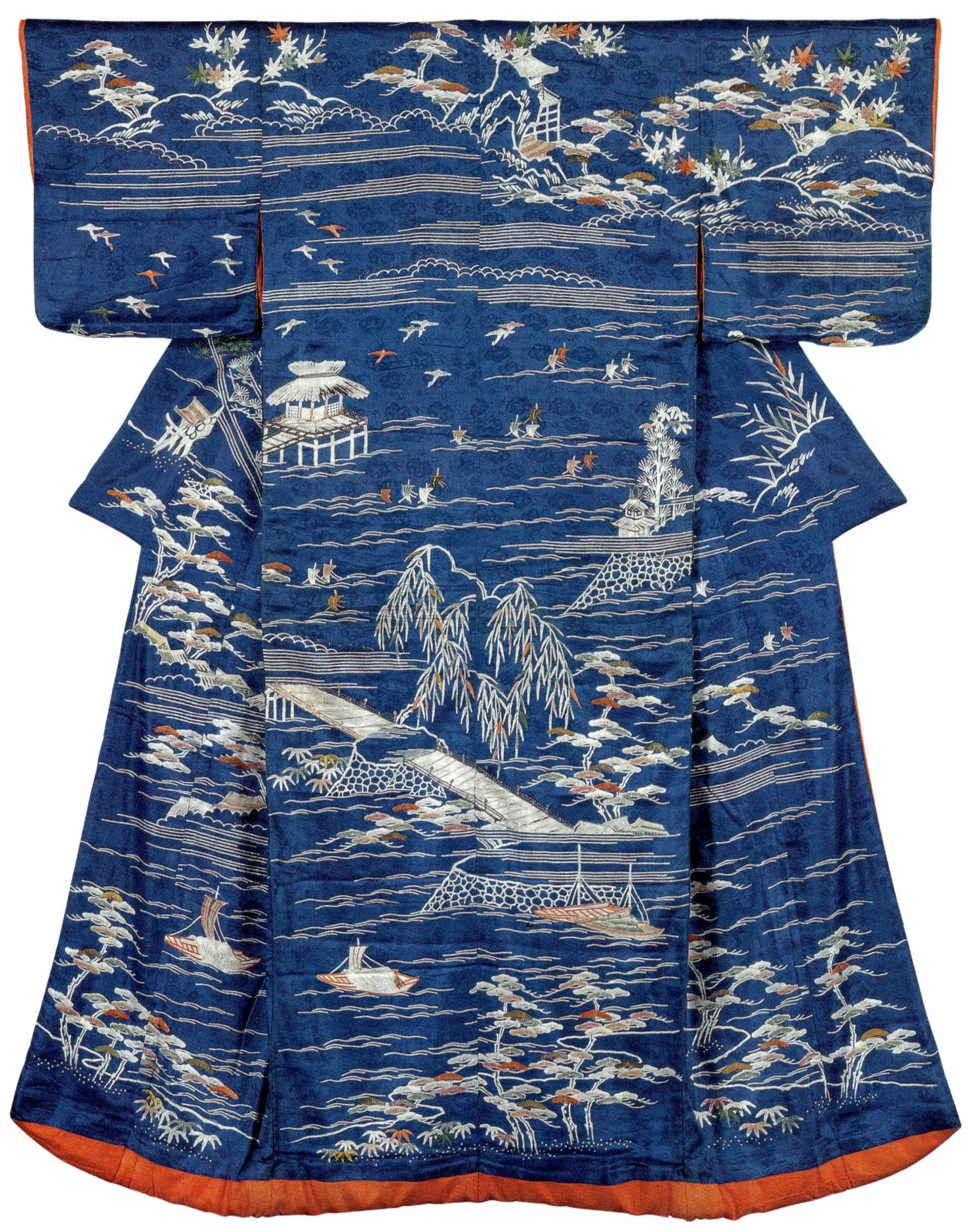

9

Artist unknown

Kosode with Eight Views of Ōmi Province Design

Mid-18th century, Edo period, 1603–1868

Yūzen-dyeing and embroidery on dark blue figured satin

155.5 × 126 cm (61 ¼ × 49 ⅝ in.)

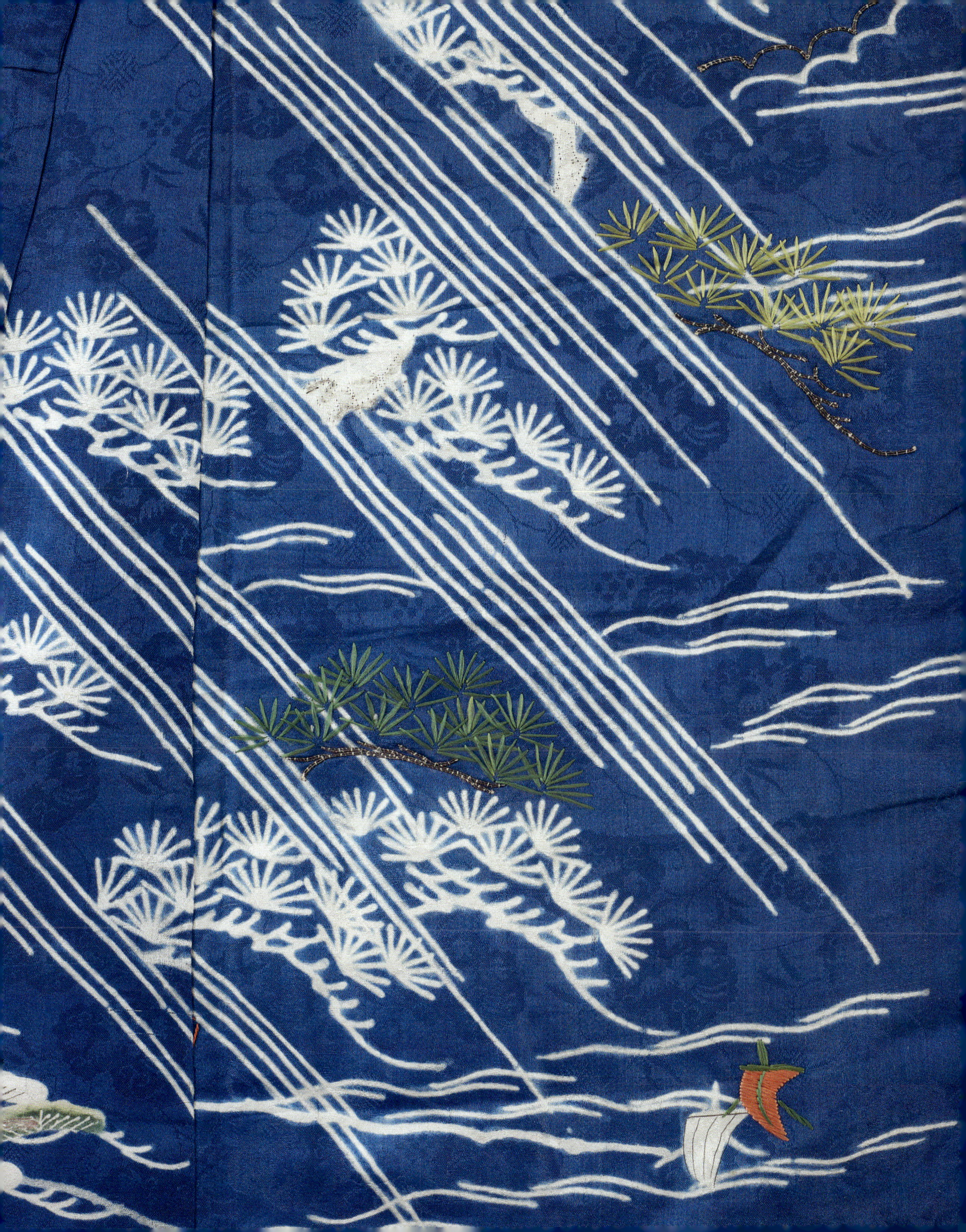

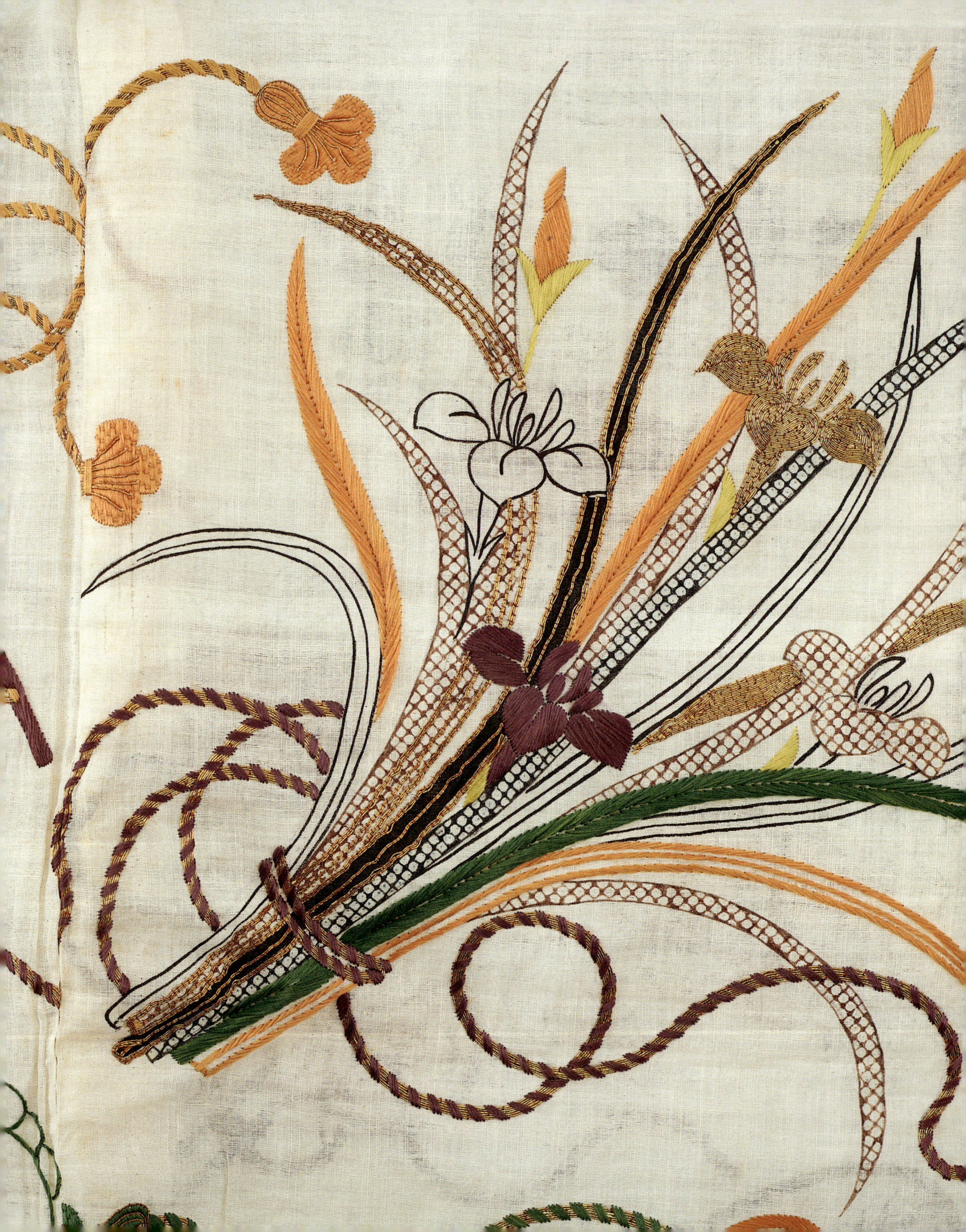

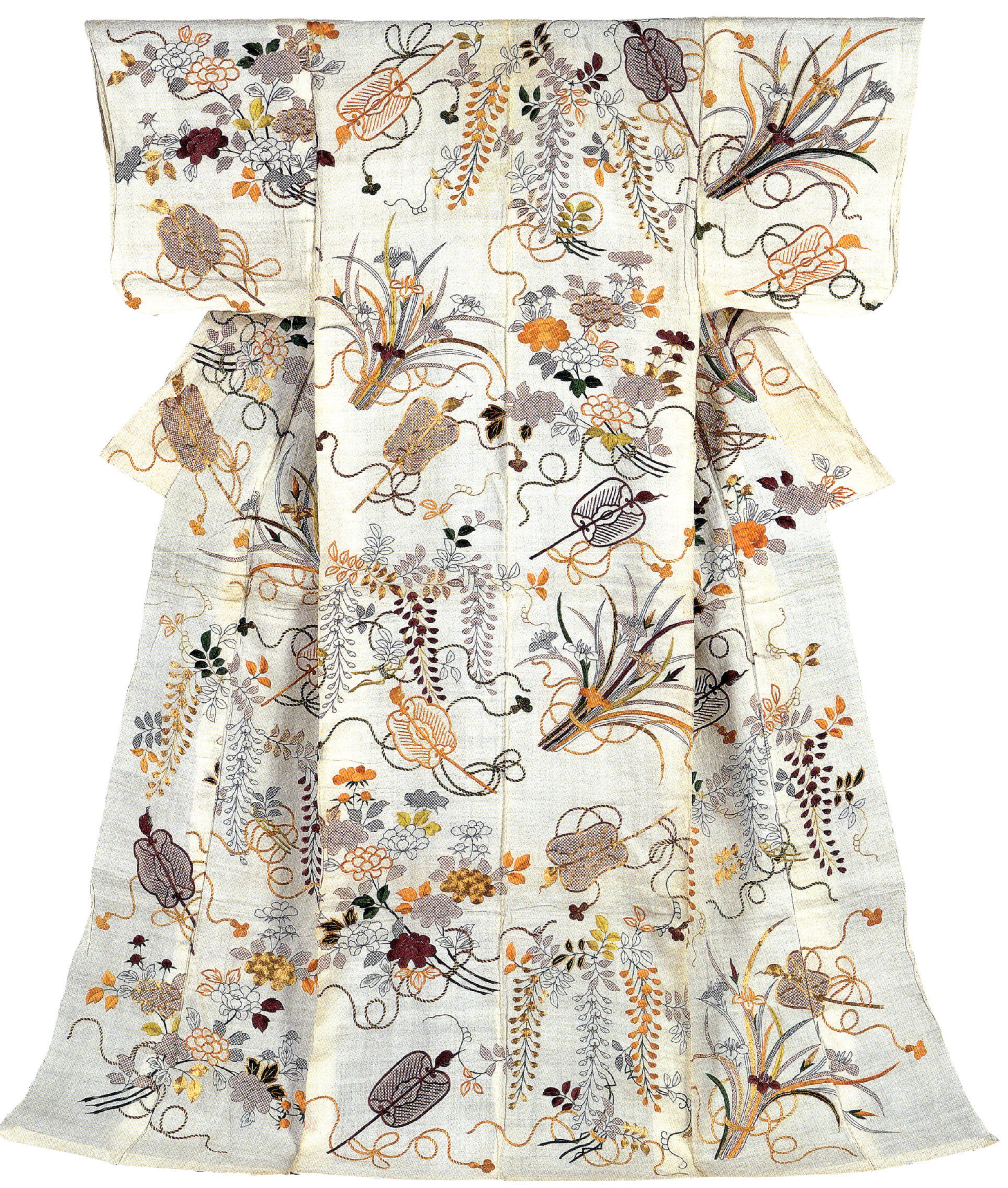

10

Artist unknown

Katabira with Chinese Fan and Flower Bouquet Design

Late 18th to early 19th century, Edo period, 1603–1868

Embroidery and stencil imitation tie-dyeing *(kata-kanoko)* on white ramie

168 × 122 cm (66 ⅛ × 48 in.)

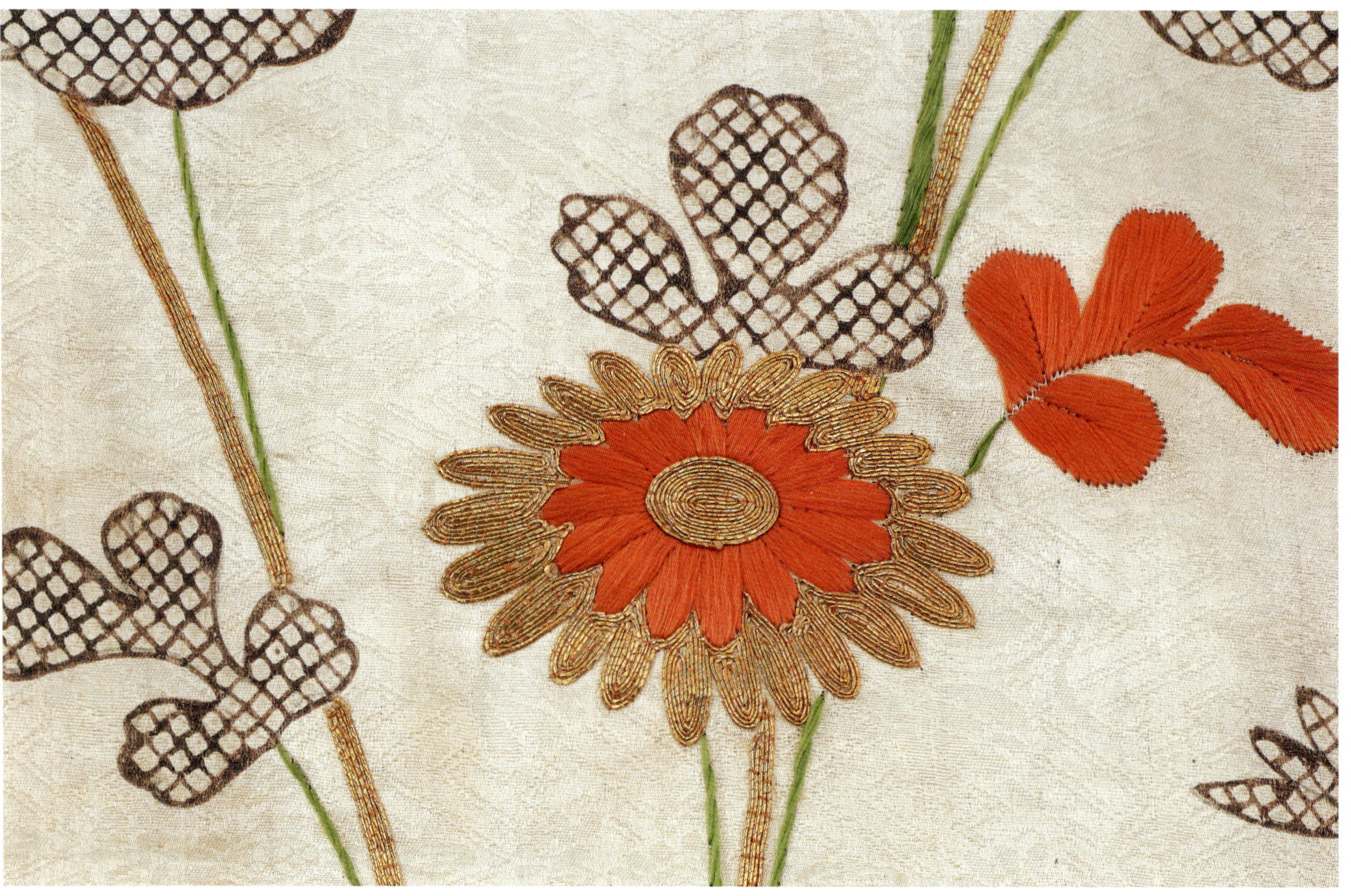

11

Artist unknown
Kosode with Tree, Chrysanthemum Plant, and Characters Design
Mid to late 18th century, Edo period, 1603–1868
Stencil imitation tie-dyeing (*kata-kanoko*), ink, and embroidery on white figured satin
148 × 120 cm (58 ¼ × 47 ¼ in.)

This stunning *kosode* has a chrysanthemum "standing tree design" (*tachiki moyō*) that extends from the hem to the shoulders. The allover chrysanthemum motif is created with stencil imitation tie-dyeing (*kata-kanoko*) that serves as the background for embroidered red chrysanthemum blossoms. Bold calligraphic Chinese characters (*kanji*) are embroidered in red and gold on the chest and shoulder sections along the back of the garment. On the front are the characters *yorokobi* (歓) and *ka* (嘉). On the back of the garment, as pictured on the opposite page, are the characters from right to left: *kiwamari* (極), *shin* (辰), *rei* (令), and *getsu* (月). These are drawn from the seven-character classical Chinese poetic sequence (Jp: *shichigon-zekku*) by the seventh-century Chinese poet Xie Yan (Jp: Shaen) included in the late eleventh-century Japanese imperial poetry anthology, *Collection of Japanese and Chinese Poems for Singing* (*Wakan rōeishū*).

Japanese poetry and literary aficionados would see the characters on this kimono as part of a literary game that invited them to identify the verse and therefore the poet. Those who correctly recognized Xie Yan's poem, given below, would have delighted in the appropriateness of the characters in celebrating the special occasion heralded by the donning of this *kosode*:

This wondrous time, these supreme months—
Joy without an end!
Ten thousand years, a thousand autumns—
Happiness that never stops.

***kashin reigetsu yorokobi kiwamari**nashi* 嘉辰令月歓無極
bansei senshū tanoshimi imada nakabanarazu 万歳千秋楽未央

(English trans. J. Thomas Rimer et al., *Japanese and Chinese Poems to Sing: The Wakan rōei shū*, New York: Columbia University Press, 1997, 230).

CS

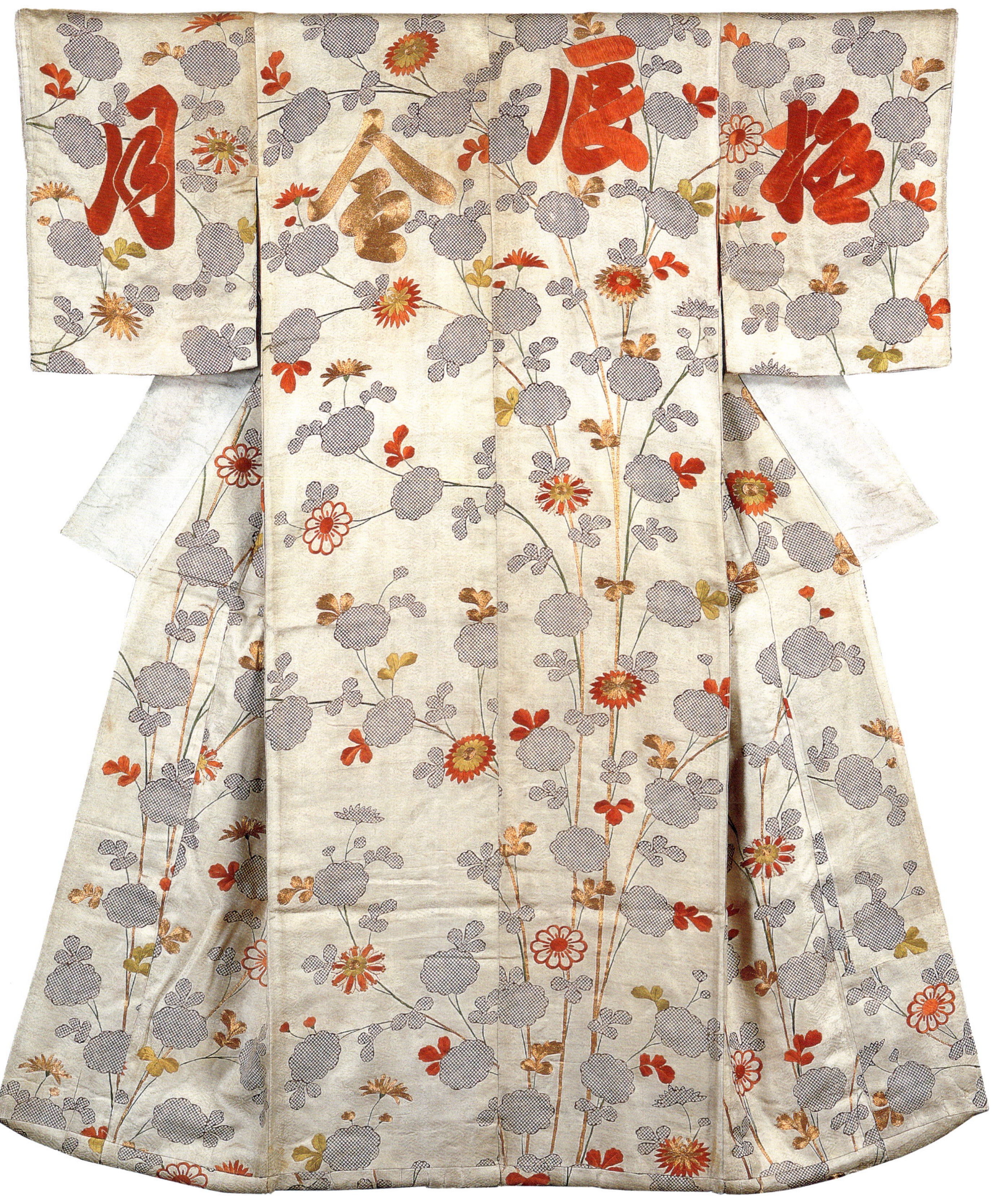

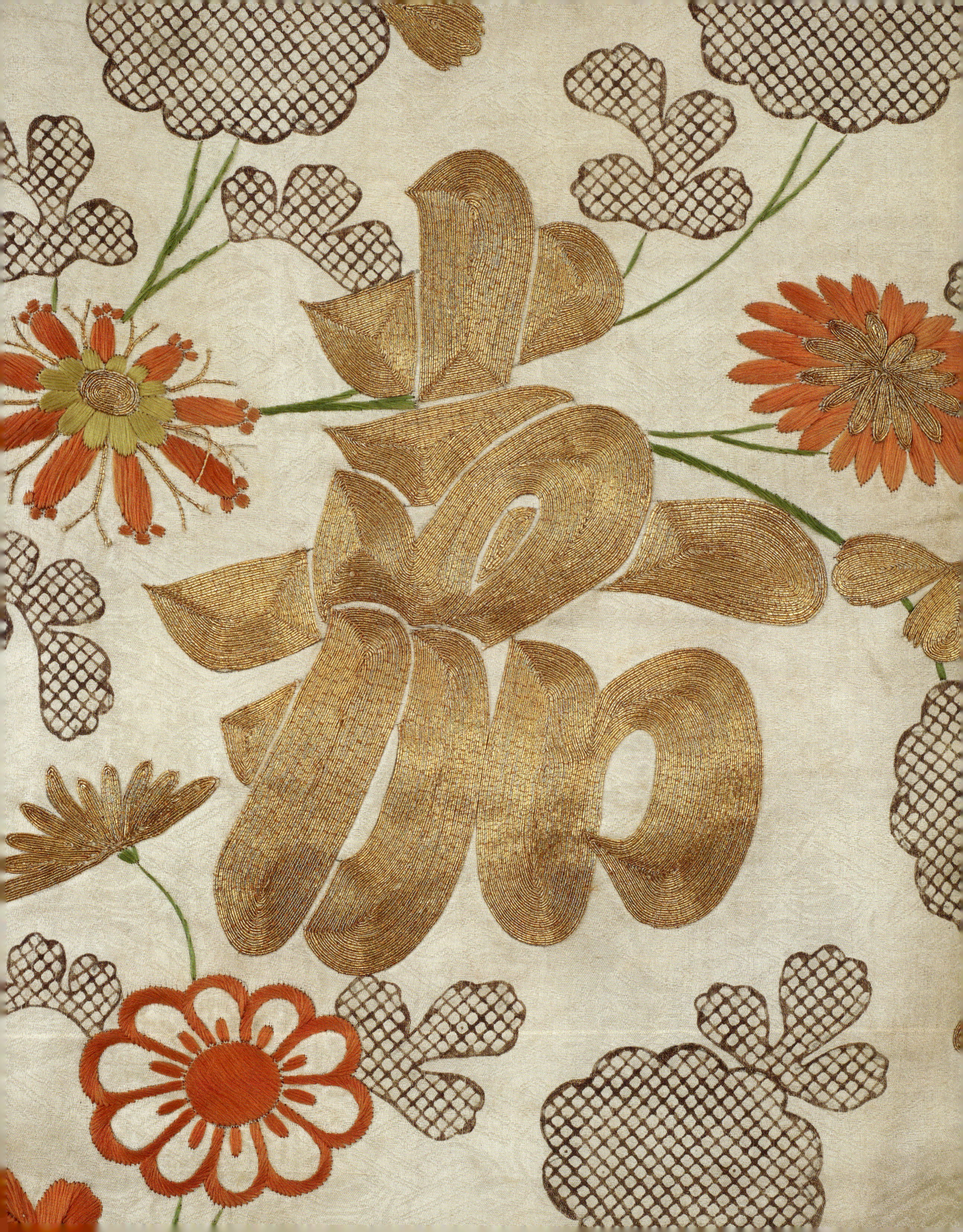

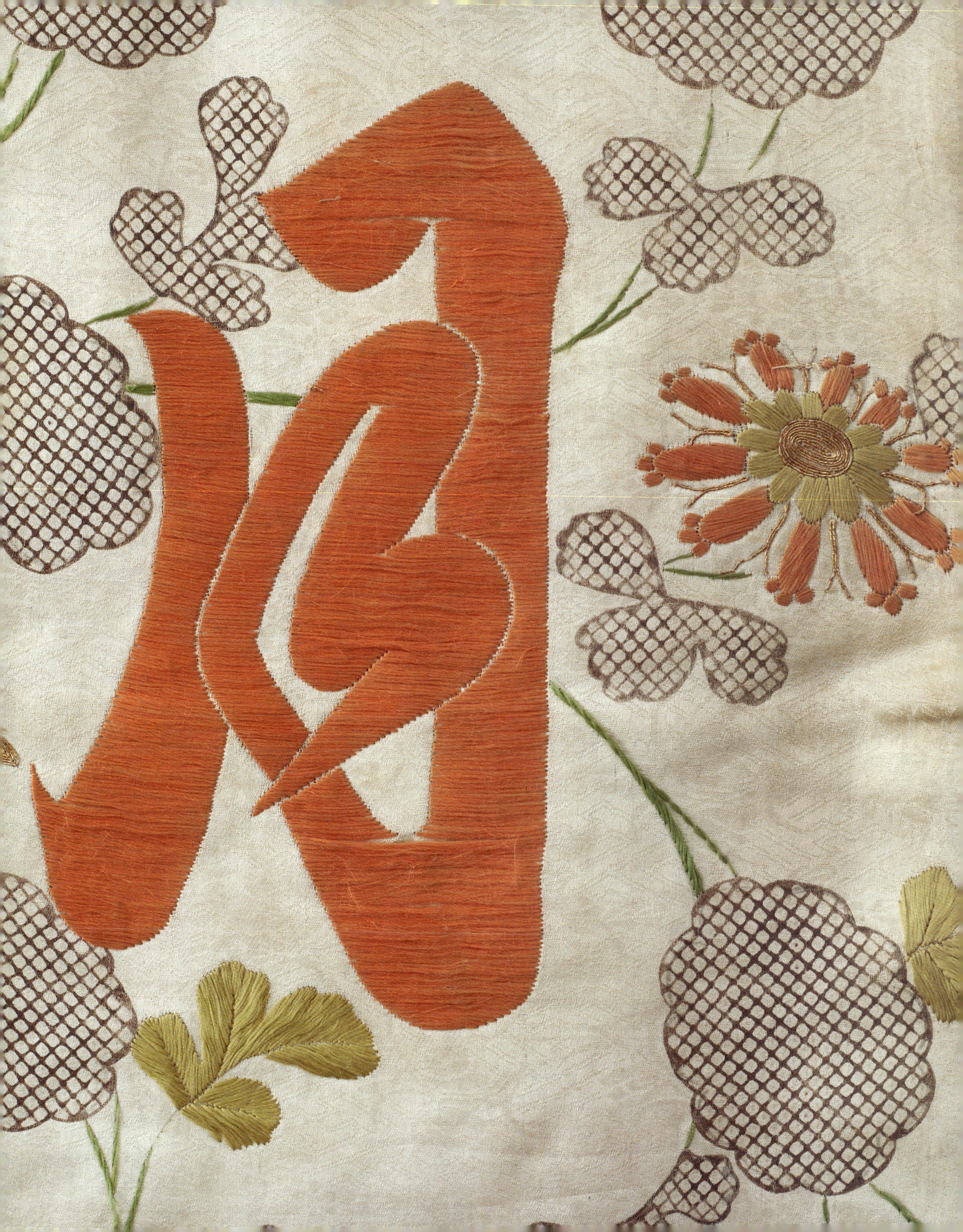

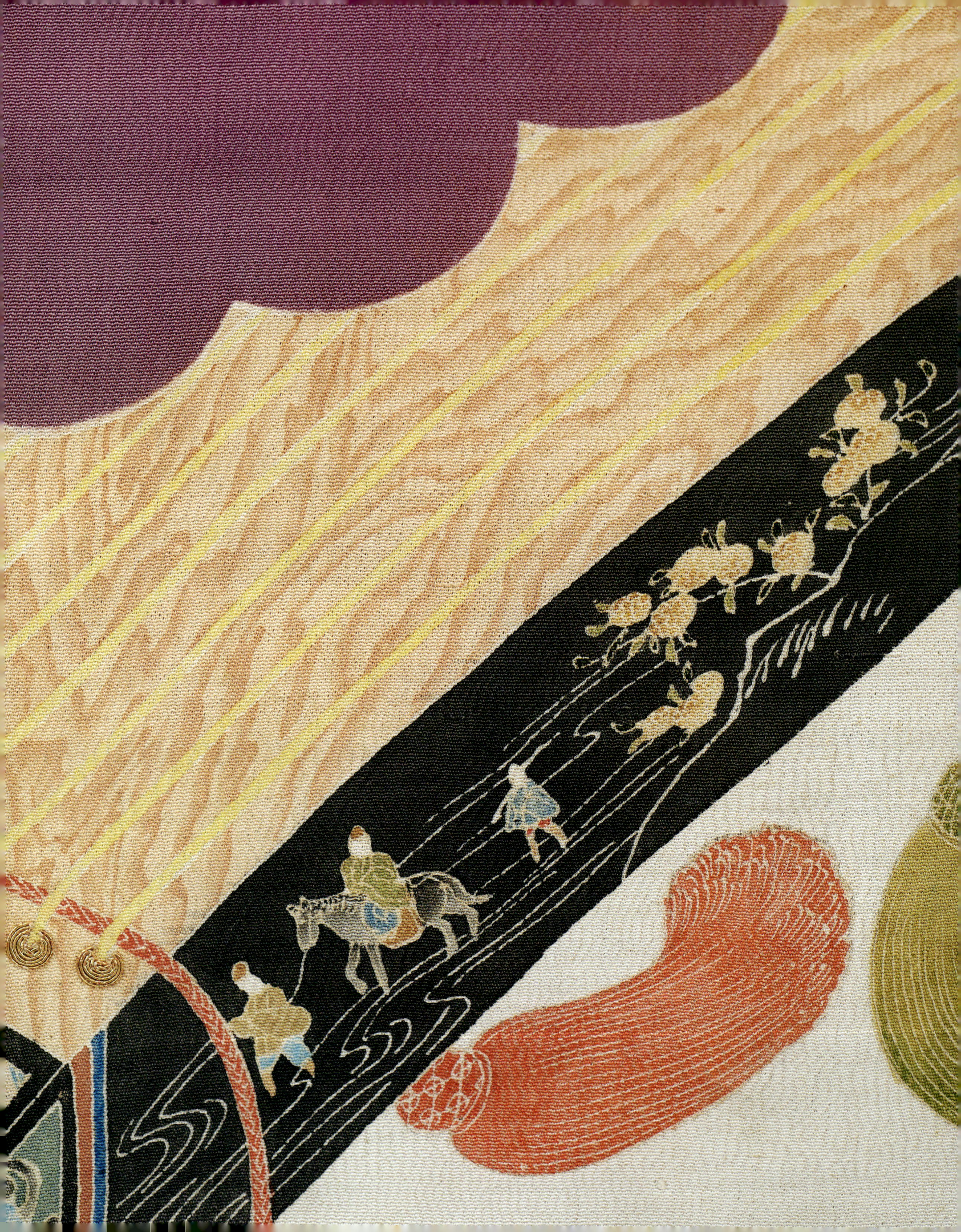

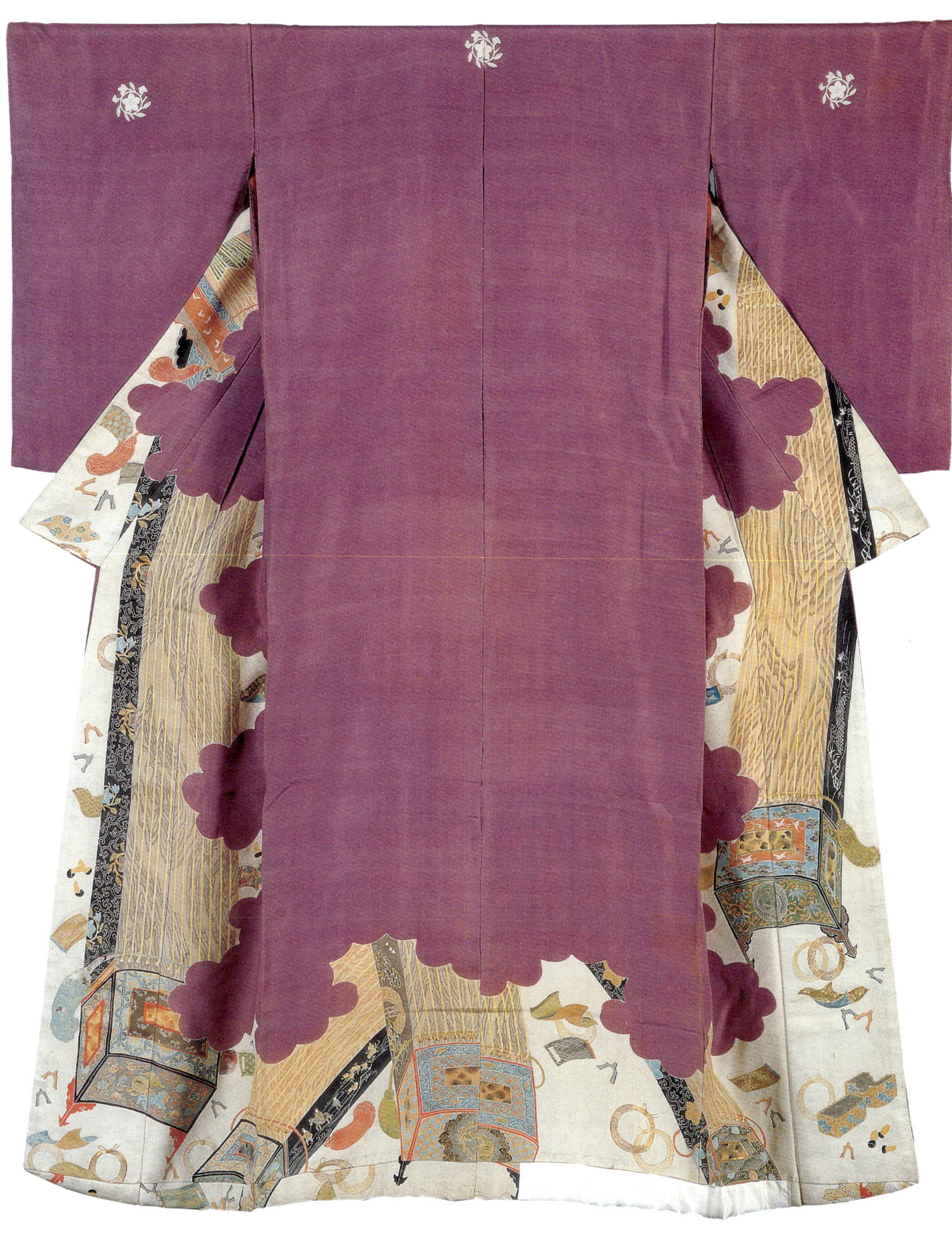

12

Artist unknown
Kosode with Koto and Cloud Design and Edge Pattern
Late 19th century, Meiji period, 1868–1912
Yūzen-dyeing and embroidery on purple silk crepe *(chirimen)*
146.3 × 118.6 cm (57 5/8 × 46 11/16 in.)

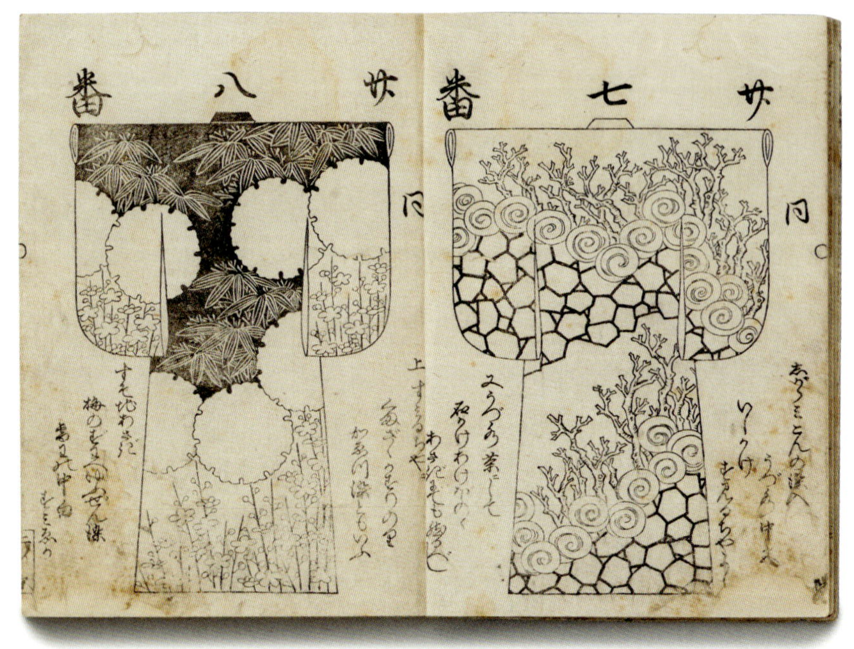

廿七番
廿八番

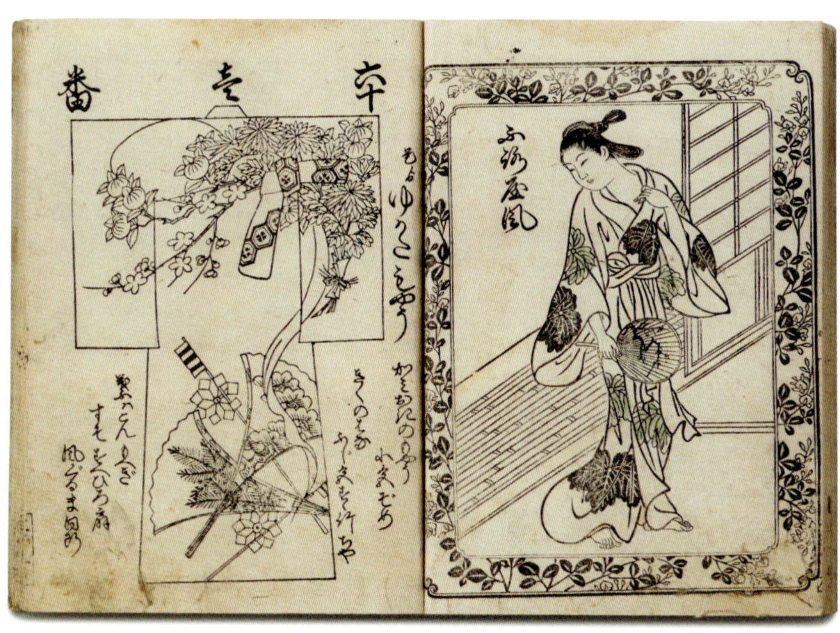

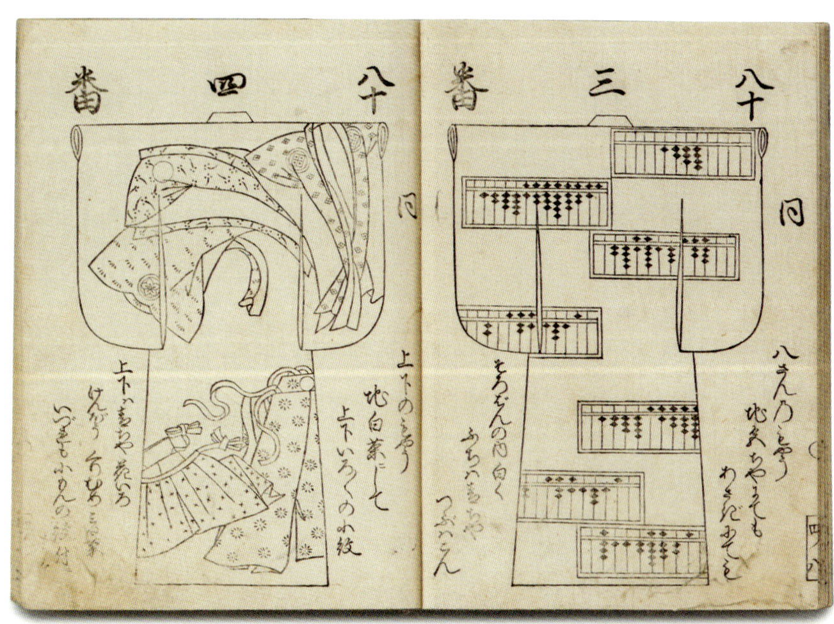

八十三番
八十四番

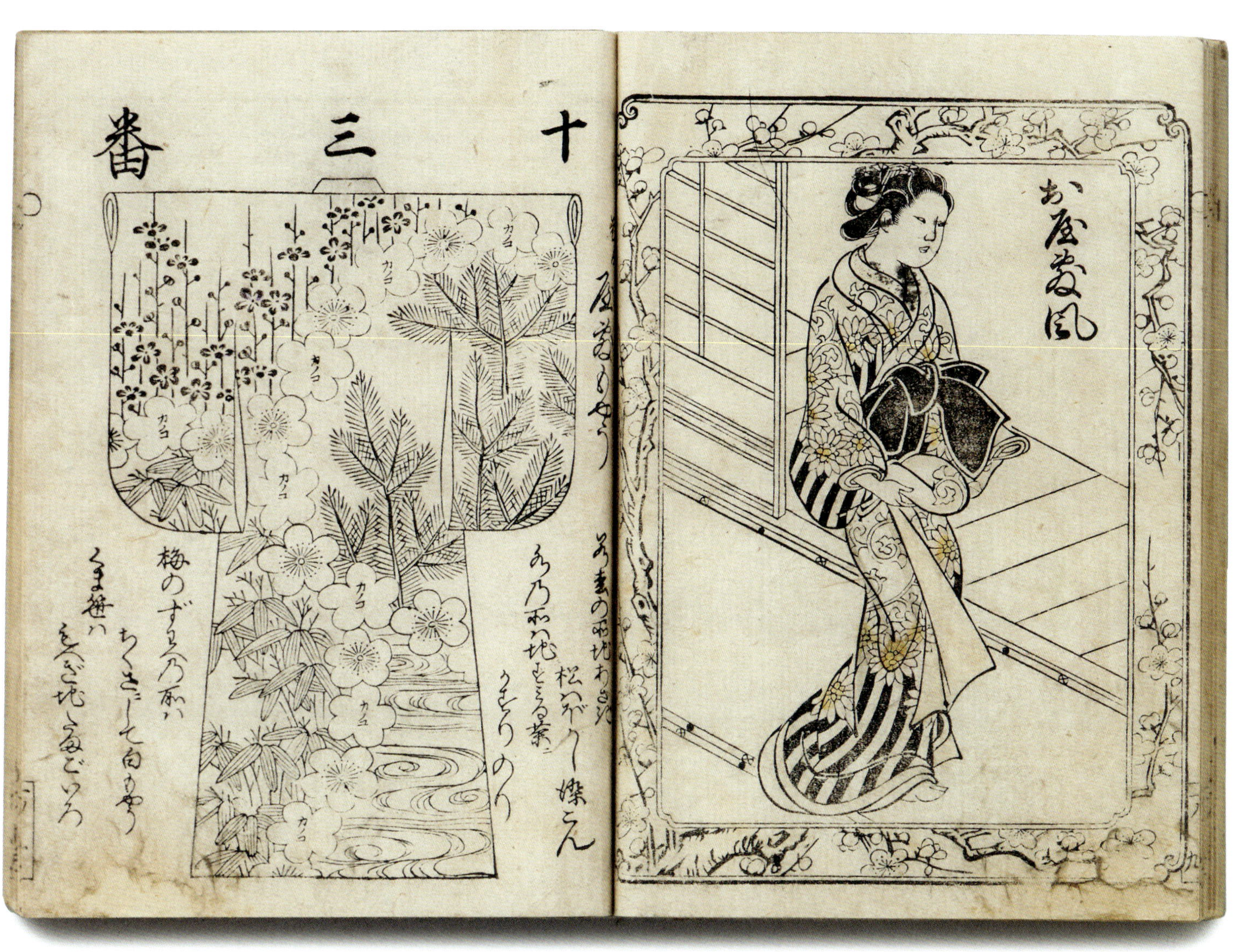

13

Nishikawa Sukenobu, 1671–1750
Patterns from the Shōtoku Era (Shōtoku hinagata)
1713, publisher: Hachimonjiya Hachizaemon
Five volumes, woodblock-printed book with black-line printing *(sumizuri)*
20.8 × 15.6 cm (8 3⁄16 × 6 1⁄8 in.)

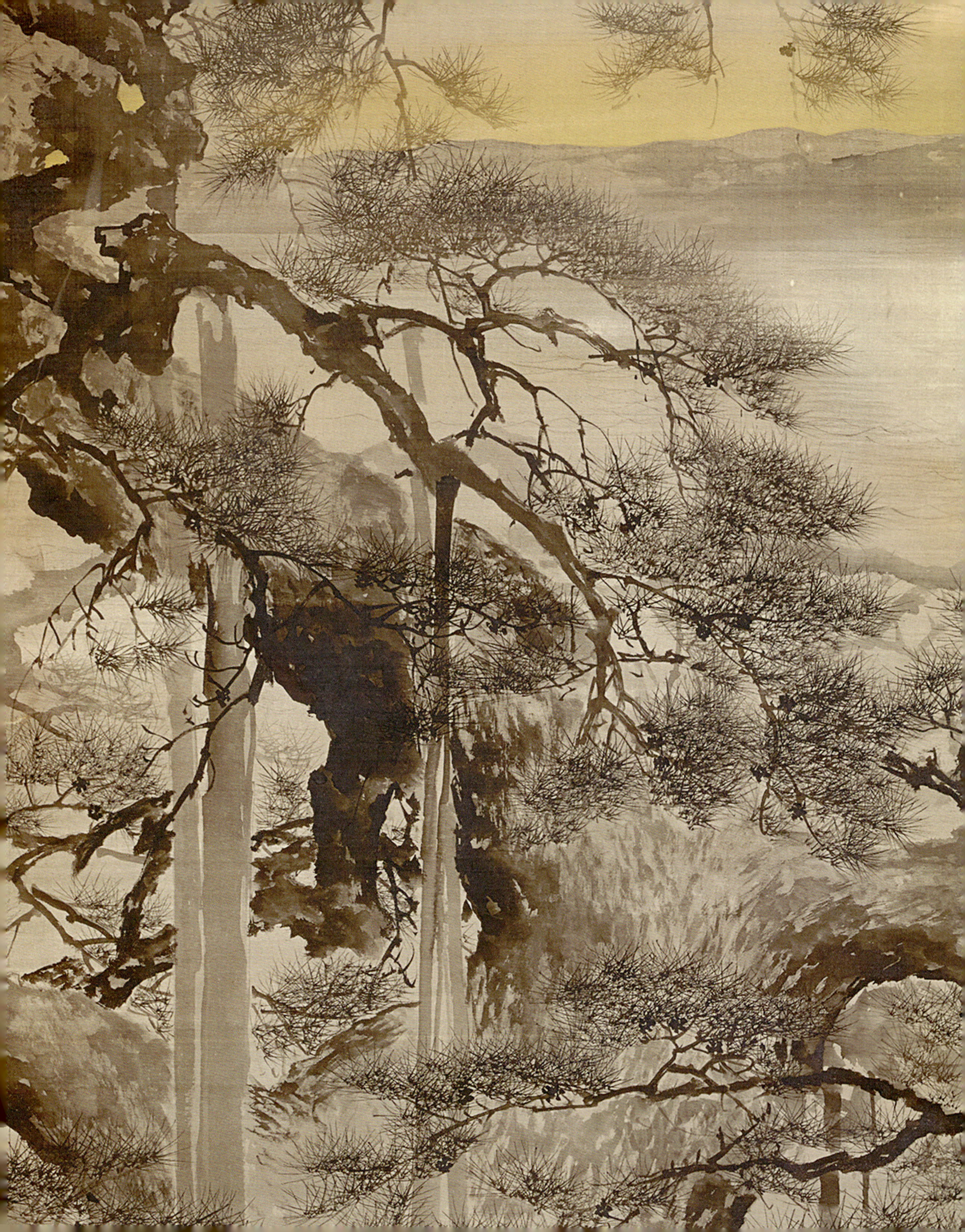

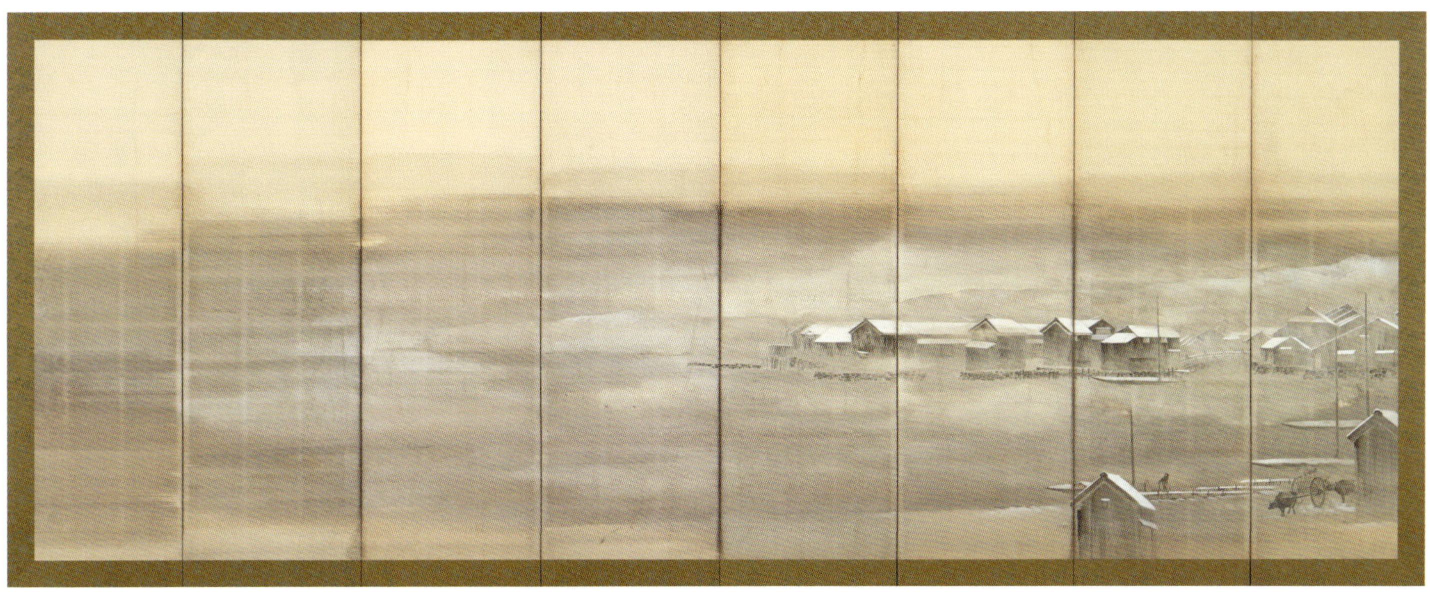

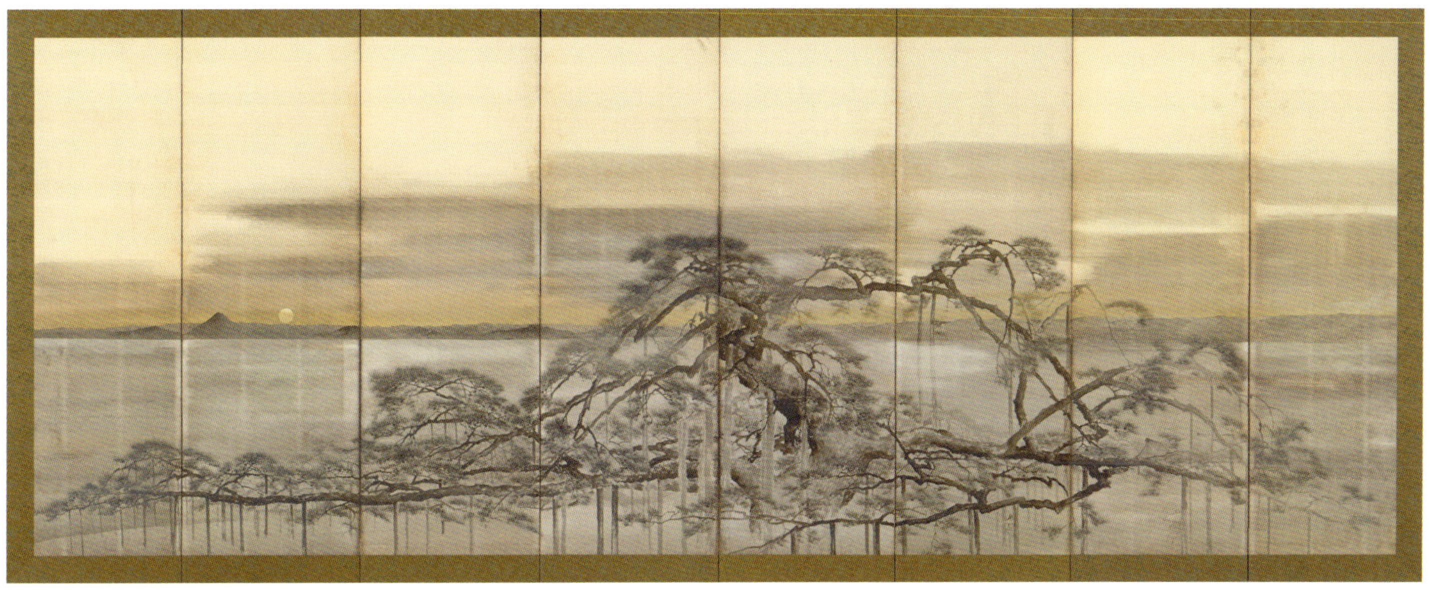

14

Kishi Chikudō, 1826–97

Karasaki

1876, one of a pair of eight-panel folding screens; ink and color on paper

158 × 422 cm (62 $^{3}/_{16}$ × 166 $^{1}/_{8}$ in.)

Ōtsu

1876, one of a pair of eight-panel folding screens; ink and color on paper

158 × 422 cm (62 $^{3}/_{16}$ × 166 $^{1}/_{8}$ in.)

(for a discussion of these screens, see Yukio Lippit's essay in this volume)

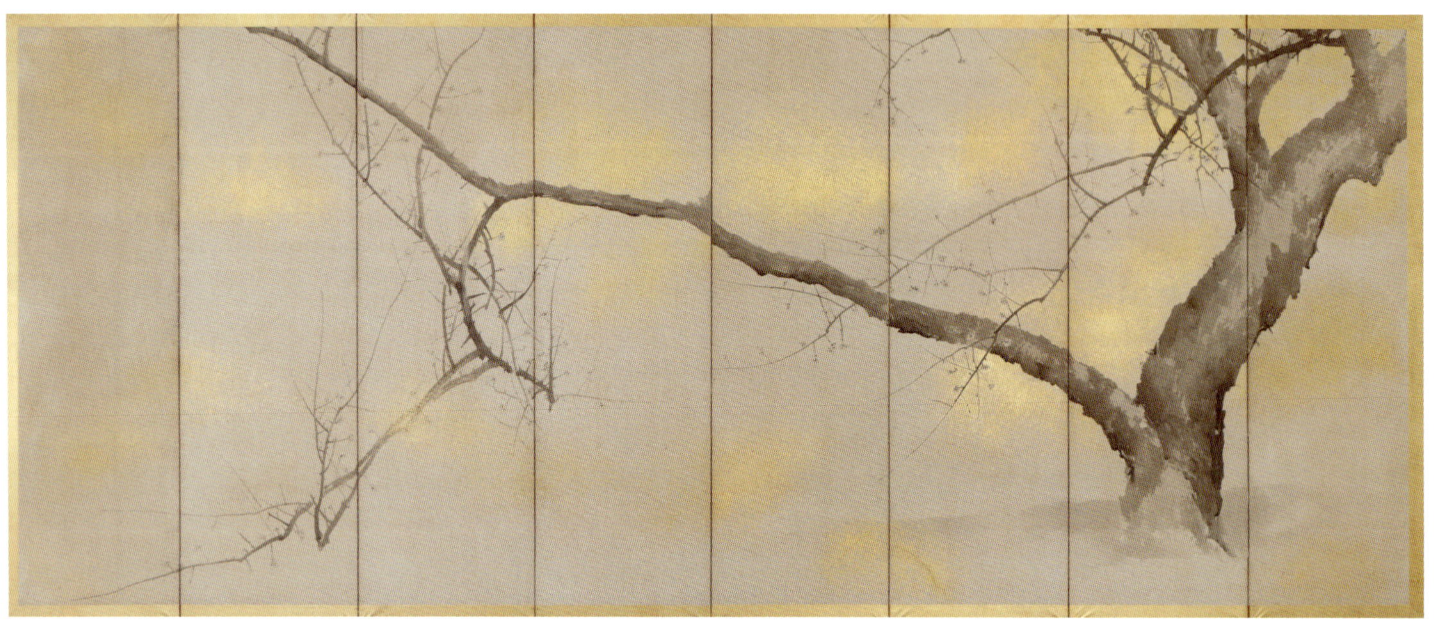

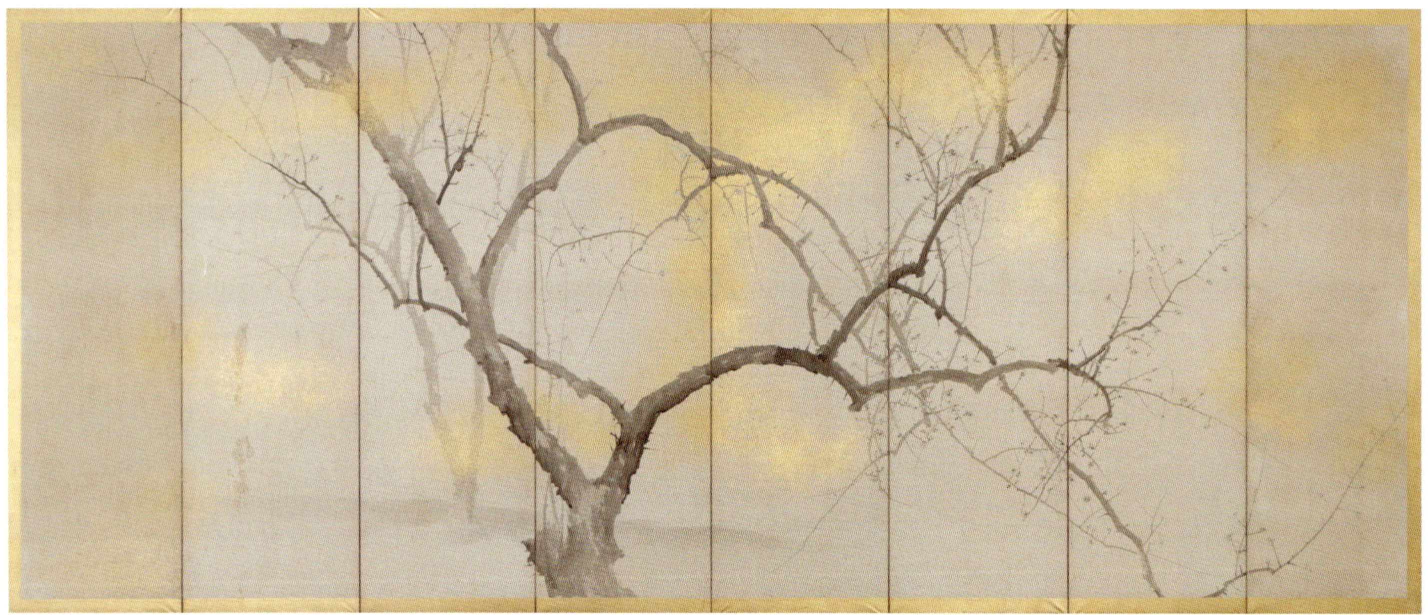

15

Kishi Chikudō, 1826–97

Plum Tree

Late 19th century, Meiji period, 1868–1912

Pair of eight-panel folding screens; ink and color on paper

158 × 422 cm each (62 3/16 × 166 1/8 in.)

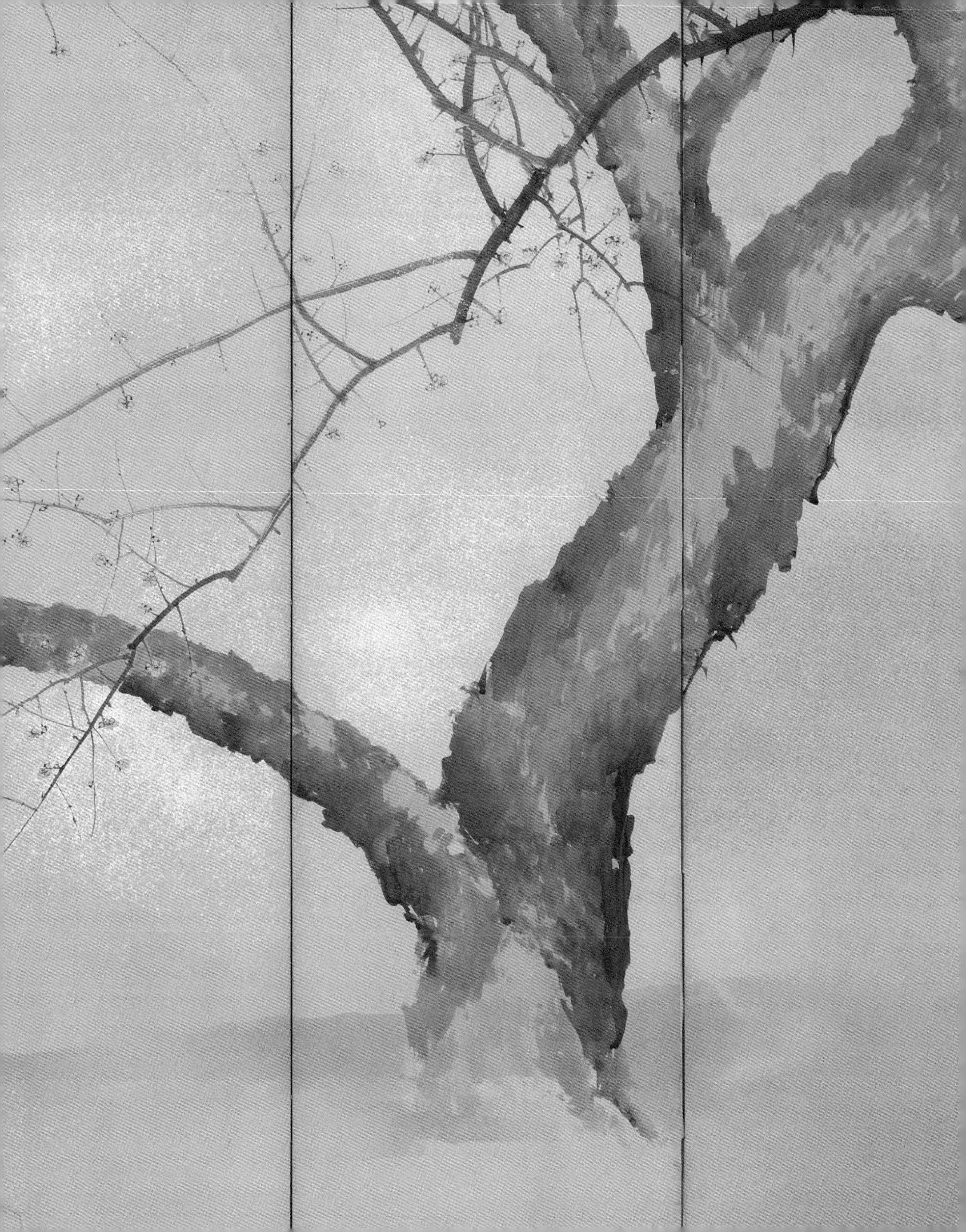

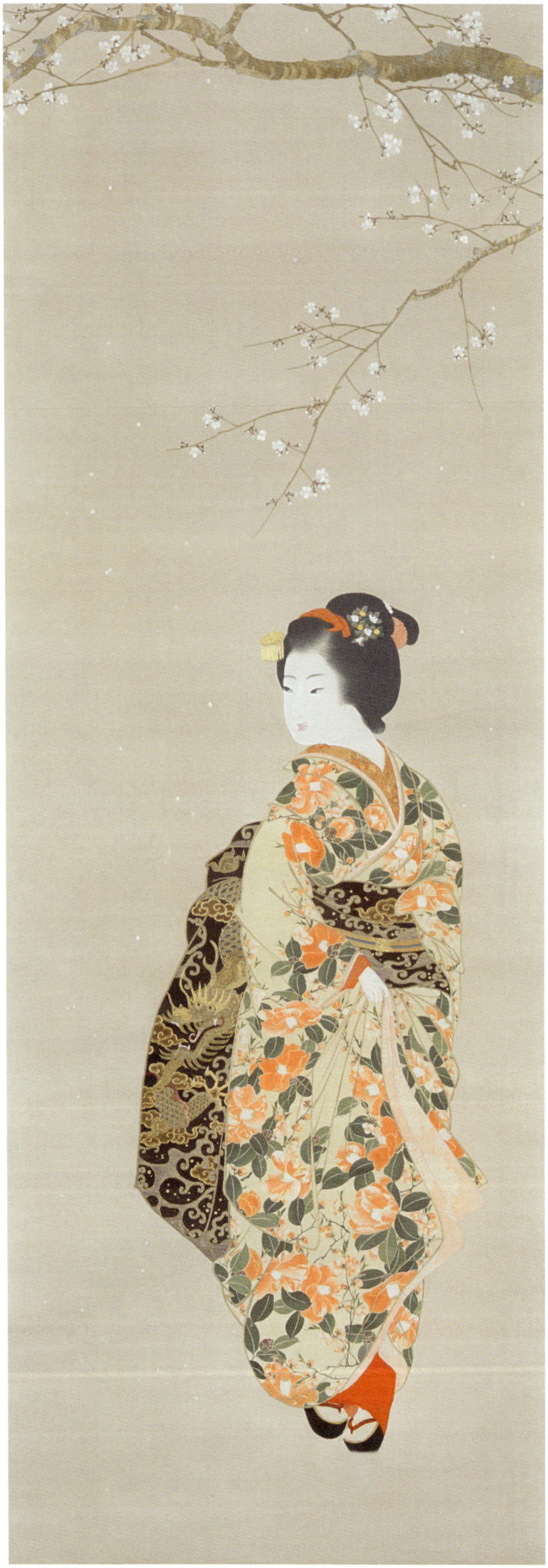

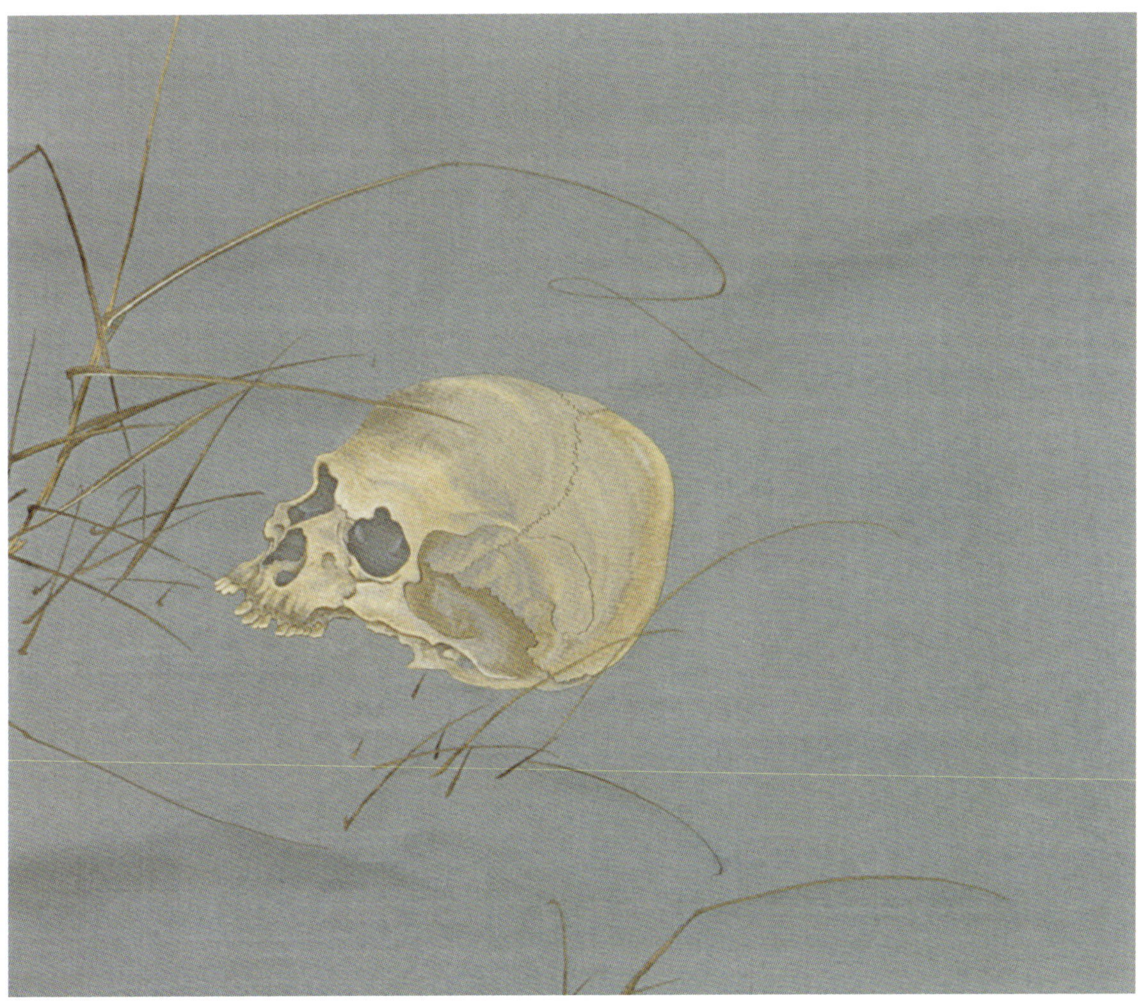

16

Kishi Chikudō, 1826–97
Yūzen dyer, Murakami Kahei, and embroiderer, Kobayashi Kyūjirō
Apprentice Maiko and Cherry Tree
1890, one of a pair of hanging scrolls; *yūzen*-dyeing, embroidery, stencil imitation tie-dyeing *(kata-kanoko)*, ink and color on silk
146.4 × 52.7 cm (57 ⅝ × 20 ¾ in.)

Skull in the Moonlight
1890, one of a pair of hanging scrolls; *yūzen*-dyeing, embroidery, ink and color on silk
146.4 × 52.7 cm (57 ⅝ × 20 ¾ in.)

The inscription on the front and back of the storage box of this delicately rendered pair of hanging scrolls is dated February 23, 1905. It was composed by the journalist, art critic, and likely close friend of Nishimura Sōzaemon XII (1855–1935), Kaneko Kinji (1851–1909). The text notes that the scrolls were based on a sketch (*shita-e*) by Kishi Chikudō, dyed by the *yūzen* craftsman Murakami Kahei, embroidered by Kobayashi Kyūjirō, and completed in 1890. During the Meiji period, a number of pieces like these were produced that had the look of paintings but were in fact embroidered works. Many examples were made for exhibitions held in the West or sent abroad as export goods. This work is unique, however, as it combines *yūzen*-dyeing and embroidery (*shishū*). At this time, *yūzen* dyers were also exploring how to create *yūzen* pieces that could be taken for paintings, as it was understood that Japanese paintings were highly valued in Europe and North America.

In Buddhism, the skull conveys the notion of impermanence—the absence of absolutes—and symbolizes the universal truth that nothing is permanent. This pair of hanging scrolls expresses the belief that all beauty, here embodied by the sumptuously dressed woman in the second scroll, will eventually decay. **NI**

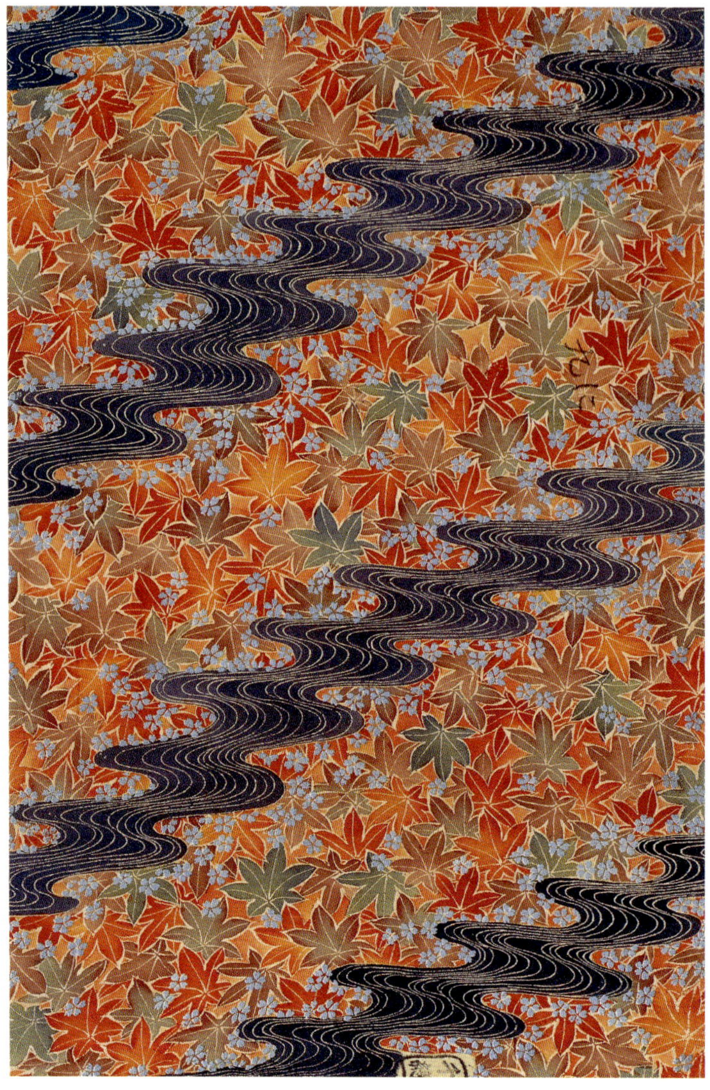

17

Imao Keinen, 1845–1924
Tatsuta River Design
1890, *yūzen*-dyed silk crepe (*chirimen*)
56.5 × 38.3 cm (22 ¼ × 15 1⁄16 in.)

During the Meiji period, Chiso was a pioneer in collaborating with several prominent Kyoto-based artists, including the *nihonga* (Japanese-style painting) practitioners Imao Keinen (cat. 23) and Sakakibara Bunsui (1825–1909) (cats. 18–19), in order to generate new patterns that were then dyed into kimono fabric samples. The introduction of imported chemical dyes from Europe in the 1860s and 1870s also allowed Chiso to develop a dyed-colored rice paste, rather than resist paste *(iro utsushi itchin yūzen)*. This could be directly applied through stencils, thereby creating the revolutionary stencil-dyed (*kata-yūzen*) process. Painterly pictorial motifs achieved by this method could now be made in multiples and enabled the use of popular designs on many kimono.

In this piece, the repeated stencil-dyed pattern of cherry blossoms and maple leaves along a flowing river represents the famous spring and autumn views of the Tatsuta River in Nara. Keinen made this for the lining of a man's *haori*, or jacket. Until the twentieth century the *haori* was commonly black but for the chic wearer the interior lining offered opportunities for a playful display of colorful designs. In the most lavish examples a celebrated painter would create a *sumi* ink painting expressly for it. **VL**

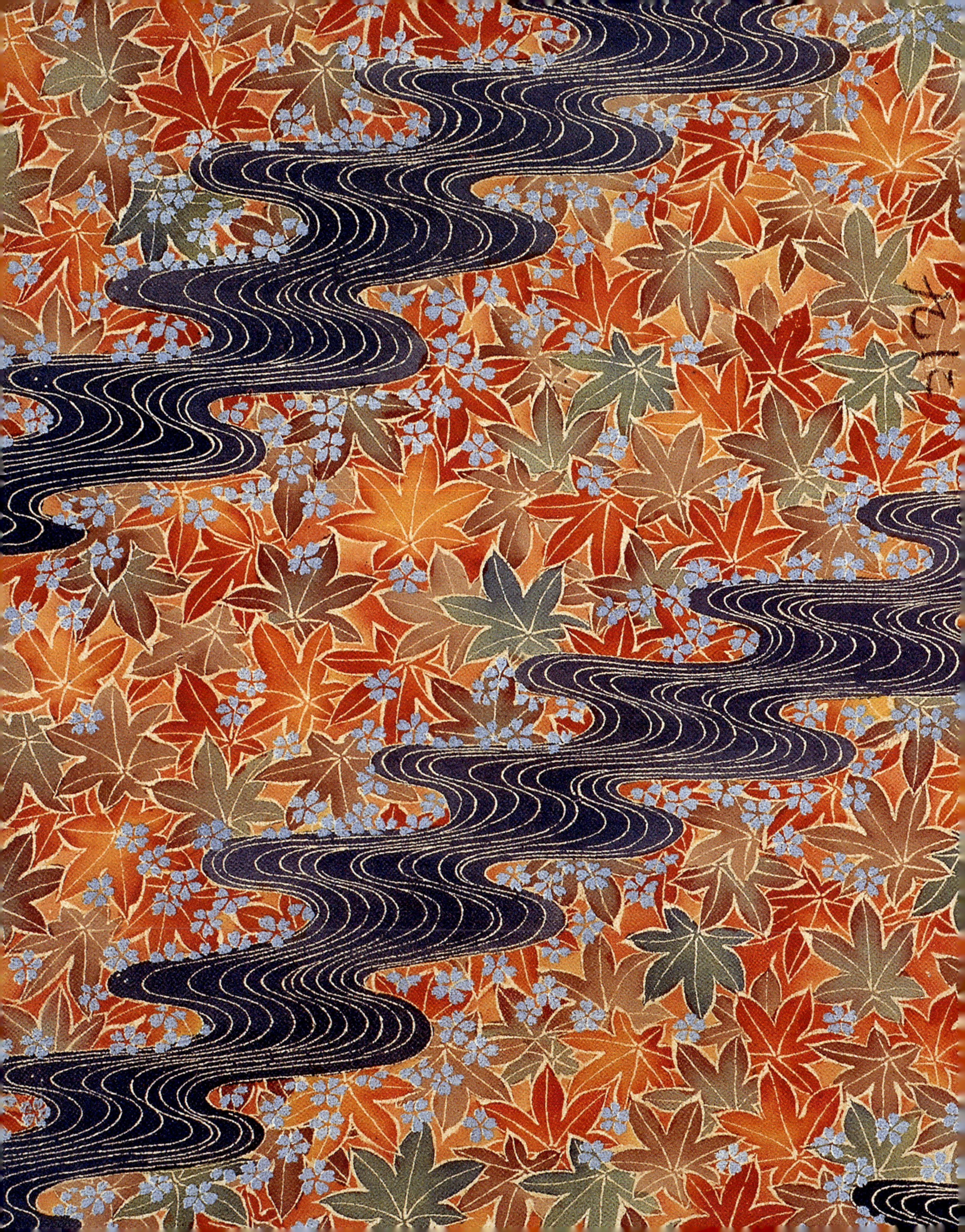

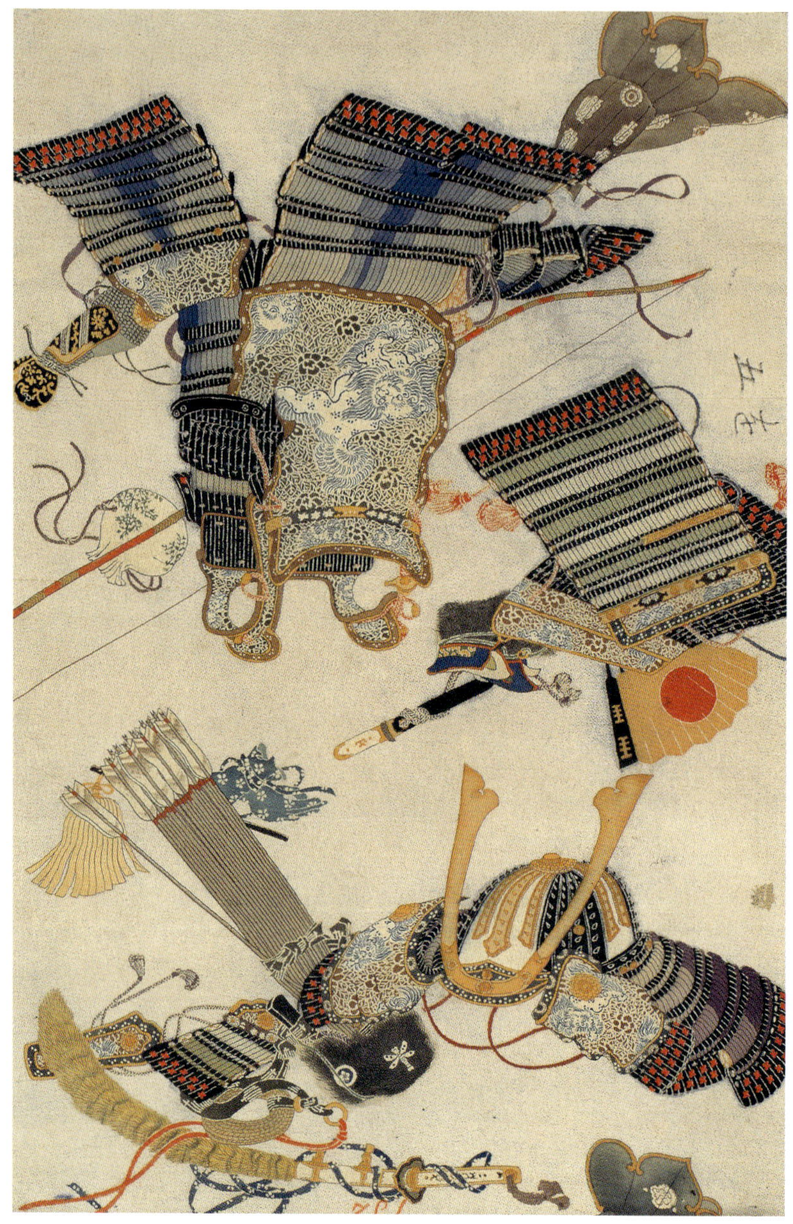

18

Sakakibara Bunsui, 1825–1909
Yoroi and Kabuto Design
1890, *yūzen*-dyed silk crepe (*chirimen*)
56.5 × 38.3 cm (22 ¼ × 15 1⁄16 in.)

This auspicious design of samurai armor (*yoroi*) and helmet (*kabuto*) by the *nihonga* artist Sakakibara Bunsui was made for the special kimono worn by boys during the celebration of *shichi-go-san*, or the life milestone ages of three, five, and seven. The year 1890, when this work was created, was especially significant with the overt patriotic sentiments of the period following the promulgation of the Constitution of the Empire of Japan in 1889 and the Imperial Rescript on Education in 1890. As seen here, kimono patterns often consist of repeated motifs that are oriented in opposite directions so that they can be adopted for both the back and front facing panels of the garment. The meticulous drawing and applied colors of this predominantly stencil-dyed kimono renders this an extraordinary work. **VL**

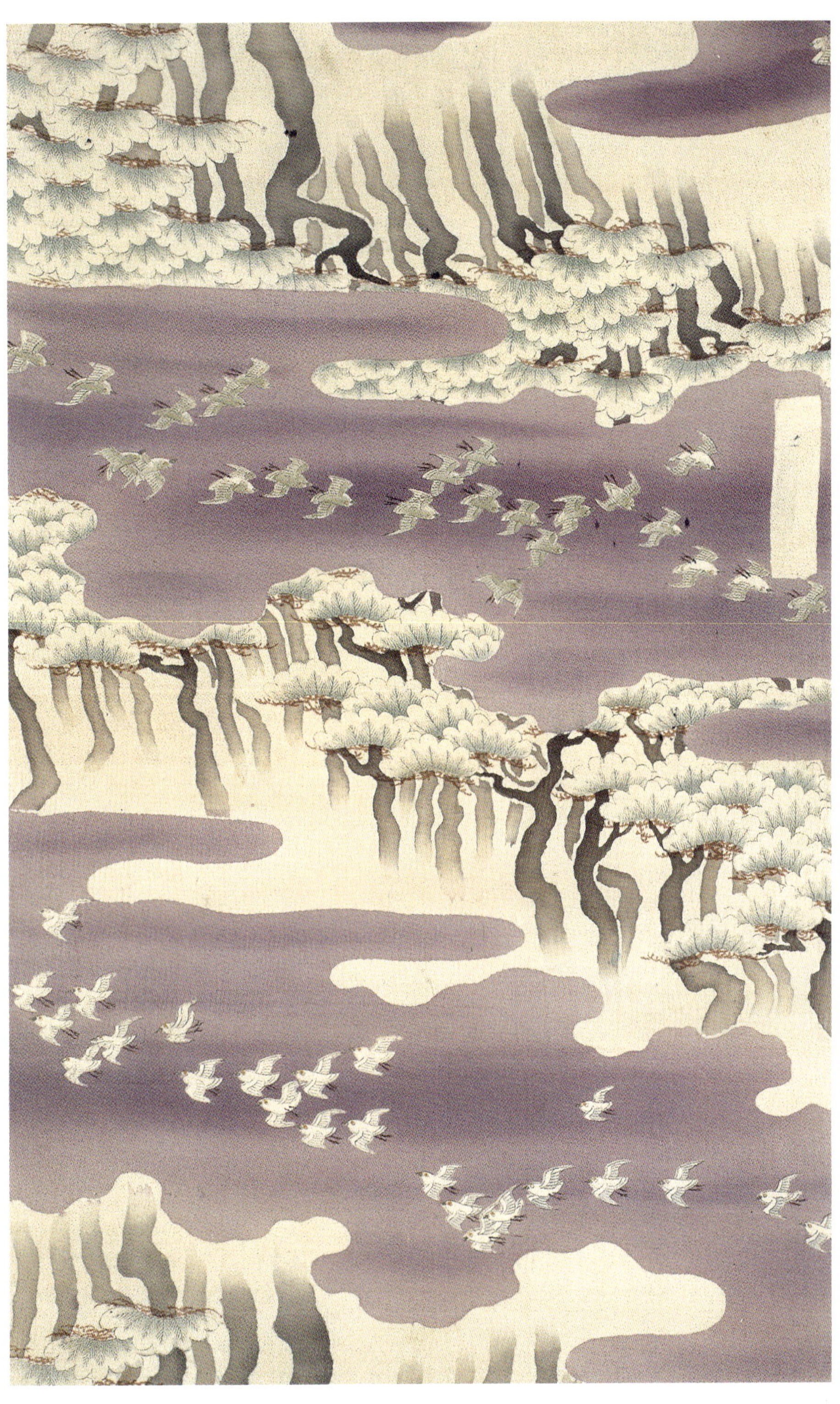

19

Sakakibara Bunsui, 1825–1909
Pine Tree and Plover Design
1890, *yūzen*-dyed silk crepe (*chirimen*)
56.5 × 38.3 cm (22 1/4 × 15 1/16 in.)

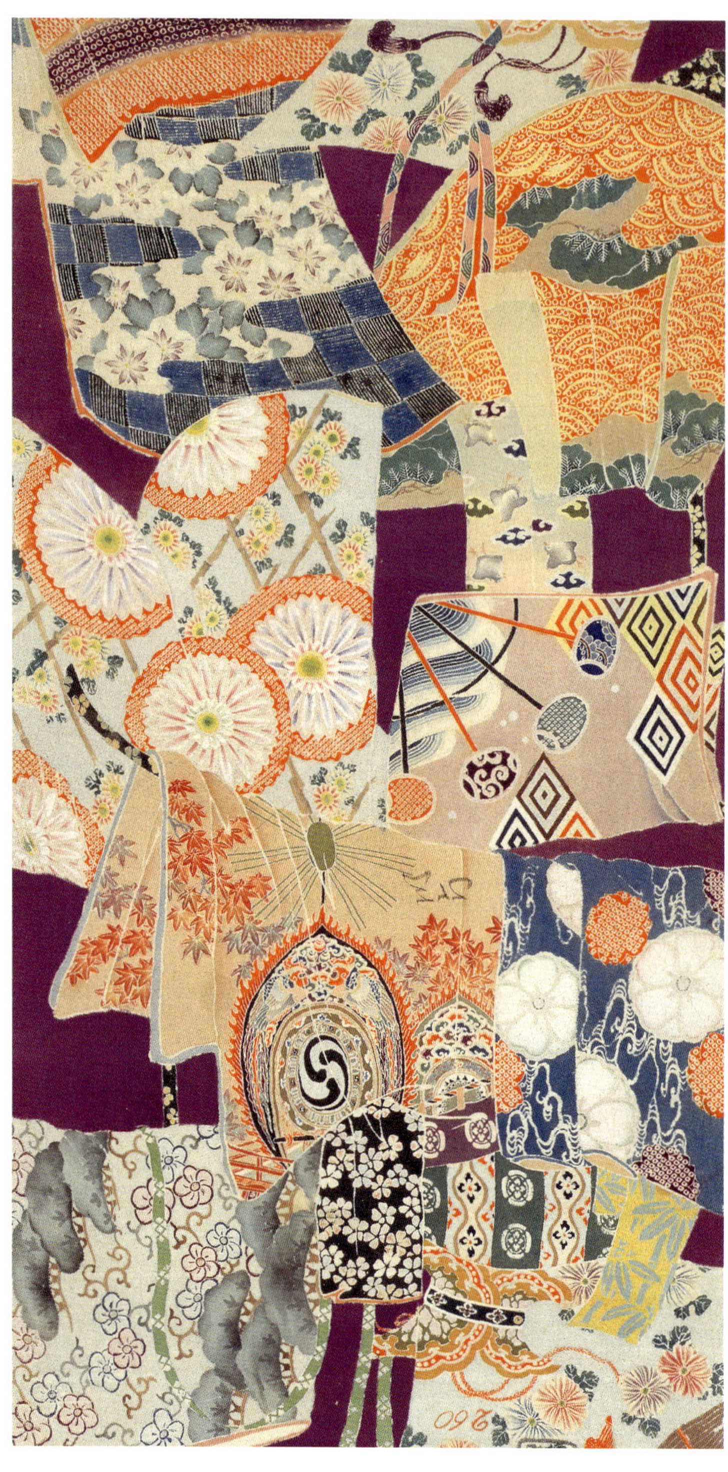

20

Fujii Gyokushū, ca. 1860–1910
A Variety of Kosode Designs
1891, *yūzen*-dyed silk crepe (*chirimen*)
75.6 × 39.2 cm (29 ¾ × 15 $^{7}/_{16}$ in.)

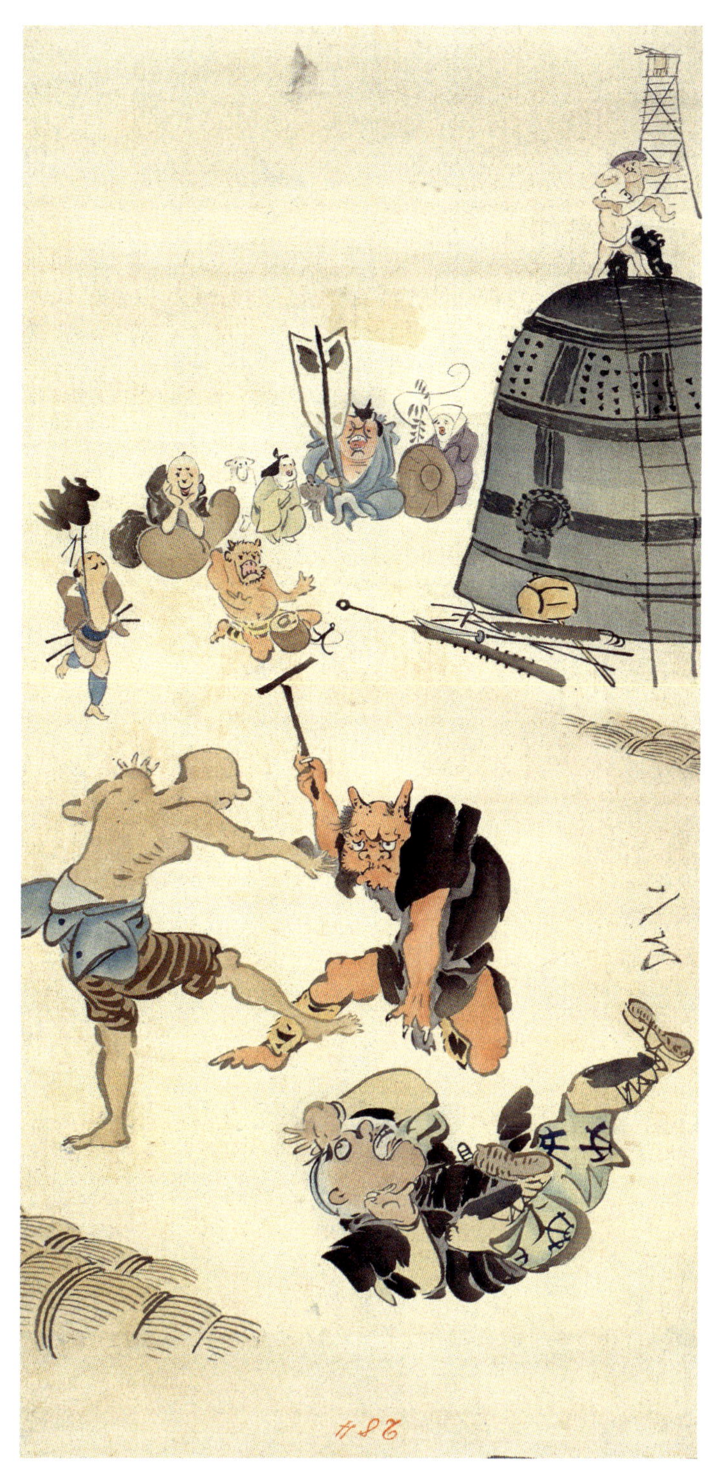

21

Kubota Beisen, 1852–1906
Ōtsu-e Design
1891, *yūzen*-dyed silk crepe (*chirimen*)
80.5 × 39.2 cm (31 11/16 × 15 7/16 in.)

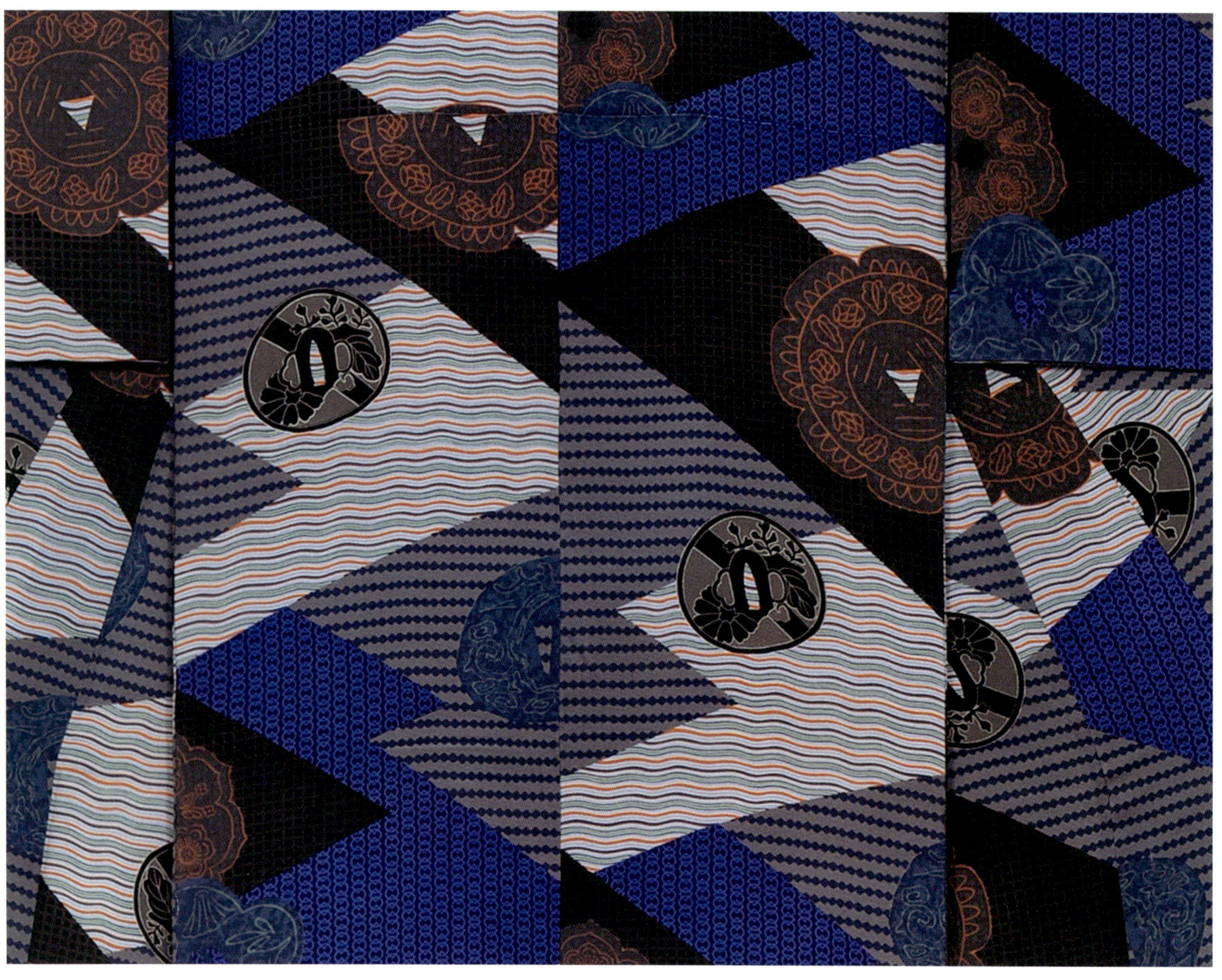

22

Yohji Yamamoto, b. 1943
Kimono with Pine Bark Lozenge and Sword Guard Design
2005, *yūzen*-dyed silk
177 × 135 cm (69 11/16 × 53 1/8 in.)

As part of the commemorative events celebrating the firm's 450th anniversary in 2005, Chiso invited the fashion designer Yohji Yamamoto to create kimono with an eye to future fashion trends. Yamamoto began his working relationship with Chiso in 1994, a period in his career when he sought to incorporate elements of traditional Japanese kimono into contemporary fashion in an approach that soon earned him international recognition. Compared to many types of dress in the West, which tend to conform to the shape of the human body, the Japanese kimono could be said to be "gender-free," and this was an important consideration for Yamamoto. He produced thirty-three unique kimono for Chiso—including the example here—that demonstrate the differences between Western dress and the kimono.

This stylish women's kimono with a masculine *tsuba* (sword guard) motif set against a sharply defined and dynamic *matsukawabishi* (pine-bark lozenge) pattern is inspired by the lining of a man's *haori*, or jacket, from the Meiji period. The notion of *iki*, often described as cool sophistication and seductive charm, is a fitting term to express the aesthetics and spirit embodied in Yamamoto's kimono design. NR

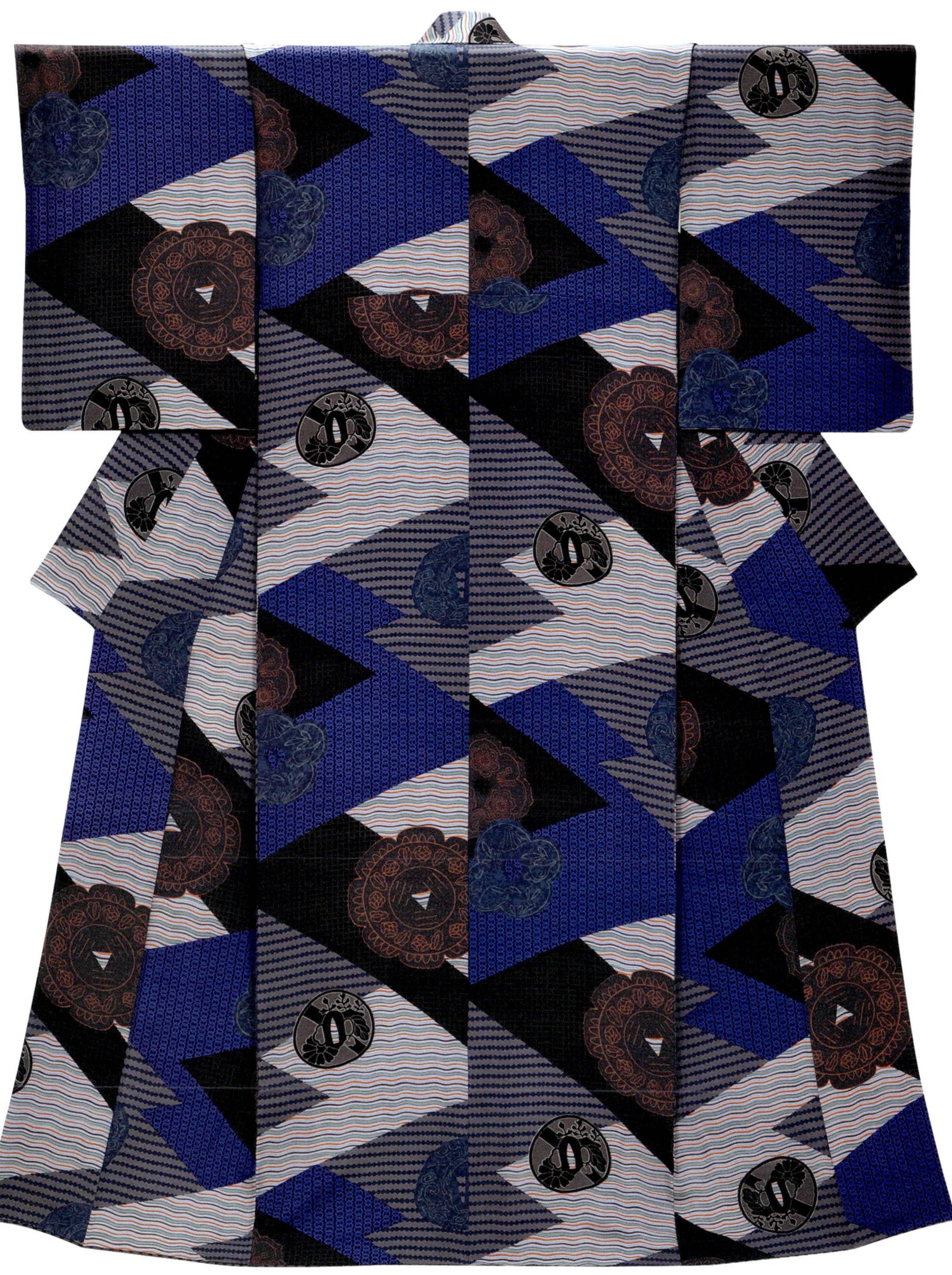

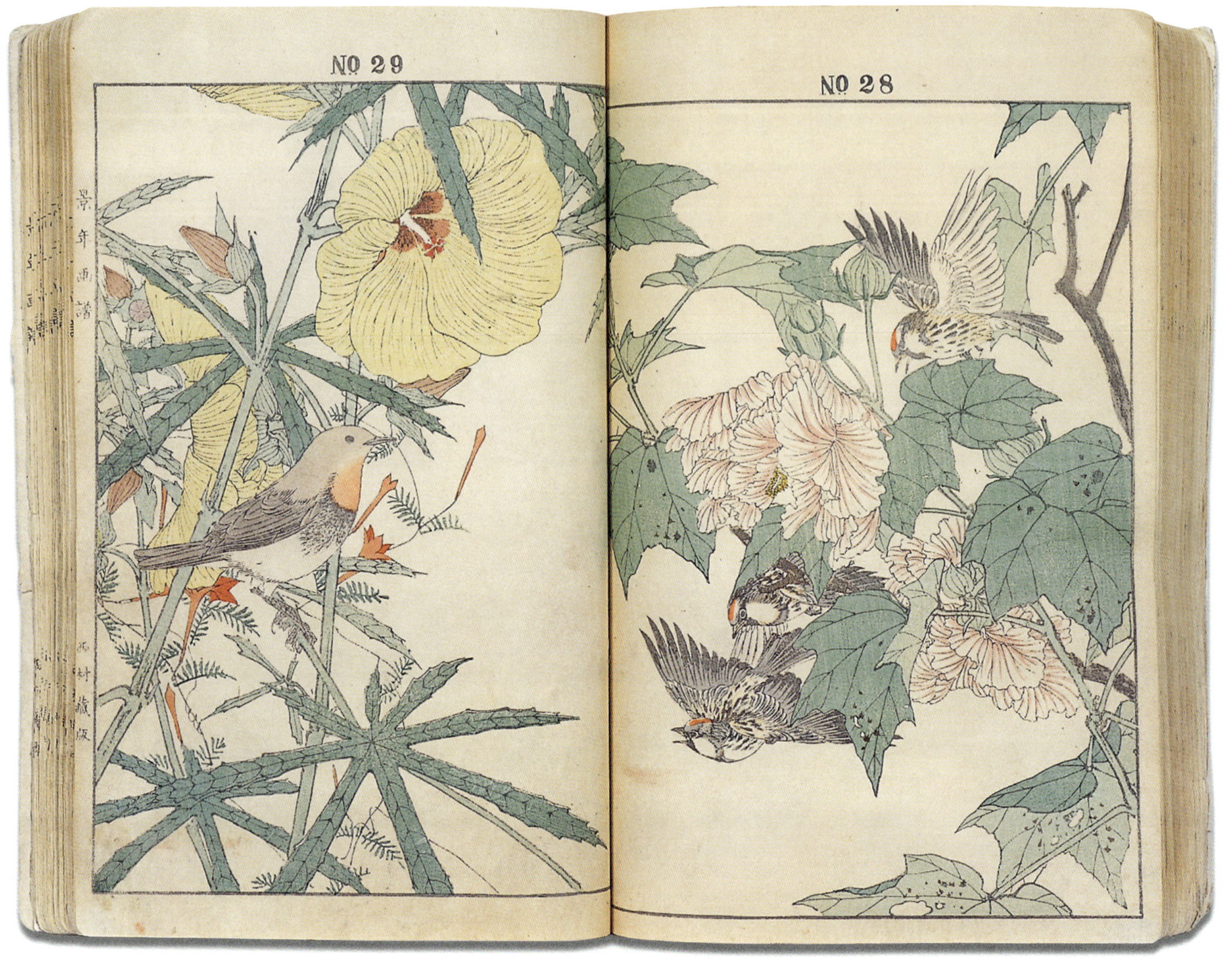

23

Imao Keinen, 1845–1924
Keinen's Painting Album of Flowers and Birds (Keinen kachō gafu)
1891, four volumes, color woodblock-printed book
(both images here are from the autumn volume)
37.5 × 25.5 cm (14 ¾ × 10 $^{1}/_{16}$ in.)

This painting album counts among the most exquisite color woodblock-printed books of the early Meiji period. A collaboration between the painter Imao Keinen and the Chiso firm, it illustrates and orders various groupings of native and non-native Japanese flowers and birds according to the four seasons. The resulting 134 images provided fine design models for artists and artisans. Keinen's book was circulated widely, not only in Japan but also in North America, Europe, and East Asia, with its success due to the artist's meticulous drawing skills, simple compositions with harmonious color combinations, and deluxe printing. **SS**

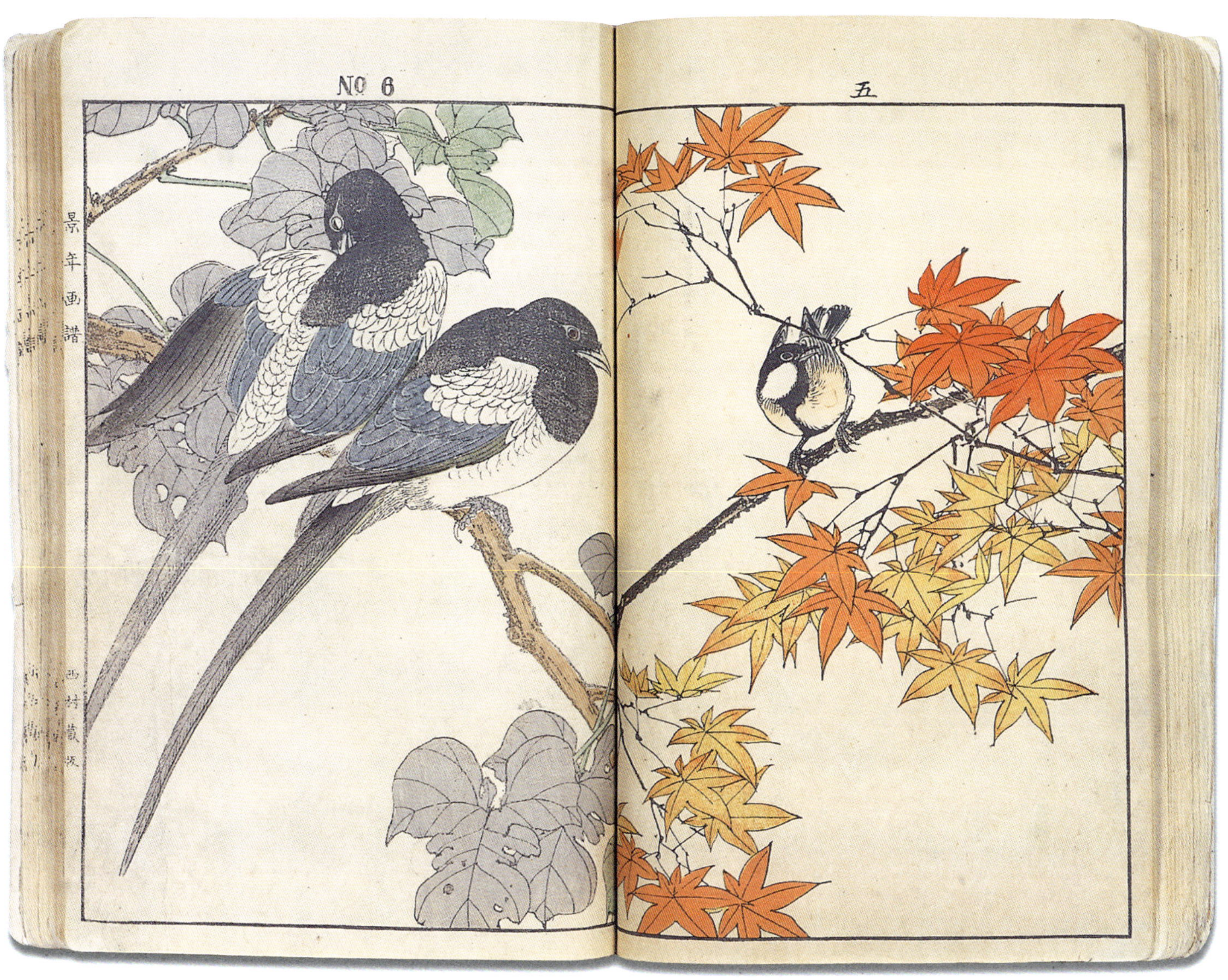
No 6
五
景年画譜
西村蔵版

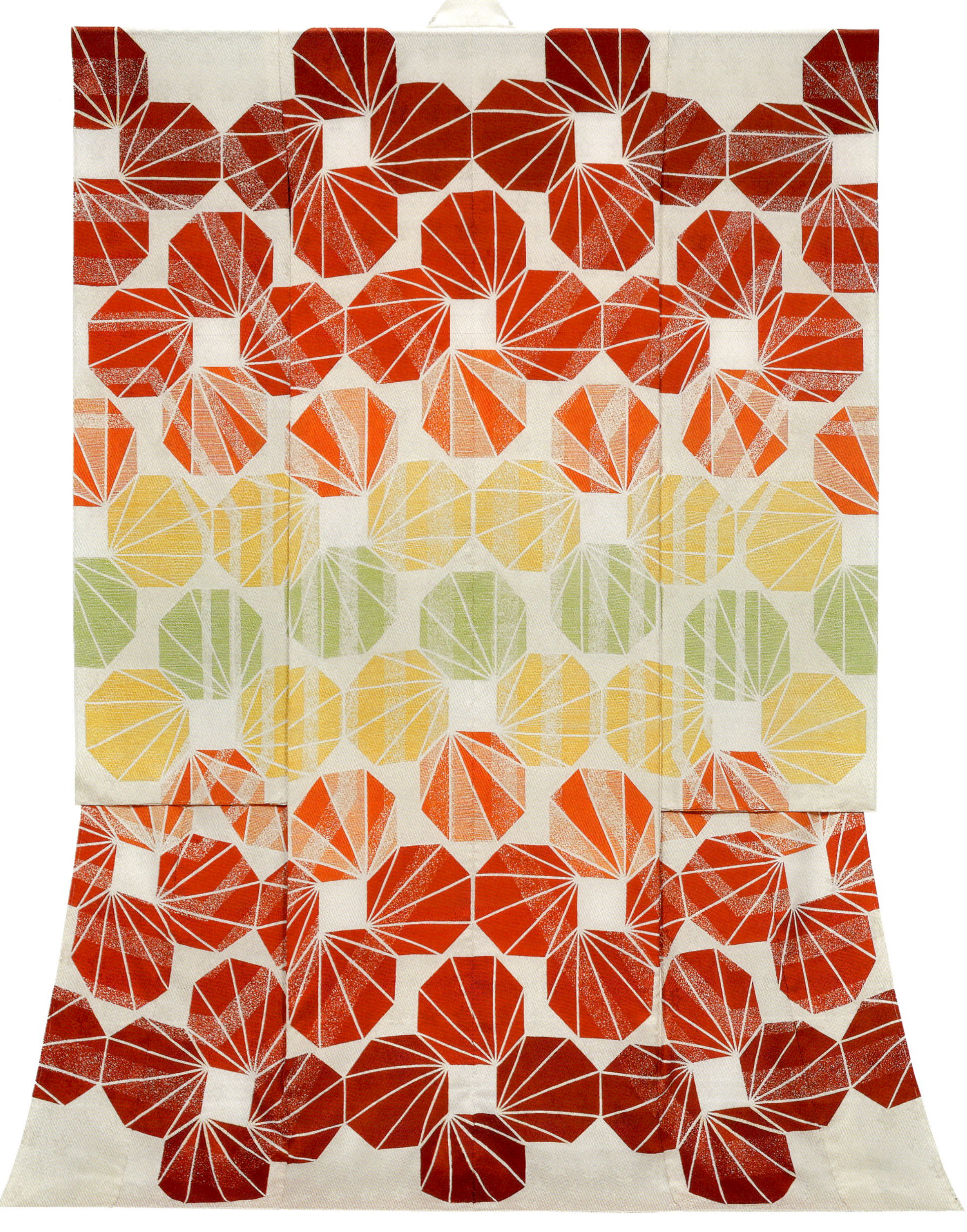

24

Chiso Co., Ltd.
Worcester Wedding Kimono
2020, barrel tie-dyeing (*okedashi shibori*), paste-resist dyeing (*yūzen*), colored flour paste-resist dyeing (*iro utsushi itchin yūzen*), threadline paste-resist dyeing (*itome-yūzen*), "snowstorm" wax-resist dyeing (*fubuki rōketsuzome*), gold leaf, and embroidery on woven silk
178 × 129 cm (70 1/16 × 50 13/16 in.), Worcester Art Museum

(for a description of the work, see the interview with Imai Atsuhiro in this volume)

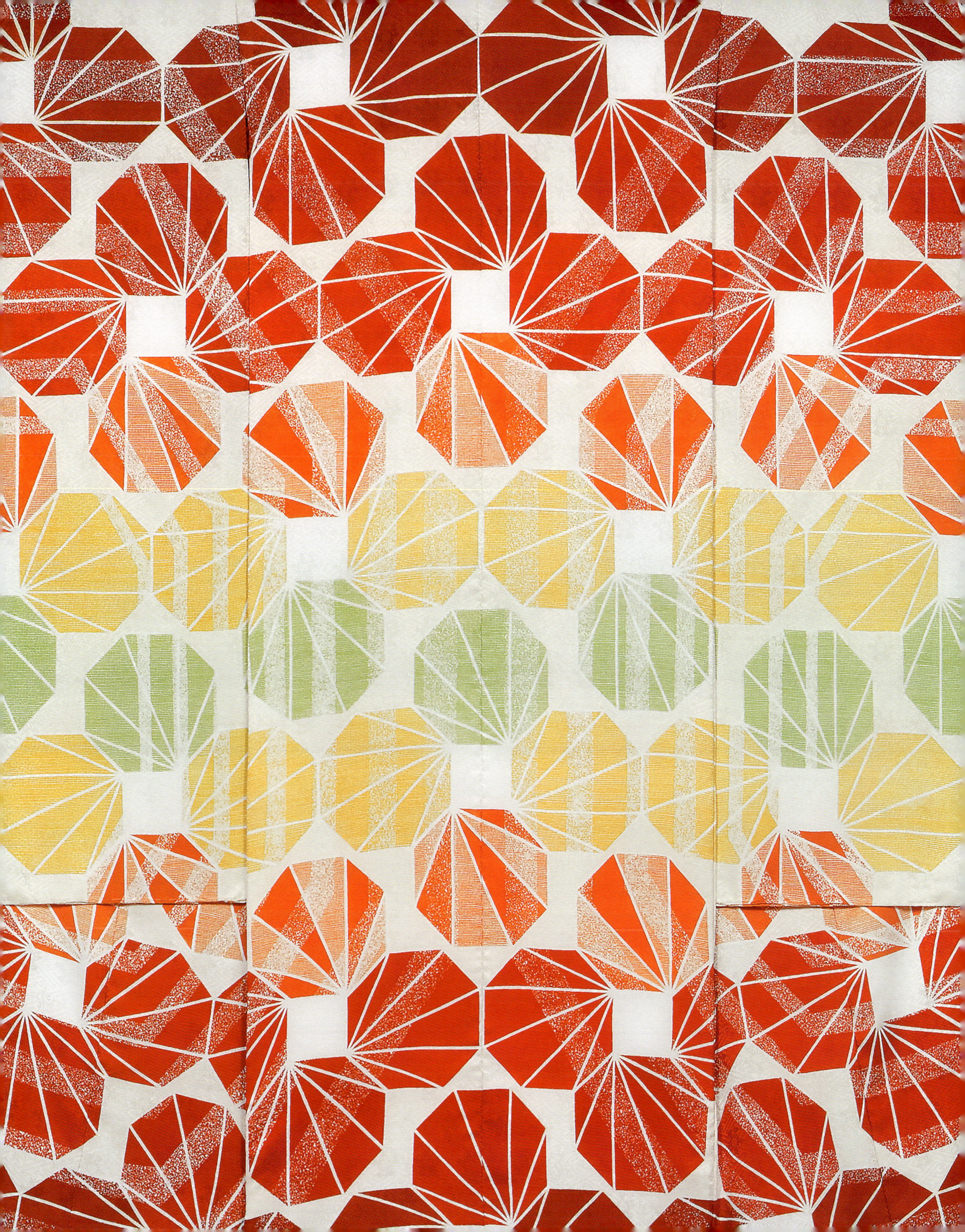

Exhibition Checklist

Cat. 1
Chiso Co., Ltd.
Uchikake with Palace Garden Design
Made for Iida Taka, the thirteenth Madame Nishimura
1913
Yūzen-dyeing and embroidery on woven silk
175 × 125 cm (68 7/8 × 49 3/16 in.)

Cat. 2
Chiso Co., Ltd.
Uchikake with Pine Leaf Design
Made for Iida Taka, the thirteenth Madame Nishimura
1913
Embroidery on woven silk
168 × 126 cm (66 1/8 × 49 5/8 in.)

Cat. 3
Chiso Co., Ltd.
Furisode with Wave and Crane Design
Made for Nishimura Tokuko, the fourteenth Madame Nishimura
1938
Yūzen-dyeing and embroidery on woven silk
171 × 128 cm (67 5/16 × 50 3/8 in.)

Cat. 4
Chiso Co., Ltd.
Furisode with Fan and Bamboo Blinds Design
Made for Nishimura Tokuko, the fourteenth Madame Nishimura
1938
Yūzen-dyeing, *kanoko shibori* tie-dyeing, embroidery, and gold leaf on woven silk
170 × 128 cm (66 15/16 × 50 3/8 in.)

Cat. 5
Chiso Co., Ltd.
Uchikake with Clouds and Pine Trees Design
Made for Nishimura Tokuko, the fourteenth Madame Nishimura
1938
Embroidery on woven silk
180 × 127 cm (70 7/8 × 50 in.)

Cat. 6
Chiso Co., Ltd.
Furisode with Mist and Fan Design
Made for Kawakami Masako, the fifteenth Madame Nishimura
1971
Embroidery and gold leaf on woven silk
163 × 126 cm (64 3/16 × 49 5/8 in.)

Cat. 7
Chiso Co., Ltd.
Furisode with Palace Garden Design
Made for Kawakami Masako, the fifteenth Madame Nishimura
1971
Yūzen-dyeing, embroidery, and gold leaf on woven silk
165 × 138 cm (64 15/16 × 54 5/16 in.)

Cat. 8
Artist unknown
Kosode with Overturned Flask Design
Mid to late 17th century, Edo period, 1603–1868
Kanoko shibori tie-dyeing and ink on white figured satin
157 × 128 cm (61 13/16 × 50 3/8 in.)

Cat. 9
Artist unknown
Kosode with Eight Views of Ōmi Province Design
Mid-18th century, Edo period, 1603–1868
Yūzen-dyeing and embroidery on dark blue figured satin
155.5 × 126 cm (61 1/4 × 49 5/8 in.)

Cat. 10
Artist unknown
Katabira with Chinese Fan and Flower Bouquet Design
Late 18th to early 19th century, Edo period, 1603–1868
Embroidery and stencil imitation tie-dyeing (*kata-kanoko*) on white ramie
168 × 122 cm (66 1/8 × 48 in.)

Cat. 11
Artist unknown
Kosode with Tree, Chrysanthemum Plant, and Characters Design
Mid to late 18th century, Edo period, 1603–1868
Stencil imitation tie-dyeing (*kata-kanoko*), ink, and embroidery on white figured satin
148 × 120 cm (58 1/4 × 47 1/4 in.)

Cat. 12
Artist unknown
Kosode with Koto and Cloud Design and Edge Pattern
Late 19th century, Meiji period, 1868–1912
Yūzen-dyeing and embroidery on purple silk crepe (*chirimen*)
146.3 × 118.6 cm (57 5/8 × 46 11/16 in.)

Cat. 13
Nishikawa Sukenobu, 1671–1750
Patterns from the Shōtoku Era (Shōtoku hinagata)
1713
Publisher: Hachimonjiya Hachizaemon
Five volumes, woodblock-printed book with black-line printing (*sumizuri*)
20.8 × 15.6 cm (8 3/16 × 6 1/8 in.)

Cat. 14
Kishi Chikudō, 1826–97
Karasaki
1876
One of a pair of eight-panel folding screens; ink and color on paper
158 × 422 cm (62 3/16 × 166 1/8 in.)

Ōtsu
1876
One of a pair of eight-panel folding screens; ink and color on paper
158 × 422 cm (62 3/16 × 166 1/8 in.)

Cat. 15
Kishi Chikudō, 1826–97
Plum Tree
Late 19th century, Meiji period, 1868–1912
Pair of eight-panel folding screens; ink and color on paper
158 × 422 cm each (62 3⁄16 × 166 1⁄8 in.)

Cat. 16
Kishi Chikudō, 1826–97
Yūzen dyer, Murakami Kahei, and embroiderer, Kobayashi Kyūjirō
Apprentice Maiko and Cherry Tree
1890
One of a pair of hanging scrolls; *yūzen*-dyeing, embroidery, stencil imitation tie-dyeing (*kata-kanoko*), ink and color on silk
146.4 × 52.7 cm (57 5⁄8 × 20 3⁄4 in.)

Skull in the Moonlight
1890
One of a pair of hanging scrolls; *yūzen*-dyeing, embroidery, ink and color on silk
146.4 × 52.7 cm (57 5⁄8 × 20 3⁄4 in.)

Cat. 17
Imao Keinen, 1845–1924
Tatsuta River Design
1890
Yūzen-dyed silk crepe (*chirimen*)
56.5 × 38.3 cm (22 1⁄4 × 15 1⁄16 in.)

Cat. 18
Sakakibara Bunsui, 1825–1909
Yoroi and Kabuto Design
1890
Yūzen-dyed silk crepe (*chirimen*)
56.5 × 38.3 cm (22 1⁄4 × 15 1⁄16 in.)

Cat. 19
Sakakibara Bunsui, 1825–1909
Pine Tree and Plover Design
1890
Yūzen-dyed silk crepe (*chirimen*)
56.5 × 38.3 cm (22 1⁄4 × 15 1⁄16 in.)

Cat. 20
Fujii Gyokushū, ca. 1860–1910
A Variety of Kosode Designs
1891
Yūzen-dyed silk crepe (*chirimen*)
75.6 × 39.2 cm (29 3⁄4 × 15 7⁄16 in.)

Cat. 21
Kubota Beisen, 1852–1906
Ōtsu-e Design
1891
Yūzen-dyed silk crepe (*chirimen*)
80.5 × 39.2 cm (31 11⁄16 × 15 7⁄16 in.)

Cat. 22
Yohji Yamamoto, b. 1943
Kimono with Pine Bark Lozenge and Sword Guard Design
2005
Yūzen-dyed silk
177 × 135 cm (69 11⁄16 × 53 1⁄8 in.)

Cat. 23
Imao Keinen, 1845–1924
Keinen's Painting Album of Flowers and Birds (Keinen kachō gafu)
1891
Four volumes, color woodblock-printed book
37.5 × 25.5 cm (14 3⁄4 × 10 1⁄16 in.)

Cat. 24
Chiso Co., Ltd.
Worcester Wedding Kimono
2020
Barrel tie-dyeing (*okedashi shibori*), paste-resist dyeing (*yūzen*), colored flour paste-resist dyeing (*iro utsushi itchin yūzen*), threadline paste-resist dyeing (*itome-yūzen*), "snowstorm" wax-resist dyeing (*fubuki rōketsuzome*), gold leaf, and embroidery on woven silk
178 × 129 cm (70 1⁄16 × 50 13⁄16 in.)
Worcester Art Museum

Bibliography

Dalby, Liza. *Geisha*. Berkeley: University of California Press, 2008.

Dalby, Liza. *Kimono: Fashioning Culture*. New Haven: Yale University Press, 1993.

Dees, Jan. *Taishō Kimono: Speaking of Past and Present*. Milan: Skira, 2009.

Feltens, Frank. "Sartorial Identity: Early Modern Japanese Textile Patterns and the Afterlife of Ogata Kōrin." *Ars Orientalis* 47 (2017): 117–57.

Fukai Akiko. "Kimono no chikara—seiyō no deai to eikyō." In *Kimono Beauty—shikku de modan na yosōi no bi Edo kara Shōwa*, edited by Nagasaki Iwao, 35–39. Tokyo: Tōkyō Bijutsu, 2013.

Gluckman, Dale Carolyn, and Sharon Sadako Takeda, eds. *When Art Became Fashion: Kosode in Edo-period Japan*. Los Angeles: Los Angeles County Museum of Art, 1992.

Ishikawa, Masakazu, and Shin'ya Nagasawa. "Customer Experience of CHISO: The Centuries-old Business of Japanese Luxury Kimono Garments." In "Customer Experience Management/Marketing Branding." Special issue, *Science Journal of Business and Management* 3, no. 2-1, (2015): 83–91.

Jackson, Anna, ed. *Kimono: The Art and Evolution of Japanese Fashion*. London: Thames & Hudson, 2015.

Karatani, Kōjin. *Origins of Modern Japanese Literature*. Durham and London: Duke University Press, 1993.

Kyoto National Museum, ed. *Kyoto Style: Trends in 16th–19th Century Kimono*. Kyoto: Kyoto National Museum, 1999.

Li, Vivian, ed. *The Kimono in Print: 300 Years of Japanese Design*. Leiden: Hotei Publishing, 2020.

Lippit, Yukio. "The Painter-in-Attendance." In *The Artist in Edo*, edited by Yukio Lippit, 23–46. Washington, DC: Center for Advanced Study in the Visual Arts, 2018.

Lippit, Yukio. *Painting of the Realm: The Kano House of Painters in 17th-Century Japan*. Seattle: University of Washington Press, 2012.

McDermott, Hiroko T. "The Pleasure and Pain of Being the Front-Runner: The Nishimura Sōzaemon House (Chisō) in the Meiji Period." In *Threads of Silk and Gold: Ornamental Textiles from Meiji Japan*, edited by Hiroko T. McDermott and Clare Pollard, 41–52. Oxford: Ashmolean Museum, 2012.

McDermott, Hiroko T. "The Way of the Newcomer: A History of the Iida Shinshichi House (Takashimaya)." In *Threads of Silk and Gold: Ornamental Textiles from Meiji Japan*, edited by Hiroko T. McDermott and Clare Pollard, 55–65. Oxford: Ashmolean Museum, 2012.

Milhaupt, Terry Satsuki. *Kimono: A Modern History*. London: Reaktion Books, 2014.

Mori Rie. "Kindai ni okeru 'kimono' no hyōkihō to sono imi no hensen—1874 nen-1980 nen no shinbun kiji o chūshin ni—." *Nihon kasei gakkaishi* 66 (2015): 197–212.

Morrison, Michael, and Lorna Price, eds. *Four Centuries of Fashion: Classical Kimono from the Kyoto National Museum*. San Francisco: Asian Art Museum, 1997.

Museum of Modern Art Shiga, ed. *Kishi Chikudō—kindai Kyōto gadan no yo-ake*. Ōtsu: Shiga Kenritsu Kindai Bijutsukan, 1987.

Nii, Rie, and Candace Ince, eds. *Future Beauty: 30 Years of Japanese Fashion*. London and New York: Merrell, 2010.

Ōhashi Tsuneyasu. "Kishi Chikudō." In *Gashū Kishi Chikudō*, edited by Harada Heisaku et al., 169–85. Kyoto: Futaba Shobō, 1984.

Ōhashi Tsuneyasu. "Kishi Chikudō no shita-e ni tsuite." *Kyōto Kōgei Sen'i Daigaku Kōgei Gakubu kenkyū hōkoku jinbun* 28 (1979): 37–65.

Oyama Yuzuruha. "Senshoku korekushon no rekishi." In "Senshoku korekushon no keifu." Special issue, *Me no me* 505 (2018): 22–34.

Parmal, Pamela A. "The Impact of Synthetic Dyes on the Luxury Textiles of Meiji Japan." *Textile Society of America Symposium Proceedings* 474 (2004): 397–405.

Rimer, J. Thomas et al. *Japanese and Chinese Poems to Sing: The Wakan rōei shū*. New York: Columbia University Press, 1997.

Rosenfield, John M., and Shujiro Shimada. *Traditions of Japanese Art*. Cambridge: Fogg Art Museum, Harvard University, 1970.

Sapin, Julia Elizabeth. "Liaisons between Painters and Department Stores: Merchandising Art and Identity in Meiji Japan, 1868–1912." PhD diss., University of Washington, 2003.

Sapin, Julia. "Naturalism Fusing Past and Present: The Reconfiguration of the Kyoto School of Painting and the Revival of the Textile Industry." In *Kyoto Visual Culture in the Early Edo and Meiji Periods: The Arts of Reinvention*, edited by Morgan Pitelka and Alice Y. Tseng, 138–60. London and New York: Routledge, 2016.

Sittenfeld, Michael. *Five Centuries of Japanese Kimono*. Chicago: The Art Institute of Chicago, 1992.

Stevens, Rebecca A. T., and Yoshiko Iwamoto Wada, eds. *The Kimono Inspiration: Art and Art-to-Wear in America*. Washington, DC: The Textile Museum, 1996.

Stinchecum, Amanda Mayer. *Kosode: 16th–19th Century Textiles from the Nomura Collection*. New York: Japan Society and Kodansha International, 1984.

Su, Stephanie. "Weaving Art, Science, and Modern Design: *Keinen's Painting Album of Flowers and Birds*." In *The Kimono in Print: 300 Years of Japanese Design*, edited by Vivian Li, 75–88. Leiden: Hotei Publishing, 2020.

Todate Kazuko. *Nakamura Katsuma to Tōkyō yūzen no keifu*. Tokyo: Senshoku to Seikatsusha, 2007.

Tōkyō Kokuritsu Bunkazai Kenkyūjo (Tokyo National Research Institute for Cultural Properties), ed. *Meiji-ki Bankoku Hakurankai bijutsuhin shuppin mokuroku*. Tokyo: Chūō Kōron Bijutsu Shuppan, 1997.

Trede, Melanie, and Julia Meech, eds. *Arts of Japan: The John C. Weber Collection*. Berlin: Museum für Ostasiatische Kunst, Staatliche Museen zu Berlin, 2006.

Vollmer, John E., ed. *Re-envisioning Japan: Meiji Fine Art Textiles*. Milan: 5 Continents Editions, 2016.

Wada, Yoshiko Iwamoto, Mary Kellog Rice, and Jane Barton. *Shibori: The Inventive Art of Japanese Shaped Resist Dyeing*. Tokyo: Kodansha International, 1983.

Wasō Shinkō Kenkyūkai, ed. *Wasō Shinkō Kenkyūkai hōkokusho*. Tokyo: Keizai Sangyōshō Seizō Sangyōkyoku Sen'i-ka, 2015.

Woodson, Yoko, and Shigeki Kawakami. *Classical Kimono from the Kyoto National Museum: Four Centuries of Fashion*. San Francisco: Asian Art Museum, 1997.

Yamanobe, Tomoyuki, and Kenzō Fujii. *Kyoto Modern Textiles: 1868–1940*. Kyoto: Kyoto Textile Wholesalers Association, 1996.

Website:
www.tobunken.go.jp/archives

Glossary

chirimen: a plain weave, silk crepe fabric

embroidery, see *shishū*

fubuki rōketsuzome: literally "snowstorm" wax-resist dyeing; splashed wax-resist applied by hand before dyeing, and once the wax is washed away after dyeing, the areas covered, or reserved, leave a dappled effect resembling snow

fuki: the lower edge of a kimono that is attached to its lining, usually padded; used for *uchikake*

furisode: literally "swinging sleeves"; long-sleeved kimono for young unmarried women

haori: unbelted jacket for men

hinagatabon: textile pattern book

iro utsushi itchin yūzen: colored flour paste-resist dyeing technique invented by Chiso that allows the colored flour paste-resist to be rubbed away from the cloth after the flour dries

itome-yūzen: literally "threadlike lines" paste-resist dyeing; resisted fine lines produced from paste squeezed from a paper cone by hand to create linear designs

kanoko shibori: literally "'fawn spots' tie-dyeing"; an effect created by tightly winding tiny areas of the fabric with thread

katabira: unlined summer robe usually made of ramie

kata-kanoko: stenciled imitation tie-dyeing (see also *kanoko shibori*)

kata-yūzen: paste-resist dyeing applied through stencils

katazome: method of patterning through the use of paper stencils

kimono: abbreviation of *kirumono*, literally "thing to wear"; generic term for any clothing that after the Meiji period (1868–1912) replaced the term *kosode* to distinguish it from Western-style clothing

komon-zome: literally "'small motif' dyeing"; paste-resist dyeing of repeated tiny white motifs using stencils

kosode: literally "small sleeves"; kimono with small wrist openings originally worn by women and men as an undergarment. It became the principal outer garment for all genders and classes from the Muromachi period (1336–1573) onward, and during the Meiji period robes in this style became generally referred to as "kimono"

obi: wide belt that secures a kimono

okedashi shibori: commonly known as barrel tie-dyeing; process in which stitching is applied to create a design that is capped with a protective cover, usually made of a non-porous material such as bamboo or even plastic, to reserve the pattern when the fabric is immersed in dye

resist dyeing: method of patterning textiles in which some substance, such as paste, wax, or wrapped threads, covers the patterned areas such that the dye does not penetrate these sections of the fabric (see also *rōketsuzome*, *iro utsushi itchin yūzen*, *itome-yūzen*, *kata-yūzen*, *komon-zome*, and *yūzen-dyeing*)

rōketsuzome: wax-resist dyeing (see also *fubuki rōketsuzome*)

sarasa: a multicolored printed cotton fabric with designed patterns introduced to Japan from India via Java by the Dutch East India Company in the sixteenth and seventeenth centuries; it gradually became a generic term for imported printed cotton fabrics with patterns

shibori: technique of patterning achieved by securing the fabric against dye penetration through stitching or wrapping a part of the cloth with threads; similar to tie-dyeing (see also *okedashi shibori* and *kanoko shibori*)

shiromuku: white silk kimono worn by a bride during a wedding

shishū: embroidery technique of decorating fabric with needle and thread that was usually reserved for high-ranking women and men until the introduction of paste-resist (*yūzen dyeing*) and wax-resist (*rōketsuzome*) dyeing in the eighteenth century

uchikake: unbelted female kimono overcoat for formal occasions, principally weddings

yūzen-dyeing (yūzen-zome): paste-resist dyeing (see also *iro utsushi itchin yūzen*, *itome-yūzen*, and *kata-yūzen*)

Detail of cat. 6

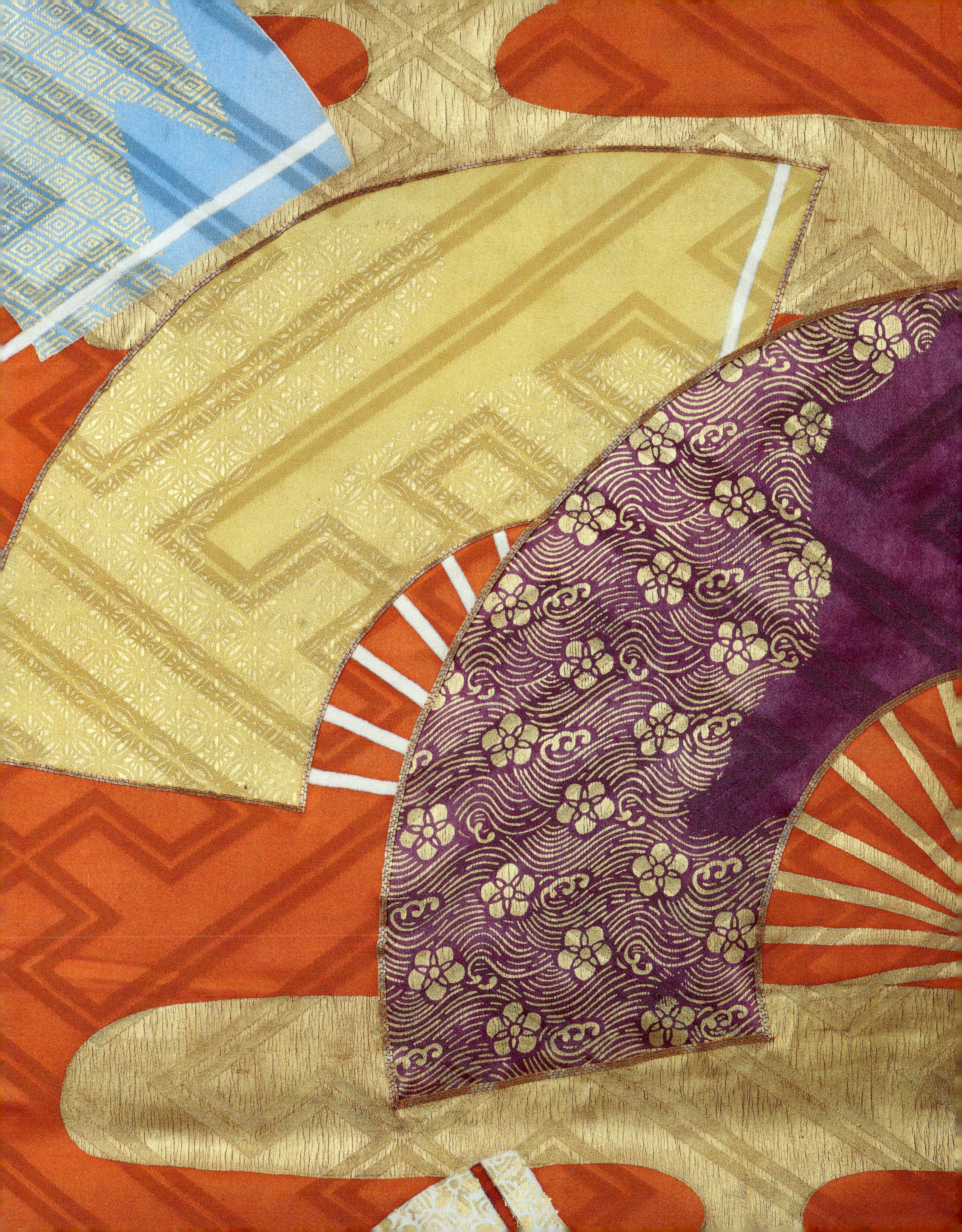

Kimono Construction

The kimono (historically the *kosode,* literally "small sleeves") has not changed its basic form since the 1600s. Kimono fashion thus references not the cut but the art on the kimono, specifically the artistry of ornamentation and patterns that are embroidered, dyed, and painted directly on its surface, as well as its coordination with other garments and accessories, such as the *obi* belt.

A single bolt of cloth for a kimono (*tanmono*) travels from one artisan studio to another, and each studio contributes their unique decorative techniques to the fabric. The entire patterned and adorned finished bolt of fabric is then cut and sewn into the kimono form such that no fabric is wasted. The standard width of the *tanmono* is approximately 40 cm (15 ¾ in.) and with kimono for women the overall length is approximately 1,200 cm (12 m or 472 7⁄16 in.). The completed kimono consists of five main panels: two panels, each covering the right and left side of the body of the garment; two panels for the sleeves; and a panel for the collar and overlapping fabric for the front.

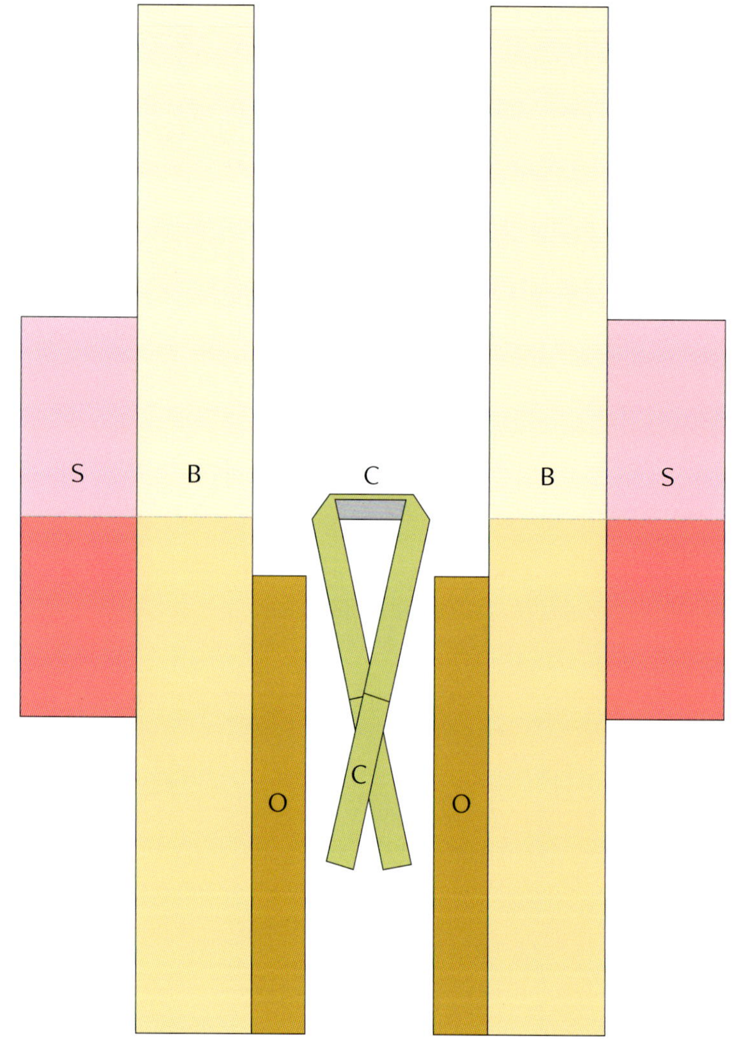

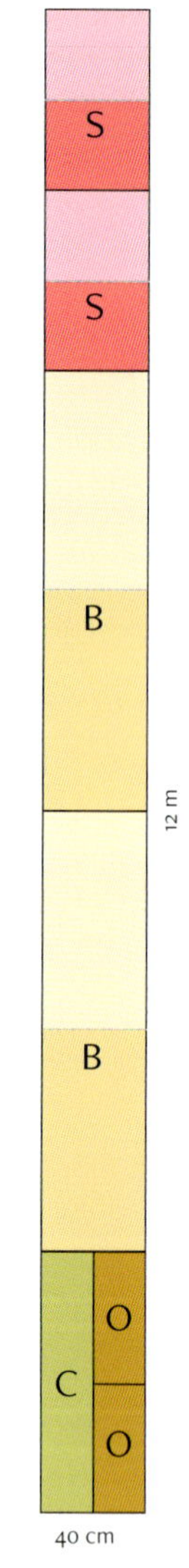

Constituent parts of a kimono: B=body; S=sleeve; C=collar; O=overlap in front.

Contributors

Monica BETHE has been engaged in the study of historical textiles, mostly from the Far East, for more than forty years. Retired from a professorship at Otani University in Kyoto and the Kyoto Consortium for Japanese Studies at Columbia University, she serves now as Director of the Medieval Japanese Studies Institute in Kyoto, primarily focused on matters related to imperial convents. Her writings on Japanese theater and traditional textiles include *Noh as Performance* (1978), as well as chapters in *Miracles and Mischief: Noh and Kyōgen Theater in Japan* (2002), *Amamonzeki – A Hidden Heritage: Treasures of the Japanese Imperial Convents* (2009), and *Transmitting Robes, Linking Minds: The World of Buddhist Kasaya* (2010).

KIKUCHI Riyo is a senior researcher in the Department of Intangible Cultural Heritage at the Tokyo National Research Institute for Cultural Properties (Tōkyō Bunkazai Kenkyūjo or Tōbunken). She specializes in the examination of various textile techniques, particularly the cultivation and processing of natural materials for textile production, and also documents traditional processes of textile creation and the maintenance of their tools. Her recently published study is the "Joint Research Report on the Spiderwort-dyed Paper Production Technique: Kusatsu Techniques that Form the Backbone of Textile Dyeing Technology" (Tōbunken, October 2018).

Vivian LI served as associate curator of Asian Art and Global Contemporary Art at the Worcester Art Museum from 2015 to 2019 and is currently the Lupe Murchison Curator of Contemporary Art at the Dallas Museum of Art. As a complement to *Kimono Couture: The Beauty of Chiso,* she also organized the exhibition and accompanying catalogue *The Kimono in Print: 300 Years of Japanese Design* (2020) drawn from the Worcester Art Museum's important John Chandler Bancroft collection of woodblock prints. She has contributed to various publications, including the *Oxford Art Journal, Yishu*, and the forthcoming anthology, *Postwar—A Global Art History, 1945–1965*.

Yukio LIPPIT is the Jeffrey T. Chambers and Andrea Okamura Professor of the History of Art and Architecture at Harvard University. His research and teaching interests center around Japanese painting of the medieval (1200–1600) and premodern eras (1600–1868), as well as the history of Japanese architecture. His books include *Painting of the Realm: The Kano House of Painters in 17th-Century Japan* (2012) and exhibition publications such as *Sōtatsu: Making Waves* (with James Ulak, 2015), *The Thinking Hand: Tools and Traditions of the Japanese Carpenter* (with Mark Mulligan, 2014), and *Colorful Realm: Japanese Bird-and-Flower Paintings by Itō Jakuchū* (2012).

NAGASAKI Iwao is an expert on Japanese textiles and has taught, published, and curated exhibitions on the subject. Formerly the curator of textiles at the Tokyo National Museum, he is currently the director of the Kyoritsu Women's University Museum (Kyōritsu Joshi Daigaku Hakubutsukan) in Tokyo; he is also a professor at that university. He has contributed to numerous international shows and publications, including *Kimono: The Art and Evolution of Japanese Fashion* (2015) and *When Art Became Fashion: Kosode in Edo-period Japan* (1992).

NII Rie is the curator at the Kyoto Costume Institute (KCI, Kyōto Fukushoku Bunka Kenkyū Zaidan), where she has worked since 1990. She has organized numerous Japanese textile exhibitions and accompanying publications, including the exhibition/catalogue *Future Beauty: 30 Years of Japanese Fashion* (co-edited with Catherine Ince, 2010) and the recent exhibition *Kimono Refashioned: Japan's Impact on International Fashion* (2018–2019), initiated by Fukai Akiko and co-organized with the Asian Art Museum of San Francisco, the Newark Museum, and the Cincinnati Art Museum.

Christine D. STARKMAN is an independent curator interested in the global, transnational, and transcultural histories of modern and contemporary art between Asia, Europe, and Latin America. She has previously worked in the curatorial departments at the Art Institute of Chicago, the Cleveland Museum of Art, and the Museum of Fine Arts, Houston. At Houston, she curated *Elegant Perfection: Masterpieces of Courtly and Religious Art from the Tokyo National Museum* (2012), *Your Bright Future: 12 Contemporary Artists from Korea* (2009), and *Where Clouds Disperse: Ink Paintings by Suh Se-ok* (2008).

Stephanie SU is assistant professor of Asian art at the University of Colorado Boulder. Her research interests include Sino-Japanese relations, global modernism, and color history. Her forthcoming book project *Colors of Modernity: Changing Aesthetics in Meiji Japanese Prints* explores the impact of the global trade network on modern Japanese prints. She co-curated the exhibition *Art Elements: Materials, Motive and Meaning* at the University of Colorado Boulder Art Museum (2019).

Photo Credits

Introduction
Figs. 1–6: CHISO
Figs. 7, 8: Vivian Li

Kikuchi essay
Fig. 1: National Museum of Japanese History
Fig 2: Tokyo National Research Institute for Cultural Properties
Figs. 3, 4: Metropolitan Museum of Art

Lippit essay
Figs. 1–4, 9, 10: CHISO
Figs. 5–8: Harada Heisaku

Interview
Figs. 1, 2: CHISO
Figs. 4, 5: Vivian Li

Plates
All images: CHISO

p.110: Kimono Construction image credit: Kim Noonan